THE 'Scottish' 4-4-0

TOM MIDDLEMASS

Foreword

The 'Scottish' school of design has regularly been identified as a distinctive feature of the British steam locomotive story by railway historians and writers and, as a publisher, I have often wondered why such an obvious theme had never, as far as I was aware, been systematically addressed in a more expanded form. In fact, I had even pencilled it in as a future title from my own pen save that the size of the task seemed rather daunting to tackle alongside my full time work. It was therefore with great delight that I received an enquiry from Tom Middlemass as to whether a book on 'Scottish 4-4-0s' would be of interest to my firm.

"Does a duck swim?" was my instant response, for I have known Tom for some years, both as a fine 'wordsmith' and a dedicated railway historian, so I knew that the product would be both well researched and highly readable. Moreover Tom is a true Scot (and proud of it) which I felt would give the properly appropriate 'flavour' to what I confidently anticipated would be a thoroughly well balanced and comprehensive work. He has not let me down.

However, when he asked me to write a Foreword, I did wonder if it was his quiet way of reacting to my suggestions in the preparation of the manuscript(!), for it was my idea to add Chapter 9 to the story and to 'Top and Tail' the work in the form of Chapters 1 and 10. As publisher, I have to thank Tom not only for agreeing so graciously to these quite considerable changes to his original idea but also for the speed at which he integrated them into the whole.

This is not the definitive story of the 'Scottish' school, for it confines attention to but one wheel arrangement — moreover one which was not even the first to be assayed by Stroudley, Jones, Drummond and Co. But I suspect that if one mentions 'Scottish' locomotives to most enthusiasts, the first image to come to mind will more often than not be a typical 4-4-0 from the pre-group period. This book tells their story in a highly entertaining fashion and it is a pleasure and privilege to write these few words by way of introduction.

David Jenkinson

© Tom Middlemass and Atlantic Transport Publishers 1994

'Pendragon Books' is an imprint of Atlantic Transport Publishers, Trevithick House, West End, Penryn, Cornwall, TR10 8HE, England. All rights reserved

Layout and Design by Barry C. Lane, Sutton-in-Craven

Set in Galliard 9pt by Ian D. Luckett (Typesetting), St. Austell, Cornwall

Reproduction and printing by The Amadeus Press Ltd, Huddersfield, West Yorkshire

British Cataloguing-in-Publication Data: a catalogue record for this book is held by the British Library

ISBN No. 0 906899 42 7

Unless annotated otherwise, all illustrations appearing in this book are from the author's private collection and the publisher regrets that copies cannot be made available to readers.

CONTENTS

Early Drummond on the Caledonian: No.115 of the small (5ft 9in) wheeled 'Gourock' bogie type, introduced in 1888 to meet GSWR competition on the Clyde Coast trains. *(BR LMR)*

Basically Drummond in principle but with cab styling by Holmes: NBR 592 Class 7ft 4-4-0 No.600, believed taken at Cowlairs in 1887.

The Stroudly-Jones 'look' on the Highland is represented by 4-4-0 No.67 *Cromartie* (originally *The Duke* — see Chapter 6). The Crewe-type front end, cab style and elaborate livery were introduced in Stroudley's time but the four-wheel bogie and distinctive chimney are Jones' contribution. *(Pendragon Collection)*

Chapter 1
SETTING THE SCENE

FROM THE MOMENT IN 1862 that William Cowan very nearly introduced Britain's first 4-4-0 tender locomotive on the Great North of Scotland Railway, and Thomas Wheatley of the North British Railway sired Britain's first inside-cylindered, inside framed 4-4-0 nine years later, the type commanded great affection in the hearts of Scottish railwaymen. The many classes which followed on all five Scottish Companies were, almost to a man, speedy, combative, and highly flexible — an ideal prescription for locomotives which had to grapple with the severe gradients and bends which hallmarked the railway system North of the Border. Even in the 1960s pre-Grouping 4-4-0s, plus additions from both the LNER and LMSR, held many a fort until internal combustion swamped the scene, in Scotland as elsewhere.

The 4-4-0 type, in fact, gained such rapid and persistent popularity in Scotland that during the 60 years which elapsed between William Cowan's initiative in 1862 and the advent of Grouping in January 1923, only six of the 24 Locomotive Superintendents who served the five Scottish Railway Companies failed to indulge in the class. Even then, Benjamin Connor, of the Caledonian Railway, had every intention in the mid-1870s of introducing a handful of inside-cylindered 4-4-0s; but illness, and premature death, left the ultimate production and detailed design of the so-called 'Dundee Bogies' to his successor in office, George Brittain. William Stroudley, on the other hand, while serving on the Highland Railway between 1865 and 1869, adhered firmly to his innate distrust of leading bogies, as did Patrick Stirling (G&SWR 1853–66) to his dislike of coupled wheels. Another Highland Railway man, Frederick George Smith, might well have built 4-4-0s, had not the 'River' fiasco of 1915 enforced his early resignation. As it was, Hawthorn Leslie & Co. later developed his proposed 4-4-0 in the form of *Snaigow* and *Durn*; and both entered traffic under the aegis of his successor, Christopher Cumming. Meanwhile, the two other 'odd men out', Walter Chalmers of the NBR and D. C. Urie of the Highland, both held office for too short a time and too near Grouping, to sponsor 4-4-0 types. That said, examination of the sundry 4-4-0s contributed by the remaining eighteen Locomotive Superintendents tells a stirring story.

Many illustrious and long serving names appear on the list, but it is universally conceded that Dugald Drummond was the real patriarch of the Scottish 4-4-0. Although he remained deeply influenced by his ten year association with William Stroudley and, consequently, never built an unattractive locomotive, Drummond, nevertheless, was astute, and far sighted enough to follow Thomas Wheatley's lead in developing the Scottish 4-4-0. It follows that his 'Abbotsford' NBR class of 1876 was a classic of study locomotive design; and on both the NBR and CR, Holmes, Reid, Lambie, McIntosh, and Pickersgill had no qualms in following his footsteps. Holmes, at once Drummond's successor and the NBR's longest serving Locomotive Superintendent, superimposed larger boilers and increased boiler pressures on what were basically Drummond designs. He also rebuilt many older engines to current standards — yet lapsed peculiarly in reintroducing the rounded Stirling cab. W. P. Reid, a North British man throughout his working life, once appointed in 1903, continued to develop established NBR traditions (in all except the Stirling cab!) and, happily, contradicted Holmes' aversion to locomotive names by making extensive use of Sir Walter Scott characters. His handsome 'Scott' 4-4-0s and (later) 'Atlantics', bearing a mix of Scott and place names, added great lustre to the NBR scene at Waverley Station and elsewhere. Meanwhile, right up to 1914 the old Stroudley/Drummond empathy still peeped forth in the bronze green livery the NBR adopted for all engines.

4-4-0s BUILT FOR SCOTTISH COMPANIES

Locomotive Superintendent	First 4-4-0 built	Numbers Built					
		NBR	GNSR	CR	GSWR	HR	Totals
COWAN, William	1862	—	33	—	—	—	33
JONES, David	1870	—	—	—	—	63	63
WHEATLEY, Thomas	1871	6	—	—	—	—	6
STIRLING, James	1873	—	—	—	22	—	22
BRITTAIN, George	1877	—	—	15	—	—	15
DRUMMOND, Dugald	1877	12	—	41	—	—	53
SMELLIE, Hugh	1882	—	—	—	44	—	44
MANSON, James	1884	—	26	—	131	—	157
HOLMES, Matthew	1886	96	—	—	—	—	96
JOHNSON, James	1893	—	6	—	—	—	6
LAMBIE, John	1894	—	—	6	—	—	6
PICKERSGILL, William	1895	—	39	48	—	—	87
McINTOSH, John F.	1896	—	—	87	—	—	87
DRUMMOND, Peter	1898	—	—	—	12	26	38
REID, William P.	1906	99	—	—	—	—	99
HEYWOOD, Thomas E.	1909	—	8	—	—	—	8
CUMMING, Christopher	1916	—	—	—	—	5	5
WHITELEGG, Robert H.	1921	—	—	—	1	—	1
TOTALS		213	112	197	210	94	826
Entered LNER & LMSR Stock (1923)		183	100	180	188	57	708
Entered British Railways Stock (1948)		94	40	72	—	12	218

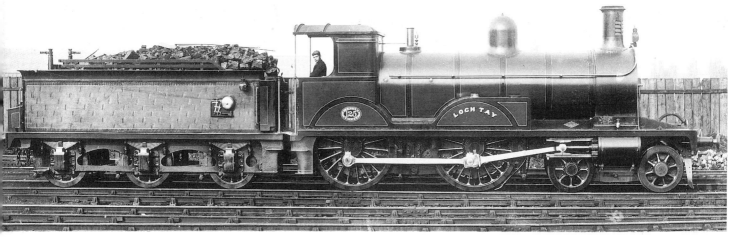

David Jones' handsome Loch Class of 1896 marked the end of the Stroudley visual influence in its 'pure' form, also the end of the outside-cylindered Highland 4-4-0 for twenty years. This is No.125 *Loch Tay*, believed to be at Inverness very soon after building. *(BR LMR)*

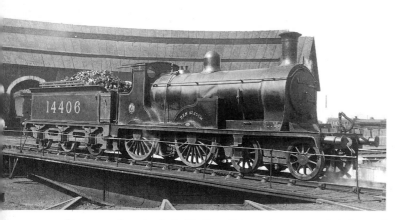

Drummond again, but this time Peter, who was much influenced by, and lived in the shadow of, older brother Dugald. This is Highland Railway 'Small Ben' No.14406 *Ben Slioch*, resplendent in LMS crimson lake in the mid-1920s and scarce distinguishable from Dugald's somewhat earlier St. Rollox product for the Caledonian.

Once he gravitated to Caledonian Railway employment in 1882, Drummond continued his highly successful 4-4-0 designs. His Stroudley-like enthusiasm for locomotive names invoked little reaction from an unsympathetic Board, but a kindred preoccupation with locomotive livery saw the CR's famous Royal Blue safely launched. During his comparatively short stay of CR office, Drummond also made a clean break with the 'Crewe' type framing which had characterised CR locomotive construction to date; and, restless to a degree, he completely modernised St Rollox Works into the bargain! Six years later, J. F. McIntosh further enhanced the CR's public image by introducing his famous series of 'Dunalastair' 4-4-0s; then crowned his 52 years of Caledonian employment by introducing Schmidt superheating on his '139' Class 4-4-0s of 1910. A later class, the '43s', employed both Robinson superheater and larger cylinders, but the CR's next Locomotive Superintendent, William Pickersgill, while content initially to follow Drummond design tradition, was rather addicted to slide valves and saturated steam. However, after experimenting with feed water heating and tinkering with saturated boilers when several 'Dunalastairs' were rebuilt, he, too, eventually subscribed to the Caledonian's new superheating tradition.

When the Highland Railway was initially formed in 1865 by the amalgamation of the Inverness & Aberdeen Junction and the Inverness & Perth Railways it acquired a miscellany of modestly powered 2-2-2 and 2-4-0 passenger locomotives, and the influence of Crewe was plain to be seen in their heavy fore-end frames. Stroudley, the HR's first Locomotive Superintendent, introduced yellow livery — his famous 'Improved Engine Green' — but it was his successor in 1870, David Jones, who took the more practical step, in 1873–75, of combatting the sharp curves of the Dingwall & Skye line by adding Adams bogies to two 1858 vintage Hawthorn 2-4-0s. The immediate success of this more flexible 4-4-0 wheelbase encouraged him to venture further with four distinct classes of 4-4-0; but not until he produced his celebrated 'Big Goods' 4-6-0s in 1894, however, did he abandon the Crewe-type front frame. Other Jones hallmarks were his Stroudley-inspired cabs, with their rounded corners and roofs, and his unique louvred chimney which, though highly functional, was never adopted by any other railway.

Once Peter Drummond took charge of HR locomotive affairs in 1897, the pattern changed radically. Not content with dropping Jones' chimney and cab, Drummond, as befitted a younger brother of Dugald, adopted inside cylinders. Continuing further with Dugald's philosophy, Peter Drummond also experimented with firebox cross water tubes and steam reversing. Both ideas were sound enough in theory, but proved to be highly unpopular with enginemen and fitters. That apart, Drummond's 'Ben' Class 4-4-0s, both 'Wee' and 'Big', were simple robust engines. The only other Highland Railway 4-4-0s, came in 1916, when Cumming sponsored the construction of three more Jones 'Lochs', and followed up one year later by introducing Walschaerts outside valve gear on his externally imposing, but quite orthodoxly principled, *Snaigow* and *Durn*.

The Glasgow & South Western Railway, also an amalgam of smaller concerns, was formed in 1850, and throughout its chequered career it employed a quite remarkable succession of Locomotive Superintendents. One need hardly add that Patrick Stirling's tenure of office from 1855 to 1869 produced nothing in the way of 4-4-0s. Next in office, Patrick's younger brother, James, continued the Stirling tradition, particularly in the way of domeless boilers, and, in 1874, perfected a steam reversing gear which was subsequently widely used on GSWR locomotives. Then, faced with designing locomotives which could handle Midland express trains between Carlisle and Glasgow, he introduced no fewer than 22 Class '6' 4-4-0s over the years 1873–77 of which No.106 was proudly displayed at the Darlington Exhibition of 1875. For good measure, he was also the first Superintendent to provide cushioned seats in 3rd class compartments. Next, in 1878, he moved south to Ashford, Kent to take up new duties with the South Eastern Railway. His replacement at Kilmarnock, Hugh Smellie, started off tentatively enough by

Manson's 'trail blazing' 4-4-0 No.11 of 1897 for the G&SWR was, by a month or two, Britain's first four-cylinder locomotive. It had the handsome lines of most Manson designs, somewhat reminiscent of those of Samuel Johnson on the Midland Railway in England, but was a little disappointing until modified — see Chapter 5. *(Pendragon Collection)*

shopping a dozen 2-4-0s. Then came two dozen 4-4-0s, still with domeless boilers. Designed for the Greenock line, and initially known as the 'Greenock Bogies', they gained great affection amongst GSWR men and were known latterly as the 'Wee Bogies'. They were immediately followed by twenty main line express 4-4-0s, the Class '153s'. Still domeless, some of them at least broke new ground by being fitted with removable extended smokeboxes, the first application of its kind in the UK. The '153s', with their sound front ends and capacity for free steaming, were an outstanding success, and worked the Glasgow Pullmans in conjunction with the Midland Railway with great distinction. Essentially practical, Smellie also enlarged Kilmarnock Works, and lowered production costs by introducing labour-saving tools, before moving on to the CR in the Autumn of 1890. The great pity was that ill health confined his Caledonian activities to a few months.

GSWR locomotive design took a completely new turn when James Manson was appointed in 1890; for the latter had already served seven years at Kittybrewster, where the 4-4-0 had long been regarded as a staple commodity. Certainly, Manson's two decades of subsequent service at Kilmarnock produced a long series of sound, handsome locomotives of that type. His first contribution, the Class '8' engines, with their domed boilers, were distinctly reminiscent of GNSR practice; albeit the 57 he built at Kilmarnock between 1892 and 1904 were designed to face far tougher tasks on the Sou' West's main line to Carlisle. Still adhering to inside cylinders, Manson then went on to develop five more classes of 4-4-0, each practically tailor-made for specific functions on the GSWR's somewhat complicated system. One class, the '14's, consisted of sixteen 'renewals' of James Stirling '6' Class engines. On the other hand, Manson's four-cylinder 4-4-0, No.11, of 1897, blazed a completely new trail — as did his superheated 4-6-0s, almost his last design, fifteen years later.

Manson's successor, Peter Drummond, thoroughly versed in St Rollox and Lochgorm ways, chose to adopt a 'big engine' policy, and the dozen 4-4-0s he produced in 1913-15, clumsy and heavy, offered a stark contrast to Manon's neat machines. Drummond's successor, R. H. Whitelegg, arrived at Kilmarnock

If not quite in the classic 'Scottish' school of styling, the two 4-4-0s of 1917, developed for the Highland Railway by Christopher Cumming, could lay sound claim to be the last new Scottish 4-4-0 design in purely conceptual terms; they were also undeniably handsome and re-introduced the outside cylindered 4-4-0 to the HR. This is the second example of the pair, *Durn*, seen as LMS No.14523 in lined black livery soon before withdrawal in 1935.

The Robinson GCR 'Director' design was, strictly speaking, an immigrant type; but those which ran in Scotland were always intended to be there and were built after the grouping purely for that purpose. This is No.6383 *Jonathan Oldbuck* on the familiar four-track stretch in Princes Street Gardens, Edinburgh, en route for Glasgow in 1926. On the parallel track, Reid NBR 4-4-2 No.9877 is in charge of an Aberdeen train. *(Ransome Wallis Collection — NRM)*

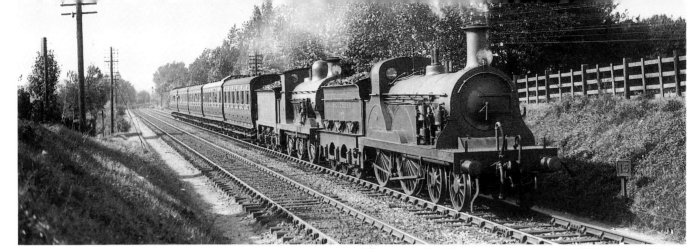

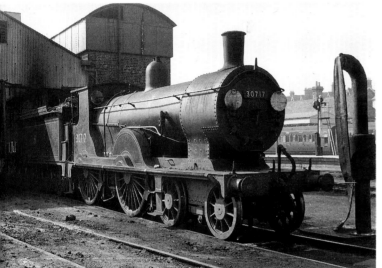

Still essentially Drummond in spite of SR superheating and BR livery: the classic LSWR Class T9 in the shape of No.30717, resting between routine duties at Wadebridge in the twilight of its life: May 1959. *(John Edgington)*

When James Stirling moved from the G&SWR to the SER, his designs hardly changed and this classic example would have looked equally at home on the 'Port Road'. It is in fact the last survivor, No.172, of his F Class (see Chapter 9) and this view was taken at an unspecified location soon before the engine was withdrawn in 1930. *(Pendragon Collection)*

in August 1918, at a difficult time in Britain's history, railway and otherwise. Apart from adding one 4-4-0 in 1921, and rebuilding Manson's four-cylinder 4-4-0 one year later, his main GSWR contribution was his intention to introduce ten standard boiler types in lieu of the 37 varieties already in use. Only three new boiler types, however, had been put into effect before Grouping descended; whence Whitelegg left to become General Manager of Beyer Peacock's Manchester Works. Meanwhile, such Manson engines as Whitelegg contrived to rebuild proved markedly unsuccessful in their new, and sadly disfigured, form.

Scotland's fifth major company, the Great North of Scotland, offered a comparatively uncomplicated 4-4-0 in 1862. Once James Manson arrived in 1883 to sweep away brass domes, copper-capped chimneys and open splashers, three subsequent successors in office, Johnson, Pickersgill and Heywood, faithfully pursued the Company's new policy of building straightforward inside cylinder 4-4-0s. The 100 which survived to enter LNER stock consisted of no fewer than fourteen different classes; though this was reduced to eleven under LNER auspices. Came 1948, and exactly 40 GNSR 4-4-0s, all of Pickersgill, Johnson and Heywood vintage, with some dating back to 1893, entered British Railways stock. Fortunately, the last survivor, No.49 *Gordon Highlander*, withdrawn in June 1958, was carefully restored to running condition, and, like the NBR's *Glen Douglas*, found a safe refuge in Glasgow Transport Museum.

It was the Great War of 1914–18, of course, which finally broke the mould of railway affairs throughout the United Kingdom. Government control, assumed perforce during that dreadful conflict, had produced such remarkable results that a Select Committee on Transport, appointed by the House of Commons in 1918, had no compunction in recommending that Britain's railways should not be allowed to return to their pre-war position. "Unification, therefore, of the railway system", it opined, "is desirable under certain safeguards, whether the ownership be in public or private hands". It was a devastating pronouncement — and, despite fierce opposition from many in the House, subsequent events, nevertheless, saw the establishment of Grouping. Thus, the 'Big Four' were born.

As far as Scotland was concerned, Grouping came none too soon. The enormous traffic involved in servicing Scottish naval bases alone, coupled with a grievous loss of skilled workmen to the Services themselves, had bled most Scottish railway companies dry. Arrears in locomotive maintenance had mounted alarmingly, and many of those locomotives which were still running were ageing too rapidly for comfort. During the years 1914–18 the five Scottish Companies had only contrived between them to build a mere 51 4-4-0s (mostly Pickersgill and Reid engines); and it was undoubtedly this shortfall which conditioned Derby and Doncaster reaction when Grouping was effected on 1st January 1923.

Nigel Gresley's initial rescue package (as described later in Chapter 7) consisted of three distinctly differing classes of 4-4-0. All three types presented former NBR locomen with new difficulties; but in the case of two of the classes these were triumphantly overcome. The third class, unfortunately, the ex-GNR Class D1 4-4-0s, proved to be beyond the pale, even for Scottish railwaymen. Derby, on the other hand, chose to pursue earlier Midland Railway tradition by introducing Compound and Class 2P 4-4-0s. Once again, problems in dealing with the unfamiliar raised their ugly head — but once more, to their undying glory, ex-Caledonian and GSWR men rose to the occasion.

One might add that when the six-coupled passenger era arrived on the Scottish scene a decade later the railwaymen of Scotland were ready and willing as ever to cope with change.

Lastly, before starting the more detailed story, it should never be forgotten that the 'Scottish' 4-4-0 was not confined to the pre-group systems north of the border. Caledonian designs were highly influential in Belgium (see Chapter 3) while an arguably much more significant contribution was made in England as a result of James Stirling's designs for the SER and Dugald Drummond's for the LSWR, both of which are covered in Chapter 9.

Chapter 2
THE NORTH BRITISH RAILWAY

HALFWAY THROUGH THE nineteenth century, at a time when new, and invariably wildly optimistic, railway concerns were springing up all over the UK, few experienced a more disastrous start to life than the North British Railway. Incorporated on 4th July 1844, and formally opened between Edinburgh and Berwick on 18th June 1846, the Company elected to acquire a near-exclusive stock of 70 R.&W. Hawthorn locomotives by 1852. Indeed, the only other engine it owned during that time was a 'high-speed' 2-2-2-0 Crampton type which was supplied by E. B. Wilson & Co. of Leeds, at a cost of £2,800, in 1849. Yet, somehow, mean-minded management contrived to offset any advantage this situation might have conferred. Poor Robert Thornton, appointed NBR Locomotive Superintendent on 6th January 1846, was, as it happened, Hawthorn-trained, yet he was consistently starved of adequate funds as he strove to maintain the undoubtedly temperamental Hawthorns in decent condition. Thus, broken axles on the double-framed machines presented a constantly recurring problem. So, too, did NBR labour relations, which were so appalling that, one day in October 1851, Thornton, goaded beyond endurance, submitted his angry resignation. From there, incredibly, things went from bad to worse; and two incompetent successors, William Smith and the Hon E. G. Petre, managed between them to bring the North British Railway to the point of mechanical paralysis by December 1855.

The NBR's fourth Locomotive Superintendent, William Hurst, took over that month. A talented and energetic man of Lancashire & Yorkshire Railway background, Hurst served his new Company well: better, probably, than it deserved. Then came one more fateful day in January 1867, when evidence of underhand financial dealings brought *him* down. Such, it should be added, was the morality of contemporary NBR management that his Chairman, Richard Hodgson, and General Manager, T. K. Rowbotham, fell with him. Nevertheless, Hurst, despite his lapse, at least introduced one important reform by persuading the NBR to end its total reliance on *English* locomotive manufacturers. He was even brave enough, in 1856, to undertake locomotive construction at the NBR's totally inadequate Edinburgh (St Margaret's) workshops; and during his regime 22 engines were turned out there. Burntisland shops accounted for two more, and private firms, mostly Scottish, subscribed 84. Soon, however, after the all-important merger between the NBR and the Edinburgh & Glasgow Railway was accomplished on 1st August 1865 the focal point of NBR domestic locomotive construction moved irrevocably across Scotland's narrow waist to the E&GR's superior workshop facilities at Cowlairs, Glasgow. NBR fortunes, meanwhile, guided by new management, gained so rapidly in confidence that in 1871 a rather astonishing agreement to join forces with the 'Auld Enemy', the Caledonian Railway, was nearly, if not quite, consummated. What a difference *that* might have made to the course of Scottish railway history!

Symptomatic of the NBR's new found prosperity, 44 applicants responded as the Company prepared to appoint Hurst's successor; and, on 1st February 1867, Thomas Wheatley was given the job. He had already spent 29 years in railway employment with the Leeds & Selby, Manchester, Sheffield & Lincolnshire and London & North Western Railways. Yet, ,despite this impressive pedigree, he, too, was destined to fall by the wayside — when revelation of *his* dishonesty brought about dismissal in October 1874. It must be conceded, though, that Wheatley left behind him a much more enhancing locomotive stock than the raggle taggle collection which greeted his arrival in 1867. The fact was that vigorous route expansion and numerous locomotive acquisitions from sundry conquests throughout the early 1860s had, in effect, endowed the NBR with a hapless mechanical miscellany.

Soon after his appointment Wheatley deduced, correctly, that a new policy of gearing new locomotive construction strictly to Company requirements was vital. So, too, was a measure of standardisation. Thus, under his markedly economical supervision the traditional copper and brass locomotive decoration of the Hawthorn and Hurst eras vanished, and new, purposeful, and quite austere-looking NBR engines began to emerge from Cowlairs and elsewhere. Wheatley even took care to rebuild ten old engines: but, more importantly, he added 185 more of his own design. The fact that 134 of these were 0-6-0 tender locomotives merely signalled a realistic appreciation of the NBR's burgeoning mineral traffic. Fife's coal mines were proving to be veritable gold mines!

Passenger services on the NBR were, for the time being, less demanding. After all, these were pre-Tay and Forth Bridge days. By dint of running powers, shrewdly obtained in 1869, North Eastern Railway locomotives were handling major traffic between Edinburgh and Berwick, and such NBR main lines as remained were being competently served by ex-E&GR Beyer 'singles' and NBR 2-4-0s. Twenty-four extremely handsome specimens of the latter genre had, in fact, been added by Hurst over the years 1861–67. True to his dictum, all had come from Glasgow builders. Dübs and Neilson supplied twelve each.

Latterly, of course, Wheatley had to turn his mind to express locomotive design. For his first cautious venture he elected to pursue the 2-4-0 tradition; and two six-wheelers he had built at Cowlairs in 1869 served the NBR well. Coincidentally, May 1869 also witnessed the emergence of the last engine to be built at St Margaret's, 2-4-0 No.38, an extensive reconstruction of a Hawthorn 'single'. Then, in 1871, came a startling development, when Wheatley introduced Britain's first inside-cylindered, inside framed 4-4-0. Thus, quite quietly, Cowlairs Works laid the foundation of a long and hallowed Scottish locomotive tradition. Despite their austere Wheatley look, Nos.224 and 264 must have created quite an impression with their close-set 6ft 6in driving wheels and widely spaced 2ft 9in solid-centred bogies. Cylinders were 17in × 24in, and a cab shelter of sorts, together with a tight six-wheeled tender and overall pea green livery, nicely lined in white, added a touch of trimness worthy of the occasion. In the event, No.264 wandered quite widely over NBR main lines. No.224 spent most of its working life in Fife.

Apart from the Westinghouse brake and what looks like a Wheatley stovepipe chimney, No.342 looks exactly as it did when it left Dübs & Co.'s Glasgow Locomotive Works in 1865. Renumbered 342A in 1889, then 877 in 1895, the 2-4-0 spent its last years handling trains in the Peebles vicinity between intermittent spells of banking at Falahill.
(Author's Collection)

No.224 is seen here as built. Ultimately, it gained immortality as 'The Diver', after plunging seaward in the Tay Bridge disaster of 28th December 1879.
(Author's Collection)

Below:
The sturdiness of Wheatley's 4-4-0 design and the durability of Cowlairs workmanship were never better exemplified than when No.224, surprisingly the little worse for wear, was fished out three months later from what should by all rights have been a watery grave.
(Author's Collection)

Rather astonishingly, involvement in the celebrated Tay Bridge disaster of 1879 by no means ended No.224's career; for the engine was speedily repaired at Cowlairs, and returned to service. Five years later, Matthew Holmes, employing a patent taken out by his cousin, W. H. Nisbet, even rebuilt the locomotive as a four-cylinder tandem compound. The experiment was not a success, however, and in 1887 No.224 was restored to two-cylinder simple form. Ten years later, a new Holmes boiler was fitted, and in May 1913 'The Diver' was renumbered 1192. Then, some *forty* years after the Tay Bridge disaster, the veteran Wheatley was sold to a Glasgow scrap dealer. Sister engine No.264 (later 1198) was scrapped that same year.

Meanwhile, as far back as 1845, the NBR had been alert enough to complement its proposed East Coast passage to the South via Berwick by obtaining Parliamentary authority to construct an ancillary south-westerly line to Hawick. It was, however, to prove an expensive exercise, for NB shareholders. First, the Edinburgh & Dalkeith Railway had to be bought, for the princely sum of £130,000. Then its 4ft 6in gauge metals had to be regauged and strengthened before the NBR could forge ahead with its new line. Latterly, one mile of new NBR construction established the vital link between Portobello and Niddrie, and the Edinburgh–Dalhousie section of the Edinburgh & Hawick Railway was duly opened on 21st June 1847. The E&DR had already been absorbed in July 1845.

No.420 is seen here after rebuild by Matthew Holmes in 1887. Though many of the latter's characteristics have been incorporated, the original Wheatley bogie and tender remain. Renumbered 1241 in 1914, the locomotive was withdrawn the following year. The last two survivors of the class, formerly Nos.421 and 423, rather surprisingly predeceased 'The Diver' by following suit in 1918. *(Author's Collection)*

Subsequent stages were neither cheap nor easy to build. Gorebridge was reached on 12th July 1847; but the next section, embracing an eight mile climb at 1:70 to reach Falahill summit, was only completed as far as Bowland Bridge ten months later. February 1849, however, saw passenger services running between Edinburgh and Newton St Boswells, and Hawick was finally reached on 1st November 1849. New engines were, of course, required to operate the NBR's second thrust south, and in 1847–48 R. & W. Hawthorn Ltd. obliged by supplying eight passenger 2-4-0s and eight heavy goods 0-6-0s. A similar 'mix' supplied a few years later were, in fact, the last locomotives Hawthorn built for the North British Railway.

Gaining access to Hawick was one thing; fulfilment of the NBR's patent ambition to reach Carlisle, 43 miles further south, was another. Vigorous legal obstruction by the Caledonian Railway made sure of that. In 1857, the threat of a Caledonian-sponsored Carlisle & Hawick Railway was bad enough; but spines must have shivered in the NB Board Room less than a year later, when the appropriate Caledonian Railway Bill sailed through the House of Commons. Fortunately for the NB, it was rejected by the House of Lords a few weeks later. Even then, the NBR Chairman saw fit to meet his Caledonian counterpart and suggest joint Company participation in building such a line. His advance was brusquely declined. By now, however, the issue of rail connection with Carlisle had become such a burning one with Border folk that the NBR Board chose to acquaint the people of Hawick with the merits of *its* proposed line *via* Liddesdale. The response was electric. Local sentiment, always more sympathetically disposed towards Edinburgh than Glasgow, swung solidly behind the NBR proposal and, despite further delaying tactics by the Caledonian, the Border Union (North British) Railways Act became law on 21st July 1859.

The men who built the Border Union Railway had no illusions as to the immense nature of the task which lay ahead of them. The creation of ten mile climb at 1:80 straight from Hawick Station was formidable enough; but, beyond that, Whitrope Tunnel, fully 1,200 yards long, had to be hacked out from difficult terrain ere the summit was reached at 1,006 feet. Cuttings through solid rock, embankments and viaducts all combined with frequent land slips to torment the contractors and labourers who toiled on unceasingly through three frightful winters. Often miles from the nearest public road, the camps which housed the labourers were invariably, but hardly surprisingly, whisky, as well as rain-sodden on pay nights! Meanwhile, construction was also proceeding from the Carlisle end, and lowland conditions there were so much more favourable that a passenger service between Carlisle and Riccarton was in operation by 2nd June 1862. Branches to Gretna and Langholm were already working. Then, on 1st July 1862, came the great day, when the NBR's first through train to Carlisle steamed proudly out of Edinburgh Waverley Station.

Any hopes, alas, that the NBR may have entertained of handling through traffic to and from the heart of England were soon brutally dashed; for a combined blockade by the London & North Western and the Caledonian Railways successfully prevented English traffic, goods and passenger alike, from exploiting the NB's new North–South route. The Midland Railway, on the other hand, would cheerfully have accommodated NBR through traffic — but *its* metals fell 60 miles short of Carlisle, at Ingleton. So, for well over a decade after its completion, the NBR's ambitious new Waverley Route was populated solely by sparsely laden local traffic. Four passenger trains, two Fast and two Slow, left Edinburgh Waverley daily for Carlisle — but never a through coach for England appeared in their midst. It seemed a sad return for the NBR's earlier enterprise in securing entry into Carlisle over 1½ miles of *Caledonian* metals, by securing a long term lease over the Port Carlisle Dock and Railway.

In 1873 Thomas Wheatley, heartened by the success of his first two 4-4-0s, added four more slightly heavier engines to NB stock. Again a product of Cowlairs, Nos. 420-423 differed only in detail from their elder sisters. The diameter of their solid bogie wheels was increased to 3ft 4in, the coupled wheelbase gained two inches, and apart from the more shapely contour which had been given to the rear splasher the only other discernible new feature was the dome, which was now situated further forward on the boiler, midway between the centres of the leading driving wheel and the rear bogie. Built with Waverley Route work in mind, Wheatley's new 4-4-0s coped comfortably enough with current traffic requirements.

In the latter half of 1874, however, one year after the introduction of Wheatley's new 4-4-0s, came events of high drama for both Wheatley and the NBR. A recently appointed NB Director, John Monteith Douglas, an accountant by profession, and incurably investigative by nature, unearthed peculiar financial irregularities in Cowlairs Works accounts. NBR Board Minutes are discreetly silent anent the report Douglas duly rendered, but due significance may be placed on the fact that Thomas Wheatley, his brother William, and the chief storeman at Cowlairs resigned their posts to a man on 20th October 1874. Ironically, Douglas himself, ever anxious to enhance staff morale, failed to be re-elected to the NBR Board once he had completed his three year stint on 15th March 1877. Wheatley, in the meantime, had obtained an appointment as General Engineer to a very modest concern, the Wigtownshire Railway. His five year appointment was renewed in August 1880, and he died in office, aged 62, on 13th March 1883.

The year 1875 brought events of even greater significance to the NBR; for not only did Dugald Drummond succeed Wheatley as Locomotive Superintendent on 1st February that year, but construction of a new Settle–Carlisle line which the Midland Railway had resolved to build was well under way. Heartened by prospects of through traffic at last, the NBR management hastened to bring its Waverley Route metals up to main

The elegant, yet purposeful lines of Drummond's new 4-4-0s emerge clearly in this Works photograph of No.479, the engine which gave the class its name. With 6ft 6in coupled wheels, 18in × 26in cylinders, and a boiler pressure of 150psi, the 44¼ ton 'Abbotsfords' could exert a tractive effort of 13,770lb. The eight built by Neilson & Co. were put to work with steam brake on the engine and Westinghouse brake on tender and train. Notwithstanding a disturbing lack of coordinating mechanism between the two systems, this arrangement persisted into the early 1890s before the Westinghouse brake was applied to all. The last four 'Abbotsfords', built at Cowlairs in 1878, had already been so equipped. (*Author's Collection*)

line standard. Conformation with contemporary Midland Railway practice also made the provision of Westinghouse brake obligatory. Thus, 4-4-0 No.421 was so fitted — the first NBR locomotive to be honoured in this fashion — and on 1st May 1876, through trains began to wend their way between Edinburgh (Waverley) and St. Pancras. Unfortunately, despite appropriate Border rejoicing, the operative word was 'wend'; for the NBR's tortuous 98 mile route posed many a challenge to locomotives and, only too soon, Wheatley's latter day 4-4-0s proved themselves insufficiently powerful to handle heavy express trains on their native soil. They simply could not cope unaided with Falahill and Hawick gradients. Desperate situations require drastic solution; thus, prompted by urgent representations from its new Locomotive Superintendent, the NBR Board agreed to commission four new 4-4-0s from Neilson & Co. of Glasgow. Drummond had, in fact, asked for six. As it was, the design was left to him, and cost was agreed with Neilsons at £3,045 per locomotive.

Dugald Drummond has provided railway historians with many a provocative anecdote. Yet, the beneficial effect of his accession on NBR affairs can hardly be overestimated. Already this 35 year old man had served the Edinburgh & Glasgow, Highland, and London, Brighton & South Coast Railways; and, curiously, a strong professional relationship he had developed with William Stroudley at each of these institutions had left an indelible impression on the otherwise diametrically opposed Scot. Drummond was as rough as Stroudley, seven years his senior, was smooth. Yet, particularly in his earlier designs, the younger man did not hesitate to emulate the master. Indeed, all through his working life, engines designed by Drummond never lacked elegance, no matter what ruggedness he chose to built into them. The very first locomotives he built for the NBR, for example — Nos.474-475, a pair of extremely handsome single wheelers — bore an uncanny resemblance to *Grosvenor*, the Stroudley LB&SCR 2-2-2 which was currently exciting attention 500 miles further south. Pursuing the Stroudley analogy even further, each Drummond 'single' bore a local name, and relied on feed water heating. The latter feature, however, was later abandoned; for Drummond, devoted disciple though he was, was soon to reveal that he had a mind of his own. Interestingly, the 'Singles' were never rebuilt, though they served the NBR to 1910.

Now 1877 was imminent and, well aware that his own rapidly growing reputation was at stake, Drummond knew in his heart that the new 4-4-0s he had so ardently recommended would have to be good. In that context it says much for the perspicacity of the man that, in preparing their design, he allowed himself to be swayed by Wheatley's example, rather than by Stroudley's well known antipathy towards bogie engines. Yet, a touch of the old Drummond/Stroudley empathy still emerged when all four Neilson 4-4-0s, shopped in 1877, were found to bear local places names. But what names they were! —No.476 *Carlisle*, 477 *Edinburgh*, 478 *Melrose*, and 479 *Abbotsford*. Drummond's insistence on bestowing place names on his new 4-4-0s may have stirred considerable controversy at the time; but one thing could not be denied — the end product was a master stroke. Powerful and speedy, his quartet not only set completely new national standards, but were destined to dominate the British express passenger scene for twenty years to come. Neilson & Co. added four more, Nos.486–489, again appropriately named, in 1878, and soon Drummond's gallant 4-4-0s were handling heavy non-stop expresses between Edinburgh and Carlisle at an average speed of 42 mph. The railway world was duly impressed and Drummond's status as a locomotive engineer soared accordingly. Cowlairs Works capped NBR's triumph by shopping one last batch, Nos.490–493, in 1878, and all but two of the class found full employment on the Waverley Route. The odd men out, Nos.486/487, were placed, new, on Aberdeen–Burntisland express service, and remained so until the fall of the Tay Bridge in December 1879 obliged them to join the others.

Next, a poor reward for the Scottish Company's enterprise in forging a second link with the South, came an unexpected, and shattering, event — Dugald Drummond's resignation from NBR service on 27 July 1882. General supposition seems to have been that Drummond was lured to St. Rollox by the substantial £700 salary increase the Caledonian Railway offered him. Alas, other factors cannot be ignored. It is known now, for instance, that at that time an investigation was also being conducted into yet another unexplained financial discrepancy in Cowlairs accounts; and one fears that this fact, coupled with the

Drummond 4-4-0 No.488, formerly *Galashiels*, passes inordinately high signals as it leads an East Coast express off the southern end of the Forth Bridge. Several Holmes touches about the locomotive, and the fact that the great bridge was only opened on 4th March 1890, suggest that the photograph was taken in the mid-1890s. Note how Drummond's original 2¼in Ramsbottom safety valves have been replaced by 3 inch lock-ups. Observe, too, that coal rails have been added to the tender, and rectangular tallow cocks, once sited below the smokebox door, have been eliminated in favour of bulbous types at the side. Later rebuilt in more radical fashion, and renumbered 1362, the locomotive, one of five 'Abbotsfords' which failed to reach Grouping, was taken out of service in September 1921. *(Author's Collection)*

NBR's uncharacteristically terse acknowledgment in Company Minutes of Drummond's defection, throws a rather different light on the subject. Significantly, no warm official compliments were paid to the departed on this occasion, and NBR Minutes confined themselves to one bleak comment: 'The resignation of Mr. Drummond, Locomotive Superintendent, is reported'. What a sad ending it was to a moment of NBR triumph!

Drummond's speedily appointed successor at £750 a year, Matthew Holmes, a man of long experience in Edinburgh & Glasgow and North British Railway affairs, and, indeed, already acting as assistant to Drummond at Cowlairs, has been described as "every inch a gentleman". A gentle gifted soul, he certainly bade his time before tampering with the Drummond heritage. Interestingly, one of his first acts was to remove all locomotive names.

By the time Matthew Holmes gained command at Cowlairs, the NBR was, in fact, quite well off for express engines. The more immediate need was for versatile and more powerful goods engines; for NBR freight traffic was beginning to overtax Wheatley's aging veterans. So, rather more than a year after assuming office, Holmes obliged with twelve general purpose 0-6-0s. The 24 more which followed in 1884–87 were still not dissimilar to Drummond's 17in 0-6-0s; but they foretold quite clearly the shape of things to come. Gone was the Drummond tender, with its outside bearings, slotted frames, underhung springs, and toolbox. Ramsbottom safety valves, too, had been abandoned in favour of independent lock-up valves. Indeed, the last dozen took matters a stage further, by featuring the rounded Stirling-type cab which was to become such a hallmark of Holmes locomotive design. Rather surprisingly, NBR locomen took kindly to the round cab, and maintained that it was less draughty than Drummond's square cab.

All these features were present early in 1884 when Holmes, flexing his biceps, designed his first 4-4-0. Like his immediate predecessors, he opted for a coupled wheel diameter of 6ft 6in. But the scale of production was grander: thus, 48 highly service-able units were turned out from Cowlairs Works over the next fifteen years. Significantly, cylinder and boiler dimensions increased as each of three distinct series emerged.

The first six, numbered 574–579, and accordingly dubbed the '574' Class, were built during June/July 1884 for Edinburgh–Glasgow express work. A shade smaller than the 'Abbotsfords', their design was, nevertheless, clearly based on a 17 inch type which Drummond had anticipated, but never built. With 17in × 26in cylinders and a boiler pressure of 140psi, Holmes' new 43½ ton 4-4-0s offered a tractive effort of 11,464lb. Westinghouse brake was provided for both engine and

train, the brake cylinder was sited under the cab and pull rods, outside the driving wheels as before, applied brake blocks to the leading edge of both wheels.

The second series of 6ft 6in 4-4-0s, 24 engines built in three batches over the years 1890–1895, left Cowlairs with 18in × 26in cylinders and a slightly larger (4ft 6¼in) boiler. Wheelbase was also increased by one foot, and a new system was adopted of placing the brake cylinder between the coupled wheels, whence a central pull thrust the brake blocks *outwards*. The first twelve were built in 1890 for the purpose of handling traffic over the newly opened Forth Bridge. Six more were added in 1894–1895 and a final half-dozen. Nos.213–218, commissioned in 1895 specifically for Waverley Route express duties, carried the additional distinction of being the NBR's first dual-fitted locomotives. All 24 engines, meanwhile, were styled the '633' Class.

The third series arrived on the scene in 1898–99 under rather different circumstances. Their construction, in fact, was a direct repercussion of NBR management's action, on 30th April 1894, in terminating the existing 1862 working agreement whereby North Eastern Railway locomotives reserved the right to work all express passenger traffic between Edinburgh and Berwick. The gesture may well have stiffened NBR pride; but it had the additional effect of sparking off an eventual shortage of NBR express engines. Thus, Cowlairs Works was required, in 1898, to fill the gap by subscribing a final batch of eighteen Holmes 6ft 6in 4-4-0s. Known as the '729' Class, they retained the coupled wheelbase of the '633s'; but, once again, cylinder and boiler dimensions were stepped up, to 18¼in and 4ft 8⅛in respectively. Holmes had already equipped the '574' and '633' Classes with his own 2,500 gallon tender. Now, with the '729' Class he provided 3,500 gallon tenders, with a six ton coal capacity. A footstep ahead of the driving wheels also made its debut on the '729s', and was soon added to the earlier classes. Handrails, too, along the boiler were now made continuous, and the provision of steam sanding gear saw the sandbox banished below the running plate. With engine weight increased to 47¼ tons and a slightly larger boiler pitched five inches higher, the Class '729s' presented a much sturdier profile than that of the two earlier series. Their tractive effort, too, offered considerable improvement at 16,514lb. Built too late to participate in the 1895 Races, they nevertheless took a prominent part in the equally competitive East Coast running, until a new agreement restoring the North Eastern Railways's former rights was signed on 1st September 1904. After that, '729' shed allocations were widespread, and covered the length and breadth of Scotland, with Carlisle, Tweedmouth, and Blaydon thrown in for good measure.

The graceful lines of a Holmes 4-4-0 were never more apparent than in this study of No.218, one of the six Class '633s' which were built in 1895 for Edinburgh–Carlisle express work. Several features of the 'Abbotsford' design have been retained; notably, the smokebox wingplates and the combined sandbox and leading splasher. Rather surprisingly, though, Holmes chose to replace Dugald Drummond's rather roomy square cut cab by introducing an unashamed version of Patrick Stirling's classic 'cut away' shelter. Equally oddly, contemporary reports suggest that NBR enginemen actually preferred this 'more manly' arrangement! The handrails which terminate behind No.218's smokebox in this view were later made continuous, as in the '729s', the third series of Holmes 6ft 6in engines. No.218, rebuilt by W. P, Reid in February 1921, graduated as LNER No.9218 (Class D31) in September 1924, and was withdrawn in July 1937. (*Author's Collection*)

In the last analysis Holmes' 48 6ft 6in 4-4-0s, despite their detail differences, offered such an intriguing range of ability that the NBR was content to rebuild the lot. The process commenced in 1911, when all six Class '574' engines were dealt with by W. P. Reid. Two years later, the NBR introduced a new alphabetical scheme of locomotive classification and, in anticipation of further rebuilding, all 48 4-4-0s were grouped under the letter 'M'. Unfortunately, the eruption of World War One upset calculations, and further rebuilding had to be postponed until March 1918. In the event, Cowlairs contrived to rebuild another 24 to Reid specification by March 1921, and Chalmers, who succeeded Reid on 1st January 1920, rebuilt the last eighteen before Grouping descended on 1st January 1923. He chose to deviate from the Reid rebuilds by removing the traditional smokebox wingplates which many NBR men swore added strength and rigidity to the frame, and replaced Holmes' gently tapered chimney with a slightly shorter straight-sided one. He also fitted helical springs on bogie and driving wheels alike in place of Holmes' previous 'mix' of laminated and helical springs. In December 1927 the LNER classified the Reid rebuilds D31/1, and the Chalmers engines D31/2.

In the year 1886, Holmes possibly had one eye on Dugald Drummond's single-wheelers, which were still performing valiantly between Edinburgh and Glasgow, when he designed his first real express engines — a series of 7 foot 4-4-0s, numbered 592–597. Built at Cowlairs during the year commencing April 1886 in anticipation of the re-opening of the Tay Bridge — an event which duly materialised on 20th June 1887 — these handsome, fleet-footed engines were specifically designed to handle through working between Burntisland and Aberdeen. Cowlairs added six more, Nos.598–603 during February/March 1888. Then, once the mighty new Forth Bridge was formally opened on 4th June 1890, with No.602 given the honour of hauling the Prince of Wales' special train, express service between Aberdeen and Edinburgh/Glasgow became a reality. As a consequence of this important development in NBR fortunes such 'seven-footers' as had found a home at Burntisland shed were now transferred to Edinburgh (St. Margaret's).

The fourth class of Holmes 4-4-0 passenger engines to emerge from Cowlairs Works were a vastly different proposition: six 5ft 7in engines, got ready in time to tackle the 100 mile long, heavily graded West Highland Railway line which was due to open between Craigendoran and Fort William in the Autumn of 1894. Although the West Highland Railway was incorporated on 12th August 1889 as an ostensibly independent concern, its real function was to act as a North British counterthrust to a satellite of the Caledonian Railway, the Callander & Oban Railway. Accordingly, the West Highland was worked by the NBR from inception, and it came as no surprise that the parent Company later absorbed it on 21st December 1908. Meanwhile, faced in 1893 with the problem of designing a 4-4-0 express locomotive which could run at obligatory moderate speeds on 75lb rails as they curved and climbed all the way to Fort William, Holmes, this time, opted for 18in × 24in cylinders and a boiler pressure of 150psi. Engine weight was 43¼ tons and the much smaller driving wheels helped to produce a tractive effort of 14,798lb. Standard 2,500 gallon tenders, with two coal rails attached, gave a useful increased capacity of 6 tons. It is doubtful, though, whether Holmes' cut-away cab offered adequate shelter to NBR enginemen as they grappled with the notoriously fickle West Highland weather.

Whatever, the first six, Nos.693–698, shopped well ahead of schedule, were taken into NBR stock in January 1894. Six more were completed that year, and Cowlaires added a final batch of twelve in 1896. While traditional smokebox wingplates and gravity sanding were still the order of the day, Holmes did deviate from the norm on this occasion by installing lever reverse gear instead of his customary vertical screw arrangement. No longer, too, were sandboxes incorporated in the splashers. All 24

Class '729' No.731, rebuilt by Walter Chalmers in January 1922, was renumbered 9731 and 2064 by the LNER in October 1922 and July 1946 respectively. The locomotive entered BR stock in January 1948, but was withdrawn in August that year without having borne its allotted number, 62064. *(Author's Collection)*

were equipped with Westinghouse brake only — until Reid had ten of them dual-fitted in 1919. During their lifetime most of Holmes' new 4-4-0s, later classified 'N', worked at some time or other on the West Highland line; but other diverse duties were also found for the class on local and residential traffic around Glasgow, main line work to Perth and Dundee, even passenger pilot activity in the Galashiels locality. Despite this apparent versatility, however, the 'West Highland Bogies', as they were known, proved to be notably deficient in adhesion and the class never earned the high respect which was accorded to Holmes' other 4-4-0s. Sixteen were withdrawn over the years 1919–1922 and, with the exception of one rather strange rebuild in 1919, the remainder, classified LNER D35, vanished by November 1924.

Like many of its sister engines, No.695 reverted latterly to miscellaneous local duties; and it was shedded at Parkhead, Glasgow when a remarkable summons emanated from Cowlairs Works very early in 1919. Totally unrecognisable as the same locomotive when it re-emerged a month or two later, No.695 had, in fact, been subjected to a complete rebuild. It now bore a new 4ft 8in Robinson-superheated boiler and the smokebox was accordingly extended. Motion, frames and cab were also renewed, and with cylinders now stepped up to 19in × 26in, tractive effort rose to 19,648lb. Subsequent performance, alas, was still inferior to that of Reid's own superheated 4-4-0s and this explains why further investment was not made in rebuilding other West Highland Bogies'. Renumbered 9695 by the LNER in March 1924 and specially classified D36, the locomotive, having lost its smokebox wingplates in 1923, was given a saturated D31 boiler in May 1936. About that time its standard Holmes 2,500 gallon tender was also replaced by one of the 3,500 gallon variety.

Came 1902 and the next NBR 4-4-0s to receive attention were Drummond's 'Abbotsfords', beginning to show their age, but so soundly constructed that Holmes decided to offer them a new lease of life; he had, of course, already introduced minor modifications. Now a complete rebuild was planned. Tragically, only six had been dealt with at Cowlairs when Holmes, sadly afflicted with heart trouble, had to retire in May 1903. The poor chap, the NBR's longest serving Locomotive Superintendent, died two months later, aged 59. In a rather ominous evocation of earlier NBR staff relationships, his successor, William Paton Reid, although already serving as Holmes' second-in-command, was obliged to serve two six-month periods of probation ere his appointment as Locomotive Superintendent was finally confirmed on 2nd June 1904. He completed the 'Abbotsford' rebuilding process by July that year.

No.218, formerly '633' Class, was rebuilt by Reid in February 1921, and is seen here, complete with typical NBR headboard, heading a Galashields train past Craigentinny early in 1922. Smokebox wingplates still remain, as does the engine's original 2,500 gallon tender. The provision, however, of a new boiler, fluted coupling rods, a large new cab, and the transfer of the Company crest from splasher to cabside are all hallmarks of Cowlair's quite recent attention. Latterly the locomotive was classified D31/1 by the LNER. *(Author's Collection)*

Rather poignantly, Holmes' last and finest 4-4-0s, his 6ft 6in '317' Class, flowered posthumously. Twelve were ordered from Cowlairs Works on 17th March 1902, but only four had been placed in traffic by the time Holmes died in July 1903. The remainder entered service in September/October that year. Boiler diameter was similar to that of the '729' Class, but a longer barrel and the flat grate Holmes favoured permitted a greater coupled wheelbase. Cylinders were larger, at 19in, and piston valves were preferred to slide valves. The first half-dozen, Nos.317–322, despatched as new to Aberdeen, were equipped with Westinghouse brake only; but Nos.323–328 were dual-fitted. Known as 'First Degree' deluxe engines from their pre-1913 NBR classification, but subsequently classified 'K', these powerful, versatile 4-4-0s exercised their 19,434lb tractive effort in due course on every NBR main line; sometimes double-heading, other times taking charge of heavy long distance expresses. Contrary to traditional NBR practice, however, none were ever rebuilt.

NBR Class '729' No.739 lost its smokebox wingplates when it was rebuilt by Chalmers in September 1922. Seen here as LNER class D31/2, at Kittybrewster shed, No.9739 displays additional features it acquired after being transferred to the LNER's Great North of Scotland Section, for a second time, in September 1933. Inverurie shops have replaced the engine's tallow cups with a Detroit two-feed lubricator and, in accordance with customary GNSR practice, have added a second footstep ahead of the driving wheels. Sheet metal coal guards, also affixed at Inverurie, are higher than the coal rails themselves; though apparently this offered no increase in coal capacity. Originally a Cowlairs product of March 1898, No.9739 was renumbered 2063 in August 1946, and was withdrawn less than a year later. *(G. R. Griggs)*

The class, incidentally, also acquired unwonted notoriety one bitterly cold, snowbound evening in December 1906, when No.324, running tender-first, had the grave misfortune to collide with a stationary local train at Elliot Junction, just south of Arbroath. Ironically, the date, the 28th, was the 27th anniversary of the Tay Bridge Disaster. Whatever the speed at which No.324 was travelling created havoc amidst the prevailing weather conditions. Its fireman and 21 passengers in the local train lost their lives and driver George Gourlay survived, only to face subsequent public trial on grounds of culpable homicide. During somewhat muddle proceedings, suspicions were raised that Gourlay had been drinking; but many still think that the driver was unfortunate to receive a five month prison sentence. Whatever the true merits of the case, a stigma attached itself to Holmes' '317' Class 4-4-0s, and almost to the end of their days these fine locomotives were frequently referred to by some NBR men as the 'Gourlay engines'. Holmes memories could well have done without that.

Holmes' successor at Cowlairs, W. P. Reid (a distant relative of William Paton, the Edinburgh & Glasgow Railway's first Locomotive Superintendent), a man who devoted his entire working life to the NBR, has been rightly hailed as a major architect in modernising his Company's locomotive fleet. Yet, in truth, he was really forced into this position by intransigent management; for, basically intent on continuing Matthew Holmes' policy, he had hardly taken his seat at Cowlairs ere the NBR directorate began to hector him on the matter of providing larger and more powerful locomotives. Intense passenger service competition from the Caledonian Railway plus increased loading demands on the NBR had, it seemed, made the provision of new and heavier North British stock essential.

Entirely at the mercy of management — indeed, often subjected to near-humiliating treatment by his Board — Reid, invoking the assistance of the North British Locomotive Co.'s Hyde Park Works, offered a suitably imposing reply in July/August 1906 by shopping fourteen truly massive 'Atlantics'. Interestingly, not only did he elect to override Holmes' aversion to locomotive names, but many of the names chosen for Reid's new monsters, e.g. *Aberdonian, Bon Accord, Auld Reekie*, had a ring about them which lifted the hearts of NBR men. Then, reverting to domestic construction, Cowlairs Works followed up within months with twelve rugged, unnamed, 'Intermediate' 4-4-0s, eminently suitable for the NBR's burgeoning fast perishable traffic. From then on superheating, larger locomotives, bigger boilers, and shrewd rebuilding of older engines became part and parcel of contemporary

The last phase. Under LNER jurisdiction more than half of the D31s worked on the GNSR Section at some time or other. Originally NBR Class '729' No.768, this Chalmers rebuild of December 1921 received LNER number 9768 in June 1924. Then, renumbered 2076 in October 1946, the locomotive entered BR stock in July 1948 as No.62072. Stationed latterly at Bathgate, it was, however, obliged to give up its BR number in favour of a new Peppercorn 2-6-0, and was rechristened 62283 in June 1949. Proud possessor, at least, of a BR smokebox numberplate, and second surviving D31/2, it worked on until February 1951. *(Author's Collection)*

NBR locomotive practice. Reid's first 4-4-0s, meanwhile, Nos.882–893, out-shopped between October 1906 and January 1907, postulated a combination of 19in × 26in cylinders, 5ft 0in saturated boiler, a working pressure of 190psi, and 6ft 0in coupled wheels. The resultant punch which this gave the 'Intermediates' (21,053lb) enabled them to cope comfortably with express freight and passenger traffic as required. Initially, most were allocated to Eastfield shed, Glasgow, where they were the last class of NBR locomotive to have the well known Cowlairs Incline rope guide affixed to their leading bogies. The practice, of course, was discontinued once rope haulage was abandoned in November 1908. Two 'Intermediates' entered service at Berwick and one at Montrose, whence long distance express goods traffic occupied their respective energies. This gambit was so successful that several were soon transferred to St. Margaret's shed for similar duties. Ere long they became familiar sights at both Newcastle and Carlisle.

The undoubted success of the 'Intermediates' was enough to persuade Reid and his Locomotive Committee to initiate production of two very similar 4-4-0 types in 1909. The only perceptible changes were that large 4,235 gallon, 7 ton tenders were now fitted to all, thereby adding 6 tons to overall working weight. One of the two new classes employed 6ft 6in driving wheels, and was given 19in cylinders.

With 18in × 26in cylinders and 4ft 4in diameter boiler, Holmes' new '592' Class 4-4-0s weighed 45¼ tons. Initially all were fitted with Westinghouse brake only, but five of the class were additionally supplied with vacuum brake by 1908. Smokebox wingplates were retained even after the whole class was rebuilt in 1911, by which time too, a leading footstep had been added. Now classified 'N', the 7ft locomotives were employed on much more local duties later in NBR life; No.600, for instance, operating from Eastfield shed, had frequent occasion to visit St. Enoch Station, Glasgow on exchange traffic for the G&SWR Section of the LMSR. Duly rebuilt in May 1911, the engine lost its wingplates in September 1925, and was eventually withdrawn as No.9600 (LNER Class D25) in September 1928. (Author's Collection)

Middle:
This stately view of No.603, obtained at Fort William in 1923 illustrates the changes which overtook the '592s' once all twelve were rebuilt by Reid in 1911. The original engines were held in such high regard that new non-standard boilers were specially constructed for the occasion. Accordingly, the lock-up safety valves are now located above the firebox. The large side-windowed cab also favoured by Reid combines with Holmes' graceful tapered chimney to add a completely new perspective to the locomotive, while the deployment of air-sanding gear has ensured that sandboxes now lie beneath the running plate. Coupling rods, too, are fluted, the handrail along the boiler is continuous, clasp brakes now engage both sides of the driving wheels and combination ejectors have replaced the non-lifting type. All this was accomplished for an additional engine weight of one tone. Cab doors have also been added, but the original 2,500 gallon, four ton tender has been retained. Allocated to Fort William at Grouping, No.9603, by now LNER Class D25, later moved to Hawick shed, and was withdrawn from there in March 1928. (R. D. Stephen)

Lower right:
The prototype engine No.592, when new, was proudly exhibited at the Edinburgh International Exhibition from 6th May to 30th October 1886, and carried brass replicas of her exhibition medal right up to 1911, when she was rebuilt. Getting the locomotive from NBR territory at Newington Goods Yard to the Exhibition site at the Meadows presented something of a problem; and ultimately No.592 travelled both ways, *under its own steam*, on temporary track which was laid along Edinburgh streets — and was lifted again once the engine passed! Such spectacular progress must have occasioned pardonable pride in those NBR men who witnessed the Caledonian and Highland Railway exhibits being towed, rather more lamely, by traction engines along Lothian Road! Employed on Stirling–Edinburgh service after rebuilt in June 1911, the NBR locomotive received LNER No.9592 in January 1925, and is seen here, liveried in early LNER green, at Eastfield shed, Glasgow, where it found regular employment latterly as Cowlairs shunting pilot. Despite new ownership, its old square NBR class 'N' plate still enjoys pride of place below the cab rail — as, indeed, it continued to do until withdrawal came in September 1932. (Author's Collection)

This Works photograph of No.695, one of the first six 'West Highland Bogies' reminds us of the slender lines of the 4-4-0s which were expected to cope with harsh schedules on the West Highland line. Half a dozen Drummond 'Abbotsfords', rebuilt by Holmes and Reid in 1902 and 1904, had to stand in latterly for the erring '693s' up to immediate pre-World War One years. After that, Reid's 6ft 'Intermediate' 4-4-0s held the fort pending the introduction of his famous 'Glens'. *(Steamchest)*

Transferred to Eastfield shed in 1931 and employed subsequently on a variety of West Highland and Devon Valley duties, No.9695 amassed a quite remarkable total mileage of 1,695,688 before being withdrawn in May 1943. Even then, this interesting 'one off' veteran was used for a further nine months as a disabled locomotive in ARP exercises before it was finally scrapped in February 1944. It is seen here at Eastfield early in 1935. *(Author's Collection)*

One cannot help feeling that Holmes' handsome rebuild, in July 1902, of No.479, the once-famous *Abbotsford*, might even have met with Dugald Drummond's approval — except, possibly, for the Stirling-type cab. The engine's original boiler has been replaced by a 4ft 8¼in in type already being used by Holmes' '729' Class, and the diameter of the cylinders has been slightly increased to 18¼in. Sandboxes, now operated by compressed air, have been moved below the running plate, faceplate injectors have replaced the original non-lifting type and, for the nonce, plain coupling rods suffice. The classic Drummond tender, with its underhung springs, remains untouched, except for the additional of two coal rails.

Initially employed on light Waverley Route expresses, and later diverted to West Highland work, No.479 and her sister rebuilds were relegated from 1910 onwards to 'stopping passenger' duties in and around Central Scotland. Grouping found the class 'M' engine, since numbered 1324 on the NBR's Duplicate List, at Haymarket shed. Allotted LNER No.10324, and classified D27, as opposed to the Reid rebuilds, which were styled D28, the one time *Abbotsford*, withdrawn in December 1923, did not live long enough to carry either LNER number or livery. *(Author's Collection)*

When Neilson & Co. built No.487 (Works No.2385) in October 1878, the locomotive entered service bearing the name *Montrose*. Then, just over a year later when the collapse of the Tay Bridge ordained its transfer to Waverley Route duties, Stroudley/Drummond logic was applied, and No.487 was renamed *Waverley*, Rendered nameless by Holmes, it is seen here at Eastfield shed shortly after being rebuilt by Reid in July 1904. Alterations as in the Holmes rebuild have been duly reproduced; but provision of a large side-windowed cab has succeeded in adding a distinctly puissant element to the locomotive's appearance. Duplicated listed as No.1361 in December 1919 — and latterly one of seven 'Abbotsford' survivors at Grouping — the engine acquired running No.10361 and D28 classification under LNER auspices. One of the two last survivors, it went to the breakers in September 1926. *(Steamchest)*

Life for the seven 'Abbotsford' rebuilds which entered LNER stock was short. By the end of 1924 all three surviving Holmes rebuilds had vanished, and only two Reid rebuilds remained. Part of Haymarket shed's allocation, D28 Nos.10361 and 10387 both found employment handling stopping trains in and out of Edinburgh. Then, very late in the day, No.10361 broke loose from its Edinburgh environment to serve local passenger needs in the Glasgow area. This picture reminds us of the green livery which was borne by LNER passenger engines at that time. Fate dealt equably with the two veteran D28s — for No.10361 was condemned on 17th September 1926, and a similar sentence came No.10387's way three days later. *(Author's Collection)*

One of the '317s' shopped after Holmes' untimely death, No.323, dual-fitted to meet Midland Railway requirements, offers a dramatic set-piece at Waverley Station as it leaves on a 2.15pm express for Carlisle and the South. Always held in high regard by NB men, these 52 ton engines coped admirably with main line demands. Original working pressure was 200psi, though Reid later reduced this to 190psi. Their tenders, typically late-Holmes in pattern, had a useful capacity of 3,525 gallons, and held seven tons of coal. The really surprising innovation in Holmes' last design, however, was the large side-windowed cab he introduced. Shorn of its wingplates, somewhat unusually at St. Margaret's shed in May 1922, No.323 was duly designated LNER class D26, and allotted No.9323. So swift, alas, was the locomotive's withdrawal, that it was still carrying NBR livery when the end came in February 1923. *(Author's Collection)*

No.9325, seen here around 1924 passing Craigentinny on an Edinburgh–Galashields train, fared only marginally better than No.323. A Waverley Route engine practically all its life, it lost its smokebox wingplates at Grouping; but at least it had the consolation of receiving a smart new LNER green livery. One of six '317s' which ended their days working on Edinburgh–Airdrie–Glasgow service, No.9325 acquired a modicum of distinction by being the last D26 to be withdrawn — in July 1926.
(Author's Collection)

The 6ft 6in engines, later NBR Class 'J', were first in the field; and Nos.895–900 emerged from the North British Locomotive Co.'s Hyde Park Works (Works Nos.18856–61) in the Autumn of 1909. Boiler pressure was 190psi, tractive effort 18,434lb, and their large tenders eminently suited their early mission in life — that of handling express trains, non-stop and otherwise, between Edinburgh and Carlisle. In an inspired stroke of imagination they were given names from the writings of Sir Walter Scott and, as this policy was pursued when ten more were later turned out by Cowlairs, the nickname 'Scotts' soon attached itself to these fine engines. For a brief period in 1911 one of the original batch, No.897 Redgauntlet, ran with a Phoenix smokebox superheater. Results, however, were unsatisfactory, and the locomotive soon reverted to its original saturated condition. By that time 'Scotts' were also being freely employed on major Edinburgh trains to Perth, Aberdeen and Glasgow.

While the NB Locomotive Co. was engaged in building the NBR's six 'Scotts', Cowlairs Works occupied itself with the construction of twelve new Reid 6ft 4-4-0s. Duly shopped between October 1909 and February 1910, unnamed, and inevitably styled 'Intermediates' again, these new additions to NBR stock were basically a mixed-traffic version of the 'Scotts'. Apart from the reduced diameter of the driving wheels, the only other differences were a boiler pressure of 180psi and an enhanced tractive effort of 19,800lb. These new 'Intermediates', later also NBR Class 'K', soon found employment on duties similar to those already being handled by their slightly older sisters; though they were distributed rather more widely throughout the NBR system. As before, they handled goods and passenger traffic with equal expedition.

An interesting diversion occurred in 1910, when No.867 of the ilk, under test, more than held its own against Highland Railway 4-6-0 Skibo Castle. Such heartening results convinced the NBR Board that the Company's 4-4-0 policy was well worth pursuing. Latterly, under LNER auspices, all twelve D33s were superheated between 1925 and 1936; thrifty Scots policy having first ensured that each original saturated boiler was thoroughly worn out! Repaint also saw the whole class running in LNER green livery. The glory, however, was short-lived — for the economies of 1928 soon reduced them to black secondary passenger livery.; Renumbered 2455–2466 in 1946, ten of the class reached BR ownership two years later; but only one, No.62464, managed to hold out for any reasonable time — and then only to September 1953.

Also in 1910, the NBR Board, never one to rush headlong into new locomotive construction, opted to examine more closely the merits of the four-coupled type which, it had firmly resolved, were best suited to meet the demands of the Company's winding and heavily graded main lines. Accordingly, a 'Scott' and an 'Intermediate' were duly matched, between April and June, in exhaustive trials between Edinburgh and Perth. A close study of the results produced authorisation to build six more 'Scotts'. The NB Locomotive Co. was again approached on the matter, but fought shy of the stipulated price of £3,000 per engine — whereupon the task was passed, more in hope than sorrow, to Cowlairs Works. Rising handsomely to the occasion, the latter not only shopped the requisite six 'Scotts' between September and November 1911, but added four more the following month for good measure! Variously numbered, the Cowlairs engines again carried glorious Sir Walter Scott names. Specification was, of course, as before. So, too, was their eventual evolution, under LNER auspices, towards superheating and removal of the Westinghouse brake. In 1914 No.359 Dirk Hatteraick was fitted with a Weir feed water heater and pump, but the apparatus was removed five years later.

In February 1911, after careful reflection on the potential benefits of superheating, NBR Directors decided that two more engines of the 'Scott' class, presently being constructed at Cowlairs, should be fitted with Schmidt superheaters. It was a bold decision — but one the NBR had no cause to regret; for, equipped with 20in × 26in cylinders, and with their superheated boilers pitched, of necessity, a few inches higher than previously, the new 'Scotts', Nos.363 and 400, turned out in the latter half of 1912, truly epitomised a final superb development of Drummond's 6ft 6in 'Abbotsford' 4-4-0s. Relative engine weight had only increased by 29%, to 57¼ tons, but tractive effort had been stepped by 35%.

Having sampled Schmidt and Phoenix superheaters, the NBR directorate then elected, in 1912, to enter into agreement with the Superheater Corporation Ltd. to employ Robinson superheaters in future. Thus, confident orders were issued to Cowlairs Works for the construction of fifteen more 'Scotts' and ten additional 'Superheated Intermediates'. Yet there must have been some lingering doubts, for five of the latter were shopped in September/October 1913 bearing Schmidt superheaters, while the other five followed up in December with Robinson equipment. A final development of the Reid 6ft 0in 4-4-0, these 'K' class engines were given the names of Scottish Glens. Popular, efficient, and versatile, they were classified D34 by the

Photographed in its prime, c.1923, 'Intermediate' No.885 displays a rather unusual type of NBR headboard as it prepares to leave Leuchars Junction on its circuitous journey to Scotland's capital city. Her elegant smokebox wingplates, such a characteristic feature of early Scottish locomotive construction, were removed shortly after Grouping, and the 1913 NBR classification 'L' had already been altered to 'K' in 1917. Known as LNER class D32/1 until November 1923, when it was superheated and thus graduated as class D32/2, the dual-fitted locomotive lost its clasp brakes during 1935–1936, when Westinghouse gear was removed by the LNER from the whole class in favour of steam brake on engine and tender, working in conjunction with vacuum train brake. Ten years later, No.9885 was given its second LNER number, 2446. Although the locomotive was subsequently allotted BR No.62446, it finished its days at Thornton, in September 1948, still carrying its LNER identity. The last of the class vanished in March 1951. (*S. Everard/Steamchest*)

On this occasion No.899 *Jeanie Deans* was captured near Thornton at the head of an Edinburgh–Dundee train. A sparkling NB Locomotive Co. product, the locomotive was renumbered 9899 by the LNER in October 1924, and, again, 2404 in June 1946. In January 1947 it became an innocent victim of 'dual' identity, when Cowlairs inadvertently painted the name *Jeanie Deans* on locomotive No.2403, *Sir Walter Scott*! Happily, the mistake was rectified after a few weeks. Meanwhile, the true proprietor of the name was given a shorter chimney in March 1947, and retained it until withdrawal came in August 1949. (*Author's Collection*)

Seen here heading a Dundee train at Leuchars Junction in the early 1920s, No.385 was the last-built of Reid's second batch of 'Intermediates'. Later classified LNER D33, all twelve were converted to steam and vacuum brake in the mid-1930s, at which time they also lost their clasp brakes. No.385, allotted LNER No.9385 in 1924, superheated in November 1935, and renumbered 2466 in 1946, was eventually withdrawn as BR No.62466 in October 1951. (*S. Everard/Steamchest*)

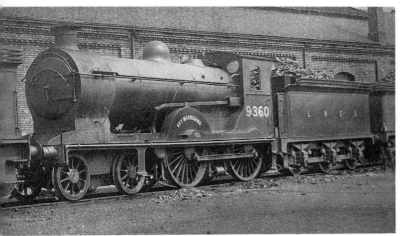

No.9360 *Guy Mannering*, a Cowlairs veteran of December 1911, seen here in LNER unlined black livery, illustrates the ultimate post-Grouping D29 appearance. The extra handrail in front of the smokebox was fitted when the locomotive was superheated in October 1930, smokebox wingplates having already vanished. Five years later the steam brake took over from Westinghouse and subsequent developments saw the vacuum standpipe repositioned centrally above the front buffer beam. Occupied on sundry local duties after World War Two, the engine was renumbered 2413 in June 1946. Life, alas, under British Railways was all too short. The advent of B1 4-6-0s in Scotland hastened the end as far as the D29s were concerned, and No.62413's final call came in August 1950. *(Author's Collection)*

No.340 *Lady of Avenel*, another 1911 Cowlairs product, was probably the most engaging of the species. In November 1925, when the locomotive was converted to Robinson superheating, opportunity was also taken to fit a Detroit four-feed lubricator. Fifteen years later her smokebox was extended by 6¾ inches in an effort to prevent smokebox door burning. Though No.9340 retained the extension until the end of her days, the experiment was not repeated on other members of the class. The single snifting valve behind the chimney was a legacy from 1942–44, when the LNER altered the previous D29 arrangement of two small valves. The locomotive, seen here at Polmont in June 1948, had been renumbered 2411 two years earlier. *(Author)*

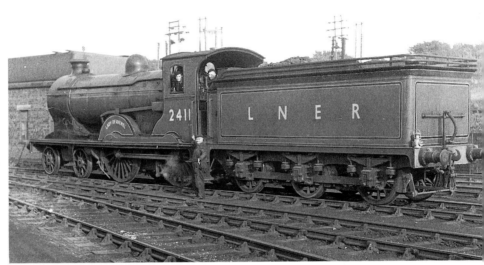

LNER, but remained affectionately known as the 'Glens' right to the end of their BR days. Thanks to the intervention of World War One, other batches were not turned out from Cowlairs until 1917–1920, but, ultimately, the class totalled 32 engines.

Next in the field came the new 'Scotts'. Duly shopped by Cowlairs between April and October 1914, Nos.409–423 carried Robinson superheaters to a man and, inevitably, introduced a rousing new batch of Sir Walter Scott names. But, as with the two earlier experimentally-fitted 'Scotts', 6ft 6in driving wheels were still employed. So, too, were 20in × 26in cylinders; though piston valves were increased in diameter from 8in to 10in. Boiler pressure remained at 165psi, as did tractive effort at 18,700lb, and 4,235 gallon tenders were again supplied. All were dual-fitted, and, despite an early post-Grouping proposal to replace the Westinghouse with steam brake, no change, in fact, was made until 1935–37.

Came 1915, and, despite the onset of a war which many innocents believed would finish by Christmas 1914, five more Robinson-superheated 'Scotts', Nos.424–28, were added by Cowlairs. These engines, and a later 1920 batch, carried rather more robustly built tenders which weighed 13 cwt heavier, at 46¾ tons. Though introduced too late to participate in non-stop Waverley Route workings, the NBR's gallant new Class 'Js' (later styled D30/2) were to handle express work expeditiously on all the Company's main lines for decades to come. On Glasgow-Edinburgh work, in particular, the ability of the superheated 'Scotts' to climb like deer up the 1:42 Cowlairs Incline with loads bordering on 370 tons endeared them greatly to the hearts of NBR men. Banking engines were, of course, provided.

The *pièce de résistance*, however, arrived in September 1947, when *Lady of Avenel* became the only ex-NBR passenger engine in post-war years to be allowed to revert to LNER green livery. Though renumbered 62411 by BR less than a year later, the 'Scott', seen here at Perth on 15th April 1949, was still wearing her green LNER mantle when the breakers summoned her in November 1952. *(Author)*

The year is 1926, and No.9400 *The Dougal Cratue*, the first of the superheated 'Scotts', heads for Edinburgh (Waverley) with its Carlisle express. Note how the NBR cab spectacles, formerly round, have been redesigned to accommodate the higher-pitched superheated boiler; and that although the locomotive is clad in LNER green, it still carries the slightly narrower dome which betokened possession of the Schmidt apparatus. For that reason, both Nos.9400 and 9363 were styled Class D30/1 by the LNER. Change, however, was imminent, for 9400 duly received a Robinson superheated boiler in August 1927. Tentatively allotted a new LNER number, 2416, in 1945, No.9400 never carried it — for, the first of the superheated 'Scotts' to be withdrawn, it was taken out of service in June that year. *(Author's Collection)*

Caught passing Craigentinny on 28th August 1926, No.9405 *Glen Spean*, now LNER Class D34, bore a Schmidt superheater when it left Cowlairs Works in December 1913. It was also equipped with hand-operated superheater dampers, but these were soon discarded. The smokebox door handrail is a legacy of Grouping. Renumbered 2473 in 1946, *Glen Spean* was duly allotted No.62473 by BR. Unfortunately, scrapped in May 1949, the locomotive never bore BR insignia. *(Author's Collection)*

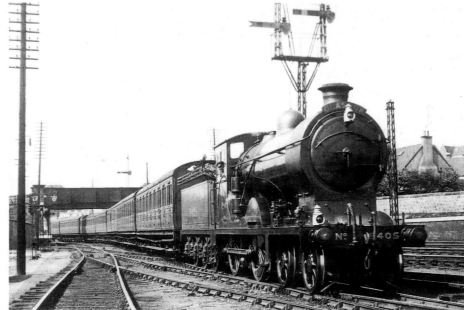

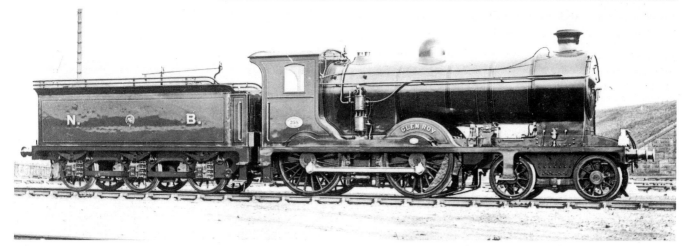

Conversely, No.258 *Glen Roy*, one of the first five to be fitted with the Robinson superheater, looks resplendent in fresh NBR livery as it poses at Eastfield shed. Smokebox wingplates are still intact, and, as yet, exhaust from the Westinghouse pump is conducted above the handrail towards the smokebox. The thin pipe looping gracefully behind the chimney was used to deliver steam to an early form of NBR ash ejector, which consisted of a 5ft 4in long two inch pipe arranged vertically within the smokebox. During 1933–34 No.9258 and sixteen other 'Glens' were fitted with drop grates and, a little later, steam brake gear replaced the Westinghouse variety. Renumbered 2470 in 1946, and 62470 in 1948, the engine latterly found a home at Perth, and worked in that vicinity until withdrawal came in May 1959. *(Author's Collection)*

The war years and their immediate aftermath were troubled ones for UK railway companies in general. Although the Government had agreed not to recruit railwaymen, thousands of men eluded this sanction by resigning from railway employment before they volunteered for the Services. It follows that heavy traffic demands and acute wartime shortages placed an additional burden on those who were left behind. Yet, despite these grave handicaps, the NBR, with noteworthy assistance from the NB Locomotive Co.'s Atlas Works, contrived to place 129 new engines in stock during the years 1915–1920. 32 of these were 4-4-0 locomotives.

The five 'Scotts' subscribed in 1915 have already been described; and one needs only add that a final batch of five, Nos.497–501, was added by Cowlairs in November/December 1920. The class now totalled 27 and except for three, withdrawn between 1945 and 1951, they worked on in LNER and BR harness well into the late 1950s. The last two, *Laird o'Monkbarns* and *Cuddie Headrigg*, both 1914 products, were not withdrawn until June 1960.

Meanwhile, the ten 6ft 'Glens', which had emerged from Cowlairs in 1913, were also making a name for themselves as NBR 'maids of all work'. Their 22,100lb tractive effort pinpointed them as particularly suitable candidates for West Highland work and now that the superheater problem had been resolved in favour of Robinson, the Company was anxious to add to their ranks. Thus, in 1917 Cowlairs built five more, then repeated the exercise in 1919. In all, 20 'Glens' were now in circulation.

In the event, W. P. Reid reached retirement age on 31st December 1919. Walter Chalmers, his chief draughtsman, succeeded him in office, with a new title of Chief Mechanical Engineer, and between April and September 1920 a final batch of twelve 'Glens' emerged from Cowlairs. Later that year came the five 'Scotts', the last 4-4-0s to be built by the NBR. The 32 'Glens', meanwhile, continued to render yeoman service wherever they were required to work on the NB system. Significantly, no fewer than 24 of them started their working lives at Eastfield shed. But they did wander. At Grouping St. Margaret's shed had eight, Thornton four and Dundee one, while the remaining nineteen were, as one might expect, stationed at Eastfield. In 1953, however, eight were despatched to BR's GNS Section in replacement for elderly GNSR 4-4-0s which had been withdrawn.

A typical scene in pre-Grouping days as a double-headed Glasgow express leaves Fort William with No.256 *Glen Douglas*, a 1913 Cowlairs stalwart, fortunately still with us, leading. Curiously, in NBR practice the pilot engine was usually placed next to the train. The maximum load for a 'Glen' between Glasgow and Fort William was set by the NBR at 190 tons, and a second 'Glen' was cheerfully hitched on as and when required. No six-coupled locomotive ever coped more doughtily with the gradients and curves of the West Highland line; yet the 'Glens' were remarkably light on maintenance. *(Author's Collection)*

No.411 *Dominie Sampson*, a 1914 Cowlairs product, was still carrying NBR livery when it was photographed at Haymarket shed on 10th September 1924. There have been changes, however. The 'pepper pot' anti-vacuum valve, formerly fixed direct on to the smokebox waist of the D30/1s, is now inverted and much more prominent; smokebox wingplates have already gone. The pyrometer 'stump', high on the smokebox, was removed immediately after Grouping and the Westinghouse exhaust outlet, seen here terminating in the upper part of the smokebox, was later lowered. No.9411 moved from Eastfield shed to Haymarket in the 1930s and, like the others, continued to deal cheerfully with whatever traffic came its way. Waverley Station, at times, was a veritable beehive of these high-spirited locomotives and, even in BR days, only one superheated 'Scott' bowed the knee before 1957. *Dominie Sampson*, as it happened, was withdrawn in May that year. *(Author's Collection)*

Cowlairs, July 1958; and No.62440 *Wandering Willie*, built there as NBR No.499 in November 1920, has come to the end of a long road. The locomotive has seen a few changes in its day. The handrail in front of the smokebox was a standard fitting on all 'Scotts' built after 1914 but removal of wingplates, including No.499's, did not commence until just before Grouping. Next, in August 1935, 9499 lost its Westinghouse brake and gravity sanding also took over. Gone, too, is the original NBR boiler — witness the two LNER Ross pops in their rectangular casing above the firebox. An Eastfield engine at Grouping, the locomotive was transferred to Hawick in the mid-1930s; and there, handling Newcastle and Edinburgh trains as to the manner born. *Wandering Willie* finished its working days. Hawick must have been a popular last post for 'Scotts' — for six others shared the same fate. *(Steamchest)*

In November 1961 the scrapping of No.62496 *Glen Loy*, the last serving D34, appeared to mark the end of NBR 4-4-0s. Mercifully, however, *Glen Douglas*, one of the original 1913 batch, had already been taken in hand by Cowlairs Works and the locomotive reappeared in August 1959, clad in NBR livery. Though not fully restored, No.256 was rendered capable of working special trains, along with other preserved Scottish engines, as required. Then, finally taken out of traffic in 1965, *Glen Douglas* found a permanent resting place in the Glasgow Museum of Transport.

And there, once more in the company of other Scottish railway veterans, she remains today: a proud symbol, to young and old alike, of halcyon days on the old North British Railway.

'I have served thee well. Farewell'. No.62495 *Glen Luss* a Cowlairs product of July 1920, might well be speaking for Scottish 4-4-0s in general as she completes one last trip from Bathgate to Glasgow before being withdrawn in April 1961. Note how the classification, D34, and the shed location have been painted on the front buffer beam in late LNER tradition. Rather remarkably, this widely travelled 'Glen' was spotted at York on 1st January 1940. *(Steamchest)*

Chapter 3
THE CALEDONIAN RAILWAY

IT IS A STRANGE IRONY of railway history that the Caledonian Railway, ultimately the most aggressively nationalistic of all the Scottish Companies, really owed its inception, on 31st July 1845, to powerful English interests who were backing what seemed to them to be the only feasible railway passage between England and Scotland i.e. that between Carlisle, Beattock, and Glasgow. Ignoring the North British Railway's contemporary bid to open up an East Coast route via Berwick, these same English interests, in supporting an Annandale project as opposed to a Glasgow camp's insistence that CR metals should find their way North via Nithsdale, rather complacently assumed that a link from Carstairs to Edinburgh would be sufficient to meet the requirements of Scotland's capital city. Both parties to what turned out to be a prolonged dispute won their point in the long run — but it was the Annandale route, with its formidable ten mile ascent between Beattock and Elvanfoot, which fell to the CR's lot. Ergo, the line from Beattock to Carlisle opened at 6.30 on the morning of Friday, 10th September 1847 and within six months connection from Carlisle with both Glasgow and Edinburgh became a reality. Calmly annexing the Scottish Royal coat of arms and motto, *Nemo. me impune lacessit,* for its own decorative use, the Caledonian Railway further emphasised its apparent Scottish ascendancy by styling itself 'The National Line'. Later, as its English running partner, the London & North Western Railway, took unto itself the sobriquet 'The Premier Line', the Caley, still shunning inhibition, advertised itself additionally as 'The True Line'. Company pride was important in those days!

The Caledonian Railway's first foothold in Glasgow was obtained at Glebe Street; then a new terminus was opened at Buchanan Street on 12th August 1849 and traffic for both North and South was handled there — until 1879, when English traffic was routed to a new station, known as Central. In 1890 and 1906 the provision of additional approach lines and a correspondingly substantial bridge across the River Clyde firmly established Central as the CR's major Glasgow station. An equivalent Edinburgh terminus, situated at the west end of Princes Street, eventually opened in 1894. But, by and large, Edinburgh remained a North British stronghold, and Glasgow persisted as the focus of CR attentions. Access to Aberdeen, fair game for both Scottish railway rivals, was pursued with unremitting zeal right up to Grouping in 1923. The CR appeared to score heavily when it absorbed the Scottish Central and the Scottish North Eastern Railways in 1865 and 1866 respectively. The NBR on the other hand, registered a bull's eye in August 1865 by gaining control of the Edinburgh & Glasgow Railway. And so the battle went on. Even later, when the NBR stole another strategic march by opening the Forth Bridge in 1890, NB access to Aberdeen still hinged on a final approach from Kinnaber Junction, using running powers over 38 miles of Caledonian Railway metals.

Strangely, for a Scottish Company, locomotive development on the Caledonian Railway — certainly up to the time of Dugald Drummond's accession in 1882 — was critically influenced by that of the Grand Junction Railway, itself a major constituent of the London & North Western Railway. Key figures here were W. B. Buddicom, Alexander Allan, and Robert Sinclair; and it was the latter, already acting as Locomotive Superintendent to the Glasgow, Paisley & Greenock Railway from 1844, who brought southern habits to the Caledonian, when he officially graduated as the CR's Locomotive Superintendent on 16th June 1849. At that time the CR's main locomotive Works were sited at Greenock. A popular leader, Sinclair also laid plans for new, and more spacious Works at St. Rollox. Just as the new Works were being prepared for occupation, however, Sinclair left CR service, at the end of 1856, to take up a similar post with the Eastern Counties Railway. His successor on the Caledonian, Benjamin Conner, appointed on 1st January 1857, duly reaped the benefit of brand new Works at St. Rollox.

Conner, previously Works manager at Neilson & Mitchell's Hyde Park Works, carried on the 'Crewe' tradition. Inclined outside-cylinders, flared smokebox, raised firebox with dome on top, underslung leading springs, slotted splashers — all remained familiar elements in early CR locomotive practice. Also a keen advocate of the use of steel, Conner even developed the 'Crewe' design far beyond that practised by its originators, by introducing horizontal-cylindered 2-2-2s in 1859. Their 8ft 2in driving wheels were the largest ever employed on British standard-gauge metals. A series of 'Crewe' type 0-6-0s, introduced in 1849 for goods traffic, had found little favour with CR management; but the success of Conner's outside-cylindered 'Improved Goods' of 1874 finally convinced the CR that six-coupled engines had a role to play in handling mineral traffic.

Meanwhile, Conner's 8ft 2in single-wheelers, beautifully liveried in Caledonian blue, were lording it on main line express work. Twelve of these handsome engines, Nos.76–87, had been shopped by St. Rollox Works during the years 1859–1865, and, though rebuilt latterly, most served well into the 1890s. Their six-wheeled tenders held 2,016 gallons of water and 3½ tons of coal.

Before long, a batch of sixteen 7ft 2in Conner 2-4-0s — ten built at St. Rollox and six subscribed by Neilson & Co., all in the years 1867–1868 — were found to be working so successfully alongside the single-wheelers that twelve more were commissioned from Neilson & Co. in 1872. For goods and less important passenger work, 2-4-0s and outside-cylindered 0-4-2s (a peculiarly popular Scottish type), all firmly based on the 'Crewe' tradition, still commanded the CR's confidence.

Unfortunately for Conner, the last five years of his tenure of office were plagued by poor health. As a consequence, his chief assistant, George Brittain, acquired valuable interim experience which was to stand him in good stead when, immediately after Conner's death, he became the CR's new Locomotive Superintendent as from 27th February 1876. Under Brittain's management new CR locomotive building policy soon abandoned both 'Crewe' front-end styling and wheel arrangements. Outside-cylinders remained; but Nos.125–129, five Neilson-built 7ft 2in 4-4-0s which emerged in 1877, clearly pointed a

This view of No.87, a St. Rollox product of 1865, illustrates how the high wheel centres of his 8ft 2in single-wheelers enabled Conner to employ horizontal cylinders. Rebuilt in 1872 and duplicate listed in 1889, No.87A was eventually withdrawn in June 1894. *(Author's Collection)*

CR 2-4-0 No.118, formerly No.467 (Neilson & Co. Works No.1383/1868), is still undeniably a Conner locomotive; but a rebuild by Drummond in 1882 has introduced many signs of things to come. Splashers have been closed, the chimney is now capped, and the dome, set further back, carries Ramsbottom safety valves. Given Duplicate No.1119 in 1912, the locomotive ran until 1915. *(Author's Collection)*

George Brittain's only 4-4-0 class, known latterly as the 'Dundee Bogies', were underboilered, and proved unsuitable for use on the main line for Carlisle. Dugald Drummond reboilered all five locomotives, but they were relegated, nevertheless, to working Dundee trains. No.127, built by Neilson & Co. in 1877 (Works No.2128), was the first to be withdrawn of these comparatively short-lived engines and was taken out of service in March 1905. *(Author's Collection)*

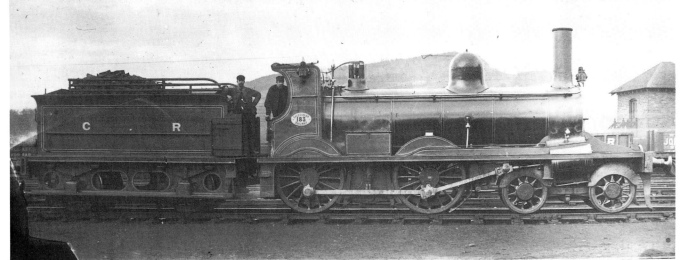

No.183, a typical 'Oban Bogie', was shopped in 1882 (Dübs & Co. Works No.1676) with cylinder dimensions of 18in × 24in, and a combination of 4ft 3in boiler and 130psi working pressure yielded a tractive effort of 13,858lb. Engine weight was perforce limited to 41 tons 11¾ cwts, and although turntable limitations also obliged Brittain to confine himself to a four-wheeler tender, the latter, weighing 24 tons, still offered a capacity of four tons of coal and 1,550 gallons of water.
(Author's Collection)

When J. F. McIntosh rebuilt all ten 'Oban Bogies' at the turn of the century he was wise enough to leave the high-sided tenders severely alone. By 1902, however, increasingly heavy loads on the Oban line obliged him to introduce replacement 4-6-0s. Seen here at Oban as LMS Class 1P, No.14103, formerly CR Nos.182/1182, was ultimately withdrawn in 1930.
(Author's Collection)

new way ahead. There was, in fact, an element of mystery about their creation; for Conner's original design postulated a 2-4-0. None the less, probably due to the fact that Brittain, in Conner's absence, influenced response to Neilson enquiries, they were duly shopped — as 4-4-0s! The pity was that the new 4-4-0s, when set against the 'Singles' on Anglo-Scottish traffic, proved to be such poor steamers that they had to be relegated to working Dundee trains. Known subsequently as the 'Dundee Bogies', all six, even when reboilered by Dugald Drummond, were still found to be unsuitable for Carlisle trains, and were withdrawn in the early 1910s.

Meanwhile, Brittain had other problems to face. Confronted, as 1880 dawned, with the difficult challenge of working the Callendar & Oban Railway's new line, which was due to open on 1st July that year, he commissioned fifteen 2-4-2Ts from Neilson & Co. Based on the LNWR's 'Radial Tanks', but uncharacteristically plagued by derailments, they soon proved, alas, to be unsuited to the steeply graded Oban metals. Fortunately, Brittain was far from being discouraged. He promptly designed a suitable 4-4-0 tender locomotive; and, known latterly as the 'Oban Bogies', ten of these excellent 5ft 2in engines were speedily supplied by Dübs & Co. On this occasion their steeply inclined outside-cylinders were, in fact, quite deceptive; for the cylinders were secured to the inside frame only — thus marking a clear departure from the CR's traditional front-end format. Close contemporaries in more ways than one with David Jones' celebrated Highland Railway 'Skye Bogies' (qv), Brittain's new 4-4-0s, met with immediate success.

By a cruel stroke of fate, Brittain's career on the Caledonian Railway was, like that of his predecessor, terminated by ill health. He had to quit office in April 1882, and, on 20th June that year, five months before Brittain submitted his formal notice of retirement, Dugald Drummond's anticipated appointment as Locomotive Superintendent was confirmed by the CR Board. His vastly enhanced salary of £1,700 per annum, twice that of Brittain's, was an accurate reflection of CR management's awareness that its locomotive stock was falling short of current requirements. After Drummond's resounding success in North British Railway harness, here, they felt, was the man who would life the 'True Line' out of the doldrums.

Drummond did not disappoint his new masters. Pausing only to reboiler quite a number of Conner's twenty-year old 6ft 2in mixed traffic 2-4-0s — thereby rendering them useful adjuncts on Carlisle–Glasgow express work — he next introduced his ubiquitous 'Jumbo' 0-6-0s. Their 18in × 26in cylinders, 150psi pressure and 5ft coupled wheels gave these astonishing engines a punch and utility value which saw their complete eventual complement of 244 safely into LMS hands, and took them decades beyond that. Typical of the man, Drummond also pronounced an unequivocal preference for the Westinghouse brake — and carried his Board with him. Again typically, he set about modernising St. Rollox Works, and lavished Royal blue livery impartially on all CR locomotives.

Then came his main line express 4-4-0s: Nos.66–75, delivered in 1884 by Neilson & Co. at a cost of £2,900 each. Basically an improved version of his NBR 'Abbotsfords',

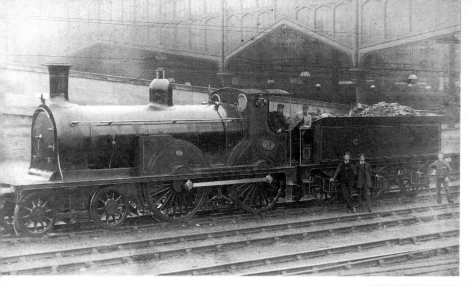

It is 2.50pm at Carlisle (Citadel) Station, as No.60, the first of the St. Rollox-built Drummond 4-4-0s, waits, surrounded by proud CR men, for its LNWR 'connection'. Note the white CR train indicator (the 'bow tie') placed ahead of the chimney, announcing to all and sundry that the locomotive will be proceeding on main line work to Glasgow via Motherwell. In course of a somewhat chequered career, No.60 was given a larger boiler in 1901, duplicate listed as No.1060 in 1916, then restored to capital stock as No.17 that same year. It received new cylinders and frames in 1917 and entered LMS stock five years later. But, withdrawn in October 1929, the locomotive never carried its allotted LMS number, 14303. *(Author's Collection)*

Drummond's new engines contrived to create an even greater sensation in the railway world. 6ft 6in coupled wheels, 18in × 26in cylinders and 150psi working pressure were all familiar ingredients by now; but Drummond's determined methods of extracting maximum advantage from steam within the cylinders produced a classic model for future CR express locomotive development. St. Rollox Works celebrated by building six more themselves during the year 1885. They bore Nos.60–65.

The Edinburgh International Exhibition of 1886 was something neither Drummond nor a vastly encouraged CR directorate could resist. Accordingly, two very special locomotives were ordered — for 'Exhibition purposes'. They cost £2,600 each. The first was the CR's immortal 7ft single wheeler, No.123. Happily, it remains with us today as a superb example of Neilson & Co.'s craftsmanship. The other was No.124, a Dübs-built 4-4-0 which, although based largely on the CR's successful '66' Class, embodied some interesting modifications. Cylinder diameter, for instance, was stepped up to 19in, a Scottish-patented Bryce-Douglas valve gear took the place of the conventional Stephenson variety and reverse gear was changed from lever to vertical screw. An increase of 1½in in the pitch of the boiler also meant that the chimney had to be shortened. Suffice it to say that the CR's enterprise was duly rewarded, and both locomotives earned a Gold Medal. In December 1887, No.124 was rebuilt with Stephenson link motion, and reverted to 18in × 26in cylinders. Named *Eglinton* in 1890 and given Duplicate List No.1124 in 1916, the 'one-off' 4-4-0 earned its keep on general service right up to withdrawal in 1925, though it never bore its allotted LMS number, 14296.

Came 1888 and Drummond turned his attention to the long standing feud which existed between the CR and the Glasgow & South Western Railway for Clyde steamer traffic. As things stood, Smellie's 'Wee Bogies' (qv), introduced in 1882–85, had given the Sou' West something of an edge in the race from Glasgow to Greenock. It follows that Drummond pleased his Board immensely when he provided a CR riposte by designing a smaller version of the Class '66' 4-4-0s. Known initially as the 'Coast Bogies', six of these 5ft 9in engines were turned out from St. Rollox Works early in 1888. Once again, standard 18in × 26in cylinders were employed. Boiler diameter and total heating surface were, however, both marginally reduced.

Once the CR's Greenock services were extended to Gourock in 1889, Drummond's 43½ ton 'flyers' really took advantage of the fact that the Caledonian route from Glasgow to the coast was much easier than that faced by its G&SWR rivals. Eventually, with three Scottish companies, the CR, NBR, and G&SWR all deploying steamer fleets in the Firth of Clyde, competition became so intense that the CR resorted to allowing passengers *only two minutes* at Gourock Pier to transport themselves

Seen rather late in life, after rebuild in 1903, duplicate listing in 1920, and still clinging to its smokebox wing plates, 'Gourock Bogie' No.1081 looks, even now, as fleet as the day she emerged from St. Rollox Works in February 1888. Nearly, but never quite, renumbered LMS 14109, No.1081 outlived many of its sisters by lasting to 1930. *(Author's Collection)*

from train to ship. It follows that a complete embargo on passenger luggage on its Clyde boat expresses became a matter of necessity, rather than one for apology!

By now Dugald Drummond was really getting into his stride at St. Rollox and construction there, in 1889, of six more Class '66' engines, Nos.76–79, 84, and 87, prefaced a series of dramatic experiments in the use of high-pressure steam. Working pressure for two of them, Nos.76 and 79, was set at 200psi for the purpose of trial against two sister engines, Nos.77 and 78, carrying 175psi and 150psi respectively. Edinburgh–Carlisle metals were chosen as the test ground. As it happened, only poor quality coal was available at the time, thanks to a miners' strike, yet No.79, one of the 200psi engines, working on short cut-off at Drummond's insistence, put up the finest performance of the series. At the conclusion of exhaustive observation, Drummond was able to claim, with conviction, that 'compounding' was an unnecessary luxury. Churchward, in later Great Western locomotive practice, implemented exactly the same belief. Meanwhile, back at St. Rollox, the persistent reluctance of Caley drivers to work 'expansively' obliged Drummond, for the time being, to revert to more modest boiler pressures. Thus, a last batch of six Class '66' 4-4-0s, variously numbered and built at St. Rollox in 1891, were shopped with a working pressure of 150psi.

No.90, one of the last batch of St. Rollox Class '66's, earned its own niche in the railway hall of fame during the 1895 London–Aberdeen 'Races', when it ran 150 miles non-stop between Carlisle and Perth at an average speed of 60mph. There were, of course, no water toughs *en route*. Drummond must have been delighted! Then, rebuilt by J. F. McIntosh in 1906, No.90 was duplicate listed in 1921. Classified 1P by the LMS and allotted No.14307, it was, nevertheless, still carrying CR No.1090 when withdrawal came in 1924. *(Author's Collection)*

LMS No.14113, shopped from St. Rollox Works as CR No.196 in July 1891, exemplifies the second batch of 'Gourock Bogies', with its 160psi working pressure and larger, Smellie-designed, boiler. Drummond tenders (3,130 gallon) were also carried by this batch. Note, however, that smokebox wingplates are no longer the order of the day. All but one of the 1891 contingent survived to enter LMS stock, whence they were classified 1P. No.14113 was one of a pair which lasted to 1930. *(Author's Collection)*

Whatever else Dugald Drummond may have had in mind in the way of express locomotives for the Caledonian Railway, we shall never know; for he occupied himself in other directions over the next two years. A new series of 0-4-4Ts were infiltrated for light branch work, more 0-4-0 and 0-6-0 saddle tanks were built and, inevitably, the CR's large existing stock of 'Jumbos' was increased. Then, suddenly in 1890, when he was at the height of his fame, professionally speaking, this restless, ambitious man elected to drop a bombshell in his employers' lap — and a Caledonian Railway Board Meeting, held on 15th April 1890, found itself confronted by his letter of resignation. An offer of a lucrative post in Australia, of all places, had, it seemed, proved too much! Ah, well, at least circumstances on this occasion appeared to be much more open than those which attended Drummond's earlier departure from NBR service. The Board genuinely expressed both 'great regret' and 'warm wishes for his future happiness and prosperity'. Presumably, however, Drummond must have forewarned his employers; for, at the same meeting, Hugh Smellie, presently Locomotive Superintendent of the Glasgow & South Western Railway, was appointed as his successor — at a much lower salary. . .

What a sad business it all turned out to be! After holding his new CR office for a few months, poor Smellie died on 19th April 1891, aged only 51. Next, Drummond's Australian venture foundered rapidly. Having burned his boats as far as subsequent Scottish railway company employment was concerned, he returned to the UK and, trading rather hopefully on his name and reputation, established the Govan firm of D. Drummond & Son. Alas, success again eluded him. Locomotive orders were hard to come by at that time and, leaving the business in charge of his sons (who later registered it as The Glasgow Railway Engineering Co. Ltd., again to little avail), Drummond was glad to slip back into harness, in August 1895, as Mechanical Engineer to the London & South Western Railway at Nine Elms. He acquired the more elevated title of Chief Mechanical Engineer in January 1905 and we shall meet him again in due course.

The Caledonian Railway Board, meanwhile, had reacted swiftly to Hugh Smellie's untimely death, and the elevation of John Lambie, the Company's Assistant Locomotive Superintendent, to the full post was ratified as from 1st April 1891. Three months later, a final batch of six 'Gourock Bogies'

No.14, one of Lambie's new 6ft 6in 4-4-0s, looks resplendent in Royal Blue as she awaits her next duty at Carlisle Station. Her 3,570 gallon tender was a particularly useful adjunct on main line duty. Rebuilt in 1905, No.14 was taken out of service in November 1920, thus failing to reach LMS stock; though three others of the class did. No.17, running between Perth and Aberdeen, put up an immortal performance during the 'Races' of 1895 — but was poorly rewarded, by being the first to go to the wall, in 1916. *(Author's Collection)*

emerged from St. Rollox Works.

John Lambie's accession at Locomotive Superintendent, even at the age of 58, opened up an interesting new phase in CR locomotive affairs. Born of a railway family — his father was Traffic Manager on the Wishaw & Coltness Railway until it was absorbed by the CR in 1848 — Lambie was very much a 'running' man, with long and wide experience of Caley locomotives and men. His instinctive concern for the latter's welfare was demonstrated clearly by the consistent manner with which he provided cab doors, longer handrails, and additional footsteps on such locomotives as he introduced. Significantly, his first contribution to CR stock, in July 1893, was a series of twelve 4-4-0Ts, neatly proportioned, and fitted with condensing gear for working in the murky depths of the Glasgow Central Low Level line. Ten similarly equipped 0-4-4Ts followed in 1895.

Between these two classes, however, came half a dozen Lambie 4-4-0s, which, although based largely on Drummond design, introduced several new features. From now on round-topped domes and neatly mounted safety-valves over the firebox were to become a Caledonian Railway hallmark. Shopped from St. Rollox Works in April/May 1894, Nos.13–18 employed

The first 'Dunalastair', proudly shopped from St. Rollox Works in January 1896, was named after the Perthshire estate of the CR's Chairman, J. C. Bunten. Then, in 1917, No.721 lost its name under the more austere leadership of W. Pickersgill. The engine survived, nevertheless, to enter LMS stock as No.14311, and lasted until 1931. *(Author's Collection)*

18in × 26in cylinders as before, but working pressure had been raised to 160psi and boiler diameter increased to 4ft 6¼in. A new flat-rimmed chimney and a wheel and handle arrangement on the smokebox door also made their debuts on this occasion; and the siting of the bogie pivot two inches ahead of centre was, in fact, to become a permanent feature on all subsequent CR bogie engines.

The next bolt of lightning to strike the Caledonian Railway in its run of misfortune came when Lambie was taken ill and died on 1st February 1895. Once again the Company's Board acted with wisdom — possibly greater than it realised at the time — by provisionally appointing another 'running' man in his place. John Farquharson McIntosh, up to then Chief Inspector of the CR's Running Department, was now 49 years of age.

The noble lines of McIntosh's 'Dunalastairs' show to advantage in this study of No.722. Interestingly, smokebox wingplates, so beloved of Dugald Drummond, have not only been retained, but have been emphasised as part of the engine's beautiful Caledonian livery. McIntosh, however, was not a devotee of double-heading and this explains why the leading drawhook offers a 'D' link only. Its position, as seen here resting against the front platform, was quite normal CR practice. Later to become LMS No.14312, No.722 outlived the prototype of the class by a good two years. *(Author's Collection)*

During the Coal Strike of 1912 'Dunalastair' No.724, formerly *Jubilee*, was equipped experimentally with Holden's oil-burning apparatus, and, as seen here, ran for a while with a 529 gallon fuel tank mounted on her tender. *(Author's Collection)*

Having worked his way steadily up, however, from fireman and driver on the Scottish North Eastern Railway to becoming Lambie's successor at St. Rollox Works in 1891, he knew Caledonian men and locomotives from the 'inside', as it were. Indeed, such was the man's sympathetic personality that he hardly needed the evidence of his right arm, maimed in the course of duty at Montrose in 1876, to earn complete respect from men and management alike. It was as well, in fact, that the CR Board confirmed McIntosh's appointment after six months' probationship: under his wise and benign leadership, the Caledonian Railway's locomotive department was to reach new heights over the next nineteen years.

McIntosh, however, was modest enough to continue the work of developing and modernising basic Drummond designs. Almost as soon as he assumed office he found himself plunged into the great London and Aberdeen 'Races'. Already, Lambie and Drummond machines were hustling excited passengers between Carlisle and Stirling at average speeds of 60mph. McIntosh added his memorable contribution, by providing 4-4-0s which could do the same — with *twice* the load! It all started with his fifteen 'Dunalastairs' as they emerged from St. Rollox Works between January and May 1896. Running numbers were 721–735, and unusually for the CR, three of the class carried names.

In this instance, McIntosh, though content to follow Drummond's basic 4-4-0 design, rejected the latter's preoccupa-tion with higher boiler pressures and expansive working. Instead, knowing his men, he offered, with his 'Dunalastairs', locomotives which could be driven 'all out', and would not fal-ter for lack of steam. 6ft 6in coupled wheels and 18¼in × 26in cylinders were normal enough CR components; but a new boil-er, pitched 7ft 9in above rail level, and much wider than normal, at 4ft 8¾in, provided a record heating surface of 1,284.45sq ft. That, coupled with a firebox area of 118.78sq ft, was sufficient to give the keenest of CR drivers their head. Significantly, too, the locomotives could be thrashed *ad infinitum*. The high-sided tenders used initially held 3,750 gallons but a year or two later, however, 4,125 gallon bogie tenders were employed; cylinders were redesigned in November 1904.

In some respects McIntosh was content to follow established Scottish locomotive practice. The bogie centre pin on his 'Dunalastairs', for instance, was sited, as always, ahead of the centre line of the bogie wheelbase. This practice, however, was abandoned by W. Pickersgill when he took charge of CR loco-motive affairs in 1914. In other fields McIntosh further elected to contradict Drummond practice by placing the 'Dunalastairs' brake pull rods *inside* the driving wheels, and their tender springs *above* the axle boxes. More significantly, 'Dunalastair' brake blocks were positioned in front of both driving and trail-ing wheels, with the clear object of reducing the stress which was so commonplace elsewhere in Scotland. Meanwhile, the fit-ting of both steam and lever reversers to McIntosh engines

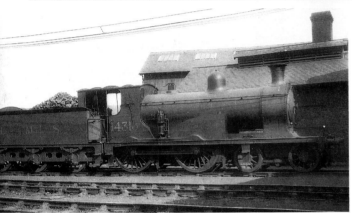

Odd man out. St. Rollox-built in 1896, No.726, later LMS No.14316, acquired a tender cab in 1917, was rebuilt in 1919, and was one of two original 'Dunalastairs' which lasted until October 1935. (Author's Collection)

'Dunalastair II' No.772 demonstrates its fleet lines shortly after being shopped from St. Rollox Works in February 1898. On the 23rd of that month the same locomotive demonstrated in course of a test run that a load of 305 tons could be handled with ease between Glasgow and Carlisle. Even the formidable Carstairs-Beattock Summit section was run at an average of 48mph. Renumbered at Grouping, and fitted with a 300 class boiler in 1933, No.14433 served the LMS until withdrawal came in April 1937. (Author's Collection)

enabled them to be moved at any time without getting up a head of steam in traditional Stirling fashion. Even in the matter of locomotive names the CR's grudging tradition was relaxed slightly, when 'Dunalastairs' Nos.723 and 724 were named *Victoria* and *Jubilee* as part of Scotland's somewhat muted contribution to nationwide celebrations in 1897. These names, however, were removed about the time that George V acceded to the throne. *Dunalastair's* name followed suit in 1917.

Heartened by the acclaim his 'Dunalastairs' received, from travelling public and Caley enginemen alike, McIntosh resolved, wisely in the event, to develop the type rather than settle for standardisation. Thus, between December 1897 and April 1898, fifteen more 4-4-0s, Nos.766–780, emerged from St. Rollox Works. The first-built, No.766, bore the name *Dunalastair II* for the next twenty years. The second last of the series likewise carried the name *Breadalbane* up to 1917, whence it was removed — only to be restored later until 1925. Whatever, in this distinctly larger version of his original 4-4-0 McIntosh lengthened the boiler by 9½in, and stepped the total heating surface up to 1,500sq ft, an increase of almost 100sq ft. Cylinder diameter, too, was increased to 19in, and a dramatic rise in working pressure to 175psi from 160psi offered a new tractive effort of 17,850lb as opposed to the 15,096lb of the 'Dunalastair Is'. Appropriately, the wheelbase of the new

'Dunalastairs' was lengthened by 12in; and sandboxes, previously an integral part of the driving splashers, were now banished beneath the running plate. Even more strikingly, new 4,125 gallon tenders were introduced. Carried on two bogies, they were the first of that type to be introduced in Scotland. The cab, too, was wider, and with Gresham and Craven sanding fitted for forward running, CR locomen had every reason to welcome McIntosh's new enterprise.

The Caledonian Railway directorate must have been highly gratified to learn in 1898 that the fame of their essentially practical Locomotive Engineer had spread to foreign parts; for that was the year when the Belgian Government approached McIntosh direct anent a supply of 'Dunalastair II' locomotives. Quite happily, St. Rollox conceded drawings and full details of the class; and, a little later, the Glasgow firm of Neilson, Reid & Co. — itself soon to become a component part of the North British Locomotive Co. — built five 'Dunalastair IIs' for use by the Belgian State Railways. Apart from conversion to right-hand drive they were practically identical to the Caledonian prototype. Their arrival and popular employment in Belgium, in fact, triggered a remarkable ten year 'McIntosh' phase in Belgian State Railways history. During that period some 720 engines, passenger, freight and mixed traffic, were built in Belgium, all clearly based on McIntosh design. A total of 95 pseudo 'Dunalastair IIs' came first, and were followed in 1902 by 140 much similar, but more powerful, 4-4-0s. Meanwhile, a 'McIntosh' class of 4-4-2T, introduced in 1899, followed the same logic and was reinforced by a later superheated class in 1905. Several hundred 0-6-0s, some saturated, some superheated — but all based on McIntosh's original CR freight design — were also introduced between 1899 and 1910. This useful class was particularly favoured by drivers and operating staff, and easily reached its diamond jubilee before withdrawals bit hard in the 1960s. Sculptures of the front end of the 'McIntosh' type 0-6-0 were even incorporated ornamentally on an overbridge at the departure end of Ostend Maritime Station.

No.14335, formerly *Breadalbane*, makes a brisk exit from Glasgow Central Station in April 1938. The Caledonian-type semaphore on the buffer beam identifies the train as one bound for Strathaven, and the Ross Pop safety valves are a relic of rebuild in 1920. The locomotive itself was withdrawn in October 1939. *(Steamchest)*

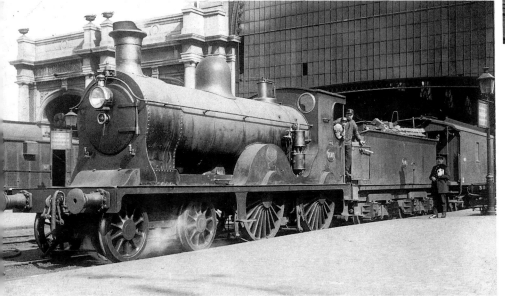

Despite its chimney capuchon and prominent headlight, Belgian State Railways 4-4-0 No.2640 has no difficulty in advertising its 'McIntosh' pedigree as it prepares to leave Brussels Midi Station in the early 1900s. *(Author's Collection)*

Hardly the type of man to rest quietly on his laurels, McIntosh, meanwhile, was drawing up plans for bigger and better 'Dunalastairs'. The fruits of his labours emerged from St. Rollox Works in December 1899 in the form of three 'Dunalastair III' 4-4-0s, Nos.900–902; and thirteen more, Nos.887–899, materialised by July 1900. Once again the traditional McIntosh machinery was employed; but so, too, was a much larger boiler. A total heating surface of 1,540sq ft was now at the disposal of Caley locomen, and an increased working pressure of 180psi yielded a tractive effort of 18,411lb. The total wheelbase was lengthened by 6in to accommodate a larger firebox. Slightly shorter bogie tenders were added. Certainly, with a full laden weight of 101 tons 3 cwt the 'Dunalastair IIIs' were easily the heaviest locomotives the Caledonian Railway had built to date. As with the 'Dunalastair IIs', several were rebuilt with superheaters in pre-Grouping years; whence cylinders were stepped up to 19½in × 26in. Total heating surface and working pressure were reduced accordingly to 1,159.3sq ft and 170psi.

The species lasted long enough for the ultimate survivor, No.894 (later LMS No.14434) to enter BR stock as No.54434 before it was withdrawn in April 1948. The prototype 'Dunalastair III', however, No.900 (later LMS No.14435), was not so fortunate; working in tandem with LMS Compound No.1176 at the head of the 7.30pm Euston–Inverness express on the morning of 25th October 1928, it ran into the rear of a freight train which had inadvertently stopped between Dinwoodie and Wamphray stations because of lubricator trou-

ble. Both express engines, thrown down an embankment, landed in an adjoining field; and, although there were no passenger fatalities, the Kingmoor-based crews of both Nos.14435 and 1176 perished immediately. The Compound proved to be repairable — but the 'Dunalastair', damaged beyond redemption, was officially withdrawn later that month.

The term 'Dunalastair III' was, of course, an unofficial one. So, too, was the designation 'Dunalastair IV' which promptly attached itself to nineteen even larger 4-4-0s as they emerged from St. Rollox Works between 1904 and 1910. In order of building they carried Nos.140–150, 923–927 and 136–138; once again, McIntosh concentrated on further enlarging the boiler. This produced a new record total heating surface of 1615sq ft. Meanwhile, a corresponding increase in water capacity to 4,300 gallons saw the combined engine and tender weight rise to 107 tons 5 cwt. The last three built were even given 4,600 gallon tenders. In light of the increased boiler pitch a more generous cab was fitted, and the long-familiar circular spectacle glasses now gave way to an almost triangular new shape. Working pressure, however, remained at 180psi. In all four 'Dunalastair' classes the regulator was of the double beat variety, and was housed in the dome.

Curiously, as with the preceding 'Dunalastair' class, the prototype 'Dunalastair IV', No.140, was also involved in a major accident — a very major one indeed, at Quintinshill, ten miles north of Carlisle, in the early morning of Saturday, 22nd May 1915. The details of this ghastly affair, the fruit of two signal-

One needs hardly add that the new 'Dunalastair IIIs' soon found employment on Glasgow–Carlisle work. In this photograph No.902 bears no headlamps; but the CR-type semaphore high on the smokebox indicates clearly that the locomotive is running on main line duty via Motherwell. *(Author's Collection)*

Fortunately, the mishap which befell sister engine No.902 in this opportunist photograph was comparatively trivial — though embarrassing enough. Derailment has not blemished the locomotive's beautiful Caledonian blue livery, and in the event, October 1939 arrived before No.902 (by then LMS No.14346) made its last sad journey to St. Rollox Works. *(Author's Collection)*

'Dunalastair III' No.14347, seen here at Glasgow Central Station in April 1938, offered continuing overtones of the 1928 Dinwoodie disaster. The locomotive, originally CR No.897, was rebuilt in typical class fashion in 1919; but when superheating and piston valves were added in 1930, opportunity was taken to incorporate the boiler from the unfortunate prototype, No.14435. Observe how, as with so many ex-CR engines, the LMS Shed Code plate was sited on the top half of the smokebox. This was possible because after 1928, it was rare for ex-CR locomotives to carry the LMS standard smokebox numberplate in that position.

(Author's Collection)

The powerful lines of McIntosh's so-called 'Dunalastair IVs' show up clearly in this fine study of No.142, a St. Rollox Works product of June 1904. Equally evident is the pride many Scottish enginemen took in embellishing the smokebox and wing plates of their locomotive charges. Later renumbered 14351, this engine served the LMS until October 1939. *(Author's Collection)*

men's negligence, have often been retailed. Suffice it, then, to say that No.140 and No.48, a superheated McIntosh 4-4-0 of later vintage, were double-heading a 600 ton down sleeping car express which, running late, arrived catastrophically on the scene one minute after a heavily laden troop train, bound for Liverpool, and hauled by No.121, another McIntosh superheated 4-4-0, had collided with a down local train which had been side-tracked, perforce, on to the up main line — and forgotten. The local train was headed by No.907, one of five splendid 'Cardean' 4-6-0s which were subscribed by St. Rollox Works in 1906.

The initial 70mph collision between the troop train and the local was bad enough, and cost the lives of two passengers. The additional impact, however, of the oncoming double-headed express on the already shattered troop train, with its wooden-underframed coaches and fully charged gas cylinders, ignited a fire which was to rage for the next 36 hours, despite utmost efforts by Carlisle Fire Brigade. The consequences were terrible

to a degree, and, mercifully, have never been exceeded in the whole of British railway history. Eight lives were lost in the express and 54 were injured. In the troop train the precise number of Royal Scots officers and men who perished in the holocaust could only be estimated at 215, for the regimental roll was lost in the flames. Meanwhile, two railway servants were also killed, and an additional 191 military men were seriously injured. As for the four McIntosh engines involved, Nos.121 and 907, battered beyond redemption, had to be withdrawn some months later, leaving Nos.140 and 48 as sole survivors. Poor McIntosh, who had retired twelve months earlier, must have been stricken to the heart to see four of his fine engines involved in such a disaster.

Only a few months old, 'Dunalastair IV' No.923 copes with the very heavy 10.00am ex-Glasgow express as it breasts Beattock Summit in April 1908. In approved McIntosh fashion a simple 'D' link, resting against the front platform, disdains assistance — in the way of double-heading at least. *(Author's Collection)*

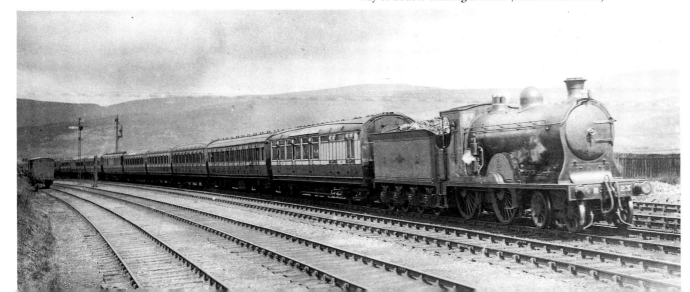

Duly superheated and fitted with 20¼in × 26in cylinders in 1917, CR No.923, now LMS Class 3P No.14438, is seen again, at Polmadie shed in 1929. One of three 'Dunalastair' which contrived to enter BR stock, No.54438 was the second last to be withdrawn, when it was removed from Dumfries depot in May 1955. By that time, like No.54439, the last survivor, it had acquired a Pickersgill chimney and six-wheeled tender. (Steamchest)

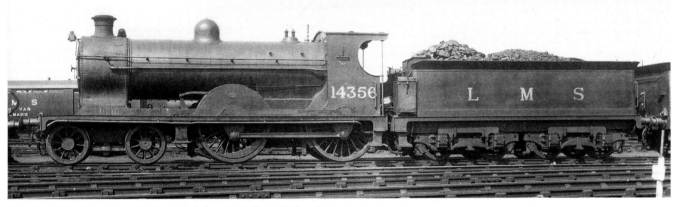

Superheated in December 1922, and duly styled Class 3P by the LMS, No.14356 (formerly CR No.147), seen here at Polmadie shed, was nevertheless erroneously numbered among the Class 2Ps, presumably because it happened to retain its original 19in cylinders. Sadly, of all the 'Dunalastair IVs' it met the most brutal end, when it was destroyed at Ladyburn during an enemy air raid in June 1941. *(Author's Collection)*

In the event two 'Dunalastair IVs', Nos.141 and 142 were rebuilt in 1905 and 1908 respectively, and all but three of the remainder, including No.140, the Quintinshill survivor, were dealt with between the years 1919 and 1926. By then, of course, superheating had arrived on the CR scene, and three of the rebuilds were so equipped. Of these, Nos.924 and 923, both rebuilt during First World War years, re-emerged with 20¼in cylinders. Strangely, however, No.147, dealt with in December 1922, was allowed to keep its original cylinders. At the other end of the spectrum, withdrawal of unsuperheated 'Dunalastair IVs' began in 1937, and ended when No.14363 (formerly CR No.137) was removed from Aviemore shed in November 1948.

In locomotive lore, the history of superheating is a venerable one. As far back as the 1830s it was realised that a rise in temperature of steam at a given pressure offered increased efficiency. The theory soon attached itself to the development of steam locomotives, and in 1839 the Newcastle firm of R.&W. Hawthorn Ltd., patented a form of steam dryer and superheater apparatus. The principle involved employment of a chamber in the upper part of a locomotive smokebox. Indeed, it extended partly round it, and a handful of Hawthorn-built locomotives were so built. By 1850, J. F. McConnell, the locomotive superintendent of the LNWR's Southern Division, was prepared to launch his first form of smokebox superheater. At that time a

French railway was also experimenting; but 50 more years were to elapse ere the first truly efficient locomotive superheater made its appearance. The work of Dr. Wilhelm Schmidt, it was developed on Prussian State Railway locomotives during 1898–99, and, finalised in smokebox form in 1901, it soon found popular acceptance all over Europe.

Scottish railways were not slow to follow the trend — and, almost inevitably, J. F. McIntosh and the Caledonian Railway were first in the field. Thus, in July 1910 No.139, originally intended to be the last of the 'Dunalastair IV' class, emerged from St. Rollox Works duly equipped with a modified form of Schmidt superheater. In this instance the cylinder diameter, too, was increased to 20in, and piston valves, placed *over* the cylinders, were employed. A total heating surface of 1,695sq ft now obtained and, in keeping with contemporary superheating practice, the boiler pressure was lowered from the previous 'Dunalastair IV' figure of 180psi to 165psi. Meanwhile, No.139 was soon tested on 220–235 ton trains and, in addition to producing a tractive effort of 18,700lb, showed a gratifying reduction of 16% in coal consumption per gross ton mile. A little later the engine could be found working the 'Grampian Corridor Express' and other crack Caledonian Railway trains as to the manner born. Duly emboldened by his success in pioneering superheating, McIntosh had four more '139' Class 4-4-0s turned out from St. Rollox Works in April/May 1911. They carried Nos.132–135.

Next, in July 1912, came five more Class '139' 4-4-0s, Nos.117–121. Again St. Rollox-built and carrying Schmidt superheaters, these locomotives, however, took matters a stage further; for their cylinder diameter had been stepped up to 20¼in, and a corresponding increase in working pressure to 170psi produced an enhanced tractive effort of 19,751lb/sq in.

The first of an historic class, CR 4-4-0 No.139 was not long out of the shops when this photograph was taken. Later numbered 14440 at Grouping, the locomotive duly entered BR stock as No.54440, and remained in service until January 1957. *(Author's Collection)*

Meanwhile, interesting new developments which were taking place in the superheater field were beginning to challenge the Schmidt supremacy. In 1911, for instance, the NBR fitted two Reid engines, No.897, a 'Scott' Class 4-4-0, and No.329, a 5ft goods engine, with Phoenix superheaters. The latter, however, was a clumsy apparatus. It took up an incommensurate amount of room in the smokebox, and also offended aesthetic considerations by requiring the chimney to be placed much further forward. After brief trials, the Phoenix superheaters were, in any case, adjudged not to have given technical satisfaction and both engines were soon restored to saturated condition. That same year, a similar experience befell the Highland Railway, when 4-6-0 No.146 *Ballindalloch Castle* was fitted with a Phoenix superheater at a cost of £225. The locomotive re-entered traffic early in 1912, only to be the subject of adverse report by June. The Highland, however, was a canny concern — and the 'Castle' retained its experimental apparatus until Cumming had it removed in 1916! The Caledonian, cannier still, kept clear of the Phoenix superheater. McIntosh, nevertheless, was still amendable to experiment. Thus, in August 1912, one last '139' Class 4-4-0, No.122, was shopped from St. Rollox — carrying a Robinson superheater. The same specification applied when eleven more 4-4-0s, Nos.39–48 and No.123 were built at St. Rollox between May 1913 and May 1914. The latter engine bore the number which happened to become available when the single-wheeler bearing it was Duplicate listed as No.1123 in 1914. Of McIntosh's 22 new superheated 4-4-0s only two, the unfortunate No.121 and No.133, withdrawn from Dalry Road shed in July 1946, failed to survive well into the 1950s.

The new superheater which was exciting such attention amongst railways in Scotland and England alike was, of course, a product of the fertile mind of J. G. Robinson, Chief Mechanical Engineer of the Great Central Railway from 1902 to the Grouping. A Swindon-trained man, Robinson had devoted himself for years to the development of steam locomotive efficiency, and he finally patented his superheater in 1911. A variation on the Schmidt superheater, Robinson's apparatus employed short return loop elements — presumably on the basis that with the long Schmidt-type elements the only real heat transference took place in the rear of the elements, while the forward portions between dome and smokebox contributed little. No doubt the eruption of war with Germany in 1914 finally sealed the fate of the Schmidt superheater as far as British railways were concerned.

Domestically speaking, the year 1914 held even greater significance for the Caledonian Railway — for J. F. McIntosh retired in May of that year, aged 68, after nearly two decades of glorious achievement. There can never be any doubt that the CR's turn of the century rise to prominence as a major British railway owed much to his influence and practical contribution. Popular, and respected by all ranks of the company he served, no man was ever more worthy of the MVO bestowed on him by King George V in 1913. He died on 6th February 1918, but the memory of his legendary Royal blue engines remains imperishable to this day.

Nominating a man to follow in McIntosh's footsteps was no enviable task; so the Caledonian Railway directorate must have swallowed hard in March 1914 when they appointed William Pickersgill. Certainly, many an eyebrow must have risen in railway circles, for Pickersgill was generally regarded as a 'small engine' man. During his twenty years with the Great North of Scotland Railway he had perpetuated the construction of inside-cylindered 4-4-0s to handle most traffic. Now, at the age of 53, he was expected to cope with the flood of naval and military traffic which would soon engulf the Caledonian Railway. A much less ebullient character than his predecessor, Pickersgill elected, perhaps wisely, to pursue (for the nonce) his new Company's distinct preference for four-coupled express locomotives. That being so, what better model could he choose than McIntosh's superheated '139' and '117' classes?

The sixteen 4-4-0s which Pickersgill eventually introduced in 1916 were undoubtedly Caledonian in pedigree — despite several changes he had incorporated in their appearance. Traditional smokebox wingplates, for instance, were no longer in evidence; much to the chagrin of many Caley locomen who swore that the wingplates, apart from being decorative, added rigidity to the main frame. Pickersgill, however, had anticipated that argument by giving his new 4-4-0s $1\frac{1}{4}$in thick frames, as opposed to the $1\frac{1}{16}$in frames which had been previously employed. He also chose to dispense with double-bogied tenders. Indeed, he devoted himself to six-wheeled tenders during the whole of his Caledonian Railway career. Similarly, a plain cast chimney became a distinct hallmark of Pickersgill locomotives. The once

Top:
No.121 was by far the least fortunate of the
McIntosh '139' Class 4-4-0s. It looks
resplendent enough in this portrait, which was
possibly obtained when the locomotive was
being run in on local passenger service. Less
than three years later, however, it was battered
beyond repair in the Quintinshill disaster of
1915. *(Author's Collection)*

Centre:
Built at St. Rollox in July 1912 as '139' Class
No.117, No.14445 obligingly poses at Perth
South shed in early post-Grouping LMS
crimson lake livery. The small steam cylinder
sited high on the smokebox side was cab
operated and controlled dampers which
protected the Schmidt superheater elements
from burning when the regulator valve was
closed. The locomotive served three masters
over a period of 40 years before being
withdrawn as BR No.54445 in December 1952.
(Author's Collection)

Bottom:
Early Grouping days at Aberdeen, as the
prototype of McIntosh's last series of 4-4-0s,
built at St. Rollox as CR No.43 in May 1913, is
prepared for duty in early LMS days, now as
No.14450. The modest steam cylinder which
formerly appeared on the smokebox side of the
Class 139s is no longer required as, with a
Robinson superheater, damper gear was now
manually operated. As BR No.54450 this
engine was one of five members of the class
which were withdrawn in 1955.
(Author's Collection)

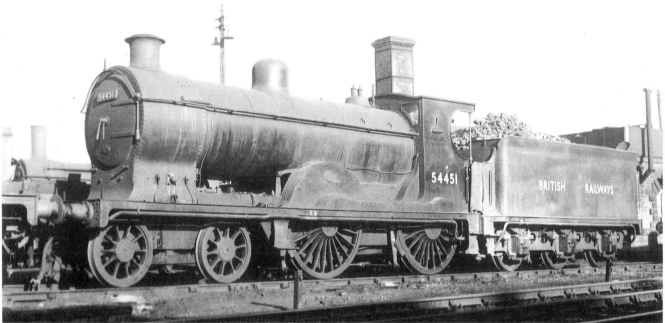

Sister engine No.54451, also one of those withdrawn in 1955, looked radically different when it was photographed at Polmadie in 1948. Smokebox wingplates have disappeared, and the provision of a plain cast chimney, Ross pop safety valves, and a 4,200 gallon six-wheeled tender are further evidence of attention by William Pickersgill, the man who succeeded J. F. McIntosh as CR Locomotive Superintendent in March 1914. Note too the changed shape of dome cover. *(J. Robertson)*

familiar built-up McIntosh chimney had gone for ever. Sturdy enough engines, the Pickersgill 4-4-0s were destined to work on solidly into the 1950s and early 1960s; though their prime function as express locomotives was curtailed only too soon by the eventual introduction of 'Royal Scots' on the Carlisle route and the slightly later employment of 'Jubilees' and 'Black Fives' on Aberdeen main line duties. Wherever they were employed, however, it remained a regrettable fact that Caley men never took the Pickersgill 4-4-0s to their hearts as they had done with McIntosh's 'flyers'.

Meanwhile, what with the severe haemorrhage of skilled men to the Armed Services and mounting arrears of locomotive maintenance, St. Rollox was a busy place in 1916. The Works there, however, did contrive to build the first six of Pickersgill's new 4-4-0s and they entered service bearing CR Nos.113–116, 121 and 124. No.121, of course, was a replacement for the

McIntosh '139' Class engine which was so tragically destroyed at Quintinshill nine months earlier. Construction of the remaining ten was farmed out to the North British Locomotive Co. and CR Nos. 928–937 (Works Nos.21442–51) duly appeared bearing the distinctive Atlas Works' oval plate on the straightened coupling rod splashers which Pickersgill had also chosen to introduce. Curiously, while the St. Rollox batch pioneered the Ross pop safety valves which were later to be adopted by the LMS, the NB Loco. Co. engines were shopped still carrying the latter day McIntosh safety valves. That apart, however, all sixteen shared the same dimensions. Cylinders were 20in × 26in, but while the large boiler tubes were in every way analogous to those previously employed by McIntosh, the employment now of Robinson Short Loop elements in the superheater reduced the total heating surface to 1,529sq ft   131sq ft less than that of the 'Dunalastair IV'. Conversely, an increase in boiler pressure to 175psi produced a tractive effort of 19,833lb. Sadly, this modest boost did not save No.124 from near ignominy in 1924 when, hauling a load of 320 tons, it competed against a Midland Compound in test runs between Leeds and Carlisle.

At this juncture, and before attempting to evaluate the true nature of William Pickersgill's contribution to CR locomotive affairs, one would do well to reflect that he entered Caledonian employment at a time when the whole nation, much less St.

Pickersgill 4-4-0 No.86 (Works No.115) was an Armstrong Whitworth product of April 1921, by which time Ross pop safety valves had been adopted as standard Caledonian Railway practice. Renumberd 14491 under LMS auspices, the locomotive had gravitated as far North as Wick by the time it was withdrawn in December 1961. *(Author's Collection)*

Right:

One of ten Pickersgill Class '72' 4-4-0s which St. Rollox Works were able to build in 1920, No.14480, formerly CR No.75, poses proudly with its crew in a northern Scottish context. Renumbered 54480 by BR, the locomotive lasted until August 1960. *(Pendragon Collection)*

In this proud photograph of No.14498, built as CR No.67 by the North British Locomotive Co. (Works No.22944) in November 1922, the cabside inscription 'P4' bears testimony to the misinterpretation which regularly (in Scotland) surrounded the second LMS attempt at locomotive power classification in 1928. In due course, the correct application of the new system (with letters as well as numbers) saw all 48 Pickersgill 4-4-0s correctly classified as '3P'. *(BR LMR)*

Rollox Works, was about to enter a prolonged period of great travail. Traffic loads grew progressively heavier as the so-called Great War wound its weary course. Years passed, and, inevitably, Caledonian maintenance and repair work mounted proportionately. Quite unable to cope because of its own shortage of skilled labour. St. Rollox even had to resort to having a number of ailing locomotives overhauled by outside contractors. It follows that when 25 of Drummond's hard-working 0-6-0s, the immortal 'Jumbos', were commandeered by the War Department in 1917 for service in Europe, little time elapsed before eleven North Eastern and Great Central 0-6-0s simply had to be sent North to ease the CR's burden. Even when hostilities ceased in 1919, the Caledonian Railway was glad to hire 50 ex-ROD type 2-8-0s from the Ministry of Transport until Government control of Britain's railways terminated on 15th August 1921. Ultimately, all 50 were disposed of in the mid-1920s. Many went to the Far East.

Pickersgill's '113' Class 4-4-0s had, in fact, been authorised in October 1914, and it was typical of the war years that they were not completed until 1916. Equally symptomatic was the fact that only 29 locomotives were built at St. Rollox during the years 1915–7. The first of these years witnessed the construction of four 0-4-4 tanks and six 0-6-0 tanks; seven more 0-6-0 tanks and the first half-dozen Pickersgill 4-4-0s followed in 1916 and over the months of November 1916 and April 1917 the emergence of his six Class '60' 4-6-0s finally broke the Caledonian inside cylinder tradition which had persisted since the days of Dugald Drummond. Handsome and quite versatile engines, the Class '60' 4-6-0s, however, were sluggish at speed, and soon earned the scornful nickname 'Greybacks' (a form of woodlouse!) from CR men who were accustomed to the whippiness of McIntosh's 'Dunalastairs'. Rather surprisingly, a further twenty were built by the LMS in 1925–6. Their main distinction was that they were the last engines to be built in a Scottish railway works (in this instance St. Rollox) either for a Scottish railway, or a division of one.

In the immediate post-war years Scottish heavy industry's trauma was such that Pickersgill must have been relieved, early in 1920, to receive authority to proceed with further construction of his rather less contentious 4-4-0s. Even so, St. Rollox Works could only handle ten, and these, given CR Nos.72–81, duly entered service between May and September 1920. This time the cylinder diameter was increased to 20½in. Boiler pres-

sure, too, was stepped up to 180psi, and the resultant locomotives yielded a tractive effort of 21,435lb. But, once more, the balance of the quite substantial order was entrusted to outside contractors. Armstrong Whitworth built ten (Works Nos.111–120) at their Newcastle works during the first half of 1921 which entered Caledonian service as Nos.82–91, while the North British Locomotive Company added a final dozen (Works Nos.22943–54) in November–December 1922. They carried CR Nos.66–71 and 92–97. There were now 48 Pickersgill 4-4-0s in existence and, together with McIntosh's superheated 4-4-0s, they were eventually classified 3P after the Grouping of 1923. In due course the McIntosh engines were given LMS Nos.14430–60 and Pickersgill's 4-4-0s received Nos.14461–508. The latter group passed intact into British Railways' hands in 1948.

As indicated previously, such prestige main line duties as the Pickersgills were able to perform were, thanks to an early influx of six-coupled LMS types, extremely brief in character. Much sooner than expected they were obliged to revert to handling the kind of semi-fast services one found around Edinburgh and Perth. Yet it must be conceded that, despite the persistent lack-lustre with which veteran Caley men view them, they performed creditably enough. Then, as the 1930s progressed (and more and more LMS Compounds and Stanier 4-6-0s flooded into Central Scotland) the Pickersgills were once more driven to seek new pastures. By the 1950s most were either working in the Highland section or handling passenger trains on the one-time G&SWR steeply graded line from Glasgow to Princes Pier, Greenock. It was on the Highland section, in fact, that the serried ranks of Pickersgill 4-4-0s experienced their one and only casualty.

The victim was No.54481, a Forres engine, and the accident occurred on the evening of 9th June 1953, some 300 yards west of Gollanfield station. The Pickersgill was approaching the spot with the 8.17pm passenger train from Inverness to Keith, when it collided violently, and head-on, with the 5.45pm freight from Keith to Inverness. Three of the enginemen were killed, and No.54481, a St. Rollox product of July 1920, was so badly damaged that it had to be demolished on site. The freight engine, No.44783, a Class 5 4-6-0, lived to fight another day.

So, too, did the remaining 47 Pickersgill 4-4-0s. But time, in fact, was running short for Scottish 4-4-0s as a species. The last McIntosh, No.54439, went to the breakers in August 1958;

Class	Number built	Date built	LMSR Class 2P	LMSR Class 3P	Last survivor(s) and date withdrawn Class 2P		Class 3P	
Dunalastair	15	1896	15 (14311–25)	—	14315/16	10/35	—	—
Dunalastair II	15	1897–98	11 (14326–36)	4 (14430–33)	14333	9/47	14433	4/37
Dunalastair III	16	1899–1900	12 (14337–48)	4 (14434–37)	14340	12/46	54434	4/48
Dunalastair IV	19	1904–10	16 (14349–55) (14357–65)	3 (14356) (14438–39)	14363	11/48	54439	8/58
'139' Class	11	1910–12	—	(14440–49)	—	—	54441	8/57*
'43' Class	11	1913–14	—	(14450–60) 11	—	—	54458	12/57
Sub Totals	87		54	32				
'113' Class	16	1916	—	16 (14461–76)	—	—	54463	12/62
	32	1920–22	—	32 (14477–508)				
Totals	135		54	80				

* '139' Class No.121 was destroyed at Quintinshill on 22nd May 1915.

One of three remaining Pickersgill 4-4-0s, No.54465 looked spruce enough as it handled a combined Railway Society Tour on Easter Monday 1962. The locomotive was doubly interesting in that when it was built at St. Rollox in February 1916 it was given CR No.121 as replacement for the McIntosh 4-4-0 which was destroyed at Quintinshill on 22nd May 1915. *(Steamchest)*

then, eight months later, came the melancholy news from Carstairs shed (64D) that No.54461, the pioneer Pickersgill 4-4-0 (formerly CR No.113) of February 1916, had been withdrawn. Considering that the locomotive had been overhauled at Inverurie only a year previously, this seemed a poor reward for the active existence it had led since — particularly when at least two of the class, Nos.54479 and 54483, each junior by four years, had been lying inert for six years or more. Indeed, by the Autumn of 1959, while nearly 100 pre-Grouping 4-4-0s remained part of Scottish Region stock, a high proportion of them lay in store at sundry locations throughout the length and breadth of Scotland. Then came the holocaust, when eleven Pickersgill 4-4-0s were officially withdrawn in October 1959 and four more went in November. By now only nineteen of the remaining 31 Pickersgills were even turning a wheel and, significantly, only six of these were located south of Perth.

Thinning of the Pickersgill 4-4-0 ranks continued relentlessly. Eight were officially withdrawn in 1960 and, with a similar fate overtaking fifteen more in 1961, only eight were left to offer the year 1962 a distinctly wan welcome. By March that year another five had gone and only three survivors, Nos.54502, 54463 and 54465, remained. The latter engine seemed particularly active and, removed temporarily from its normal Motherwell locale, it was tidied up before being sent north on Easter Monday to work a combined BLS/SLS Tour. Two vintage Caledonian coaches added a period flavour to the occasion.

As if to prove its continuing worth, No.54465 ran into Glasgow Central on 4th May that year at the head of the 6.10pm ex-Motherwell - and kicked its heels up further by running light round the Cathcart Circle. Meanwhile, of the other two survivors, No.54463, duly steamed, had already moved from Inverness to Polmadie on 20th April. Shortly afterwards it was joined by No.54502, ex-store from Beattock, and the purpose of this intriguing ploy only became clear just before Glasgow's electric Blue Train service commenced public operations on Sunday, 27th May. The Blue Trains were destined to offer Glaswegians a superb service but, as maintenance of the units was carried out at Hyndland depot, Westinghouse-braked locomotives were required to haul the sets from Smithy Lye to High Street for this purpose. Accordingly, the three Pickersgill survivors stood in to assist for a short period while two Type 1 diesels were so fitted. On 20th May, therefore, such observers as happened to be present were treated to a remarkable sight as Nos.54463 and 54465 concluded a day's trial running by climbing from Shields Junction to Cumberland Street with a nine-car electric set. No.54502 arrived rather too late to offer much assistance; but No.54465 continued to flaunt its fitness on 25th May, by working a four-coach evening rail tour over the electrified lines. It even threw in the Beith branch for good measure.

The photographer who captured No.54463 in such pensive mood at Inverness roundhouse in July 1955 had no way of knowing that the locomotive would be the last Pickersgill, and Caledonian, 4-4-0 to be withdrawn. The summons duly arrived at Polmadie shed in December 1962. *(Steamchest)*

With diesel locomotion rapidly gaining precedence in Scotland, as elsewhere, the final Caledonian 4-4-0 chapter closed later in 1962. Indeed, by the end of that year inroads were being made into the ranks of much more modern classes. Even BR 'Clans', introduced as recently as 1951, began to disappear. The three surviving Pickersgills, meanwhile, had been taken out of service some months earlier and now lay inactive at Polmadie and Motherwell sheds. Came October and the patient vigil of two of them, Nos.54465 and 54502, was brought to an end. Hope ran high amongst enthusiasts that No.54463 might, as a last resort, be retained for private preservation — but sadly, hopes came to naught — and the locomotive was officially withdrawn in December 1962.

Mercifully, the Scottish preservation movement successfully rescued reminders of the Drummond and McIntosh eras, in the form of the Caley 'Single wheeler', and two McIntosh engines, 0-4-4T No.419 and 0-6-0 No.828. Before retiring in 1925 William Pickersgill put in two years of service as Mechanical Engineer to the Northern Division of the LMS; but, alas, no physical trace remains of the many locomotives he subscribed during a most difficult decade in both national and Caledonian Railway affairs.

Chapter 4
THE GREAT NORTH OF SCOTLAND RAILWAY

INCORPORATED ON 26th June 1846, the GNSR appointed its first Locomotive Superintendent, Daniel Kinnear Clark, in October 1853. In theory, the appointment looked an impressive one, for the 31-year-old Clark was already practising in London as a consulting engineer. In the event, his association with the GNSR was to last less than two years; mainly because of Clark's stubborn refusal to take up residence in Aberdeen, as required by contract. Meanwhile, an order was placed without delay with William Fairbairn & Co. of Manchester for the supply of twelve 2-4-0 tender engines; seven passenger and five goods. Designed by Clark, all were to be additionally equipped with his patent smoke preventing device. The latter apparently worked rather well, and effected considerable fuel economy. The real trouble arose when delivery of the first locomotive was delayed until mid-1855. Thus, the GNSR's carefully laid plans to employ the 2-4-0s on occasion of the ceremonial opening of the Aberdeen–Huntly line on 19th September were thoroughly confounded. Further calamity developed shortly after the arrival of the first seven 2-4-0s — when two of them broke down almost immediately, through sheer overwork. All in all, one can imagine the GNSR Board hardly needed Clark's resignation in July 1855 to complete its discomfiture!

Possibly as much in despair as in hope, the GNSR next nominated J. F. Ruthven, the Works Manager at Kittybrewster, as Clark's successor. Poor Ruthven — his starting salary of £160 a year alone spoke volumes for the sincerity of his Company's intentions! It came as no surprise, therefore, that after ordering a few minor locomotives from outside contractors, and being involved subsequently in a fierce row over locomotive repair costs, Ruthven elected, in May 1857, to move sideways and make room for a fresh GNSR appointment. Events which followed seemed even more bizarre; for the Board's new nominee for the job of Locomotive Superintendent was none other than William Cowan, the very man who had succeeded Ruthven as Works Manager! Fortunately for all concerned, *this* new broom, however, swept very cleanly indeed. Cowan, in fact, provided the GNSR with such a fine stud of locomotives over the next 25 years that some of them were still running in the 1920s.

Rather as Wheatley did on the NBR, Cowan proceeded very cautiously at first, by importing nine 2-4-0 goods engines from R. Stephenson & Co. of Darlington. Apart from their 16in × 20in cylinders they were very similar to those already in the GNSR's possession. Unlike Wheatley, however, Cowan did not eschew the copper-capped chimney and tall brass dome which were so fashionable at the time. It follows that when the GNSR's first 4-4-0s, the Class '28s', made their debut — and they were very nearly the first of that wheel arrangement in the country — the locomotives looked very handsome in Brunswick green livery. Stephensons were again the suppliers, and nine of these 5ft 1in outside-cylindered locomotives Nos.28–36, were built over the years 1862–1864. A modest 3ft 9¾in boiler boiler worked to a pressure of 140psi, cylinders were 16in × 20in,

bogies were encased in outside springs, and a weather board provided minimal shelter for train crews. In working order each engine weighed 34½ tons, and a four-wheeled tender, adding half as much again, brought the total up to 50 tons. As the locomotives were designed for work in the Strathspey district, no doubt the sharp curves they would encounter there persuaded Cowan to adopt bogies instead of rigid wheels. Whatever, the Class '28s' served their purpose satisfactorily enough — until 1878, when No.31 burst her boiler when standing at Nethybridge station. Subsequent enquiry suggested that the boiler pressure was too high at 140psi, and the whole class was reboilered in 1880–83.

Procrastination seemed to be an integral part of contemporary GNSR life. In September 1864 Cowan requested construction of six more engines, to handle additional traffic which would be generated by the opening of the Fraserburgh branch. The branch duly opened in 1865, but, thanks to lethargy in the Board room, the six locomotives, Nos.43–48, were not delivered by Neilson & Co. until March/April the following year. Larger and more powerful than the '28' Class engines, and duly classified 'B' (later 'K'), these new 5ft 6½in 4-4-0s were provided with more modern bogies; and while cylinder dimensions had been stepped up to 16in × 24in, a working pressure of 140psi still applied. That apart, all the earlier external flamboyant features were retained. In due course, all six were rebuilt by Cowan's successors between 1889 and 1891.

Back on the GNSR, meanwhile, a decade of very stringent locomotive economy followed the construction of the Class 'Ks'. Latterly, however, Cowan insisted that he must have new engines to cope with increasing traffic and, rather grudgingly, four Class 'L' 4-4-0s were commissioned from Neilson & Co. in October 1873 for delivery in the following Autumn. When the new 4-4-0s were still not delivered by the beginning of 1875, however, enquiry revealed that Cowan had exceeded his mandate by ordering *six* engines. Again somewhat grudgingly, the Board homologated Cowan's action, and Neilson & Co. were asked to expedite delivery. The Class 'Ls' finally arrived in 1876, and entered traffic as Nos.49, 50, 54–57; No.57 was later altered to 52. In prudent Scottish fashion three were charged to capital, and three to revenue. Coupled wheels were still 5ft 6½in, but cylinders had been increased to 17½in × 26in, and larger boilers and fireboxes, working at 150psi, marked a new advance in GNSR locomotive practice. Four of the Class 'Ls' were transferred to the Duplicate List in October 1920, but all six, nevertheless, contrived to enter LNER stock, whence they were classified D47/1. Never destined to carry LNER numbers, all were withdrawn by January 1926.

William Cowan's last two classes arrived at Kittybrewster in the shape of twelve 4-4-0s. Supplied by Neilson & Co. in 1878, nine of them, styled Class 'M', had 5ft 7in coupled wheels. The other three (Class 'C'), built a month or two later and regarded by the GNSR as 'express engines', had 6ft 1in wheels; but all fol-

Above:
William Cowan's Class '28' No.29, built in 1862, is seen here in rebuilt form. Apart from the substitution of new, and more modern, bogies and the provision of a cab, the locomotive's early appearance has been faithfully retained. No.29, as it happened, was the first to be broken up, in 1905. Seven which survived to 1907 had their boiler pressure reduced latterly to 120psi; and two last survivors, though duplicate listed in 1914–15, saw the First World War out before retiring in 1920. *(Author's Collection)*

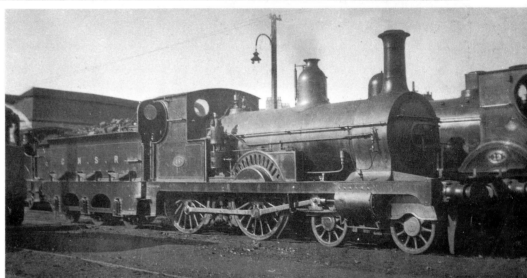

'K' Class No.48 was rebuilt in November 1889 by James Manson; but despite the provision of a new boiler the locomotive retained much of its traditional Cowan appearance. The dome, now transferred from the firebox to the barrel, has kept its original profile, clack boxes on the boiler have also survived, and a cab has been provided in lieu of the original weatherboard. The boiler handrail has also been extended, though it still remains unconnected to the straight front rail, and the original 1,800 gallon, three ton tender has been left alone. Duplicate listed in October 1920, No.48A entered LNER stock as Class 47/2, and, never renumbered, it was withdrawn in June 1925. *(Author's Collection)*

Sister engine, No.45A, running latterly with a four-wheeled 1,050 gallon, two ton tender, earned more kudos in its old age. Taken out of local service early in 1925, it was repainted in GNSR green livery. Thence it was sent, complete with a train of early GNSR carriages, to appear as item No.48 in the Centenary Celebrations at Darlington. Though the locomotive was officially withdrawn on 31st July 1925, a subsequent spell as Inverurie Works shunter raised hopes of possible preservation. Alas, it was not to be. No.45A was scrapped shortly afterwards, and the vintage coaches she had left at Darlington were sold on to the Marsden & South Shields Railway. *(Author's Collection)*

lowed the GNSR's traditional outside cylinder arrangement. However, although both classes were readily identifiable as Cowan engines, the rear box splasher was abandoned on this occasion: the cab sheets were now neatly curved. Cylinders were increased slightly to 17½in × 26in, and total working weight rose to 71 tons. But, in both classes, pressure remained at 140psi.

The Class 'Cs', in their original form, marked the end of an epoch for the GNSR; for William Cowan built no more locomotives before he retired, aged 60, in October 1883. His successor, James Manson, came from the Glasgow & South Western Railway's Kilmarnock Works and had little time for the brass and copper extravagances of GNSR locomotive practice to date. Manson also favoured inside cylinders, and he soon set about

Class 'L' No.55 (Neilson &Co. 2072/1876), with a total working weight of 69 tons 3 cwt, exceeded that of the Class 'Ks' by nearly five tons. The six-wheeled tender alone accounted for one ton of that. Initially, the only brake on the 'K' and 'L' series was a handbrake on the tender; but this was duly superseded, first by a steam brake for the engine, then by a Westinghouse brake for both engine and train. *(Author's Collection)*

The same locomotive, No.55, is hardly recognisable after rebuilt in March 1900 by W. Pickersgill. A plain cast Johnson chimney has replaced the original copper-capped one and Cowan's handsome brass dome has disappeared in favour of a plain closed variety, with Ramsbottom safety valves sited separately over the firebox. Note, too, how the boiler rail, previously terminated behind the smokebox, now curves continuously over the front. Brass beadings at running plate level have, however, been retained. So, too, has the six-wheeled tender with its outside frames and springs. At Grouping, No.55 was allotted LNER No.6855. Withdrawal in August 1924, alas, ensured that the locomotive never carried it. *(Author's Collection)*

making his mark at Kittybrewster. Thus, hardy a year elapsed before six inside-cylindered 4-4-0s, Nos.63–68, built to his design, arrived from Kitson & Co. of Leeds (Works Nos.2668–73/1884). Similar in dimensions to Cowan's 'C' class, but lighter in weight and sporting 6ft coupled wheels, they were duly classified 'A'. Westinghouse brake only was fitted, and the arch-framed six-wheeled Manson tender with which they were initially equipped carried 3 tons of coal and 2,000 gallons of water. Rebuilt between 1905 and 1912, this class, however, was subjected to considerable tender variation in later years.

In May 1885 three more Kitson & Co 4-4-0s (Works Nos.2838–40) followed smartly on the heels of the Class 'As'. To all intents a goods version of the latter, the Class 'Gs', Nos.69–71, accordingly employed 5ft 6in coupled wheels. Other dimensions were identical, except for tractive effort, which increased proportionately. All three were rebuilt with slightly larger boilers during 1905–1911, and re-emerged with engine weight stepped up by nearly five tons. Their main employment was on goods and fish traffic, particularly in the Buchan area, but they also worked main line and branch passenger trains as required.

In the year 1887 James Manson achieved the near-impossible by erecting two more 4-4-0s in the extremely cramped locale of Kittybrewster Works. The main components were purchased from various locomotive building firms. Compared to Class 'G' engines, the driving wheels of Nos.5 and 6, Class 'N' as they were known, were one inch larger at 5ft 7in, and both boiler and firebox were longer. They were also the first GNSR engines to carry names; though these were later removed by W. Pickersgill, who disapproved of the practice. Though only two in number, the Class 'N's, later LNER Class D46, handled a great

As with the Class 'L' engines, the nine Class 'Ms' looked vastly different after rebuild by W. Pickersgill between the years 1896 and 1904. Dome and safety valves have again been separated and the new boilers have a diameter of 4ft 6in, the standard adopted by the GNSR from 1897 onwards. No.51, seen here still in GNSR livery on 27th August 1923, was one of six Class 'Ls' which were rebuilt at Kittybrewster during 1896–1900. The three others, including No.58, were dealt with at Inverurie in 1903–04. No.51 eventually graduated as LNER Class D45 No.6851; but it suffered the minor indignity of having to make its way to Cowlairs Works before being scrapped in January 1927. *(Author's Collection)*

Class 'M' No.58 (Neilson & Co. 2352/1878), seen here at Elgin, illustrates the classic features of Cowan's latter day designs. As steam brake was originally provided, the presence of Westinghouse brake equipment suggests that this photograph was taken circa 1895. The more orthodox tender now adopted by Cowan had room for three tons of coal and 1,950 gallons of water. In much later GSNR, possibly LNER, days the addition of coal rails raised tender capacity to four tons. Reboilered at Inverurie in November 1903, the locomotive was withdrawn as LNER No.6858, in May 1927. *(Author's Collection)*

valves, placed above, instead of between, the cylinders, were worked by rocking shafts. This, in turn, permitted the use of 3ft 9½in bogie wheels, a practice which was to become truly characteristic of later GNSR 4-4-0s. In working order these engines weighed 41 tons 9 cwt.

Nearly 30 years later, over the years 1915–1920, all nine of Manson's Class 'Os' were rebuilt with boilers of the same size as those originally fitted. Four of them, however, were equipped with Robinson superheater, one received a Schmidt superheater and the remaining quartet remained saturated. All were classified D42 when they entered LNER stock at Grouping. In their original form the Class 'O' engines had weighed 41 tons 9 cwt. Once rebuilt, the saturated and superheated members of the class turned the scales at 44 tons and 46 tons 7 cwt respectively. The whole class lasted remarkably under LNER colours, and the last, No.6817 (Kitson & Co. Works No.3060/1888) did not bow the knee until February 1946. No.6874, the sole Class 'O' fitted with the Schmidt superheater in April 1916, reverted to Robinson superheating after Grouping, and was withdrawn from Elgin shed in May 1939. Stored for a few months at Inverurie in case of wartime need, it was cut up early in 1940.

The Class 'O's proved to be so satisfactory in service that in August 1889 the GNSR Board authorised the further purchase of six similar locomotives; this time from R. Stephenson & Co. All were delivered in 1890, but because of interim alteration, they were deployed as two distinct GNSR classes. The main difference was that GNSR Nos.12–14 (Class 'P') had 6ft 0½in coupled wheels, while the coupled wheels of Nos.75–77 (Class 'Q') were altered before completion to 6ft 6½in. The Class 'Qs', Manson's last locomotives for the GNSR, cost £2,525 per engine, £25 more than the Class 'Ps'. Meanwhile, all six engines were fitted with Westinghouse brake only and entered traffic with new style Manson eight-wheeled tenders. The latter, by dint of employing a leading bogie, with two rigid axles behind,

variety of traffic in their day. According to the GNSR Chairman of the time, the Company saved £300/£400 by having them built at Kittybrewster.

Although Manson had introduced three new classes of 4-4-0 within a period of three years, the second half of 1887 found his Directors calling for still larger engines, to cope with ever increasing passenger traffic. With further construction prospects patently futile at Kittybrewster, Manson then prepared a fourth design, and commissioned nine Class 'O' 4-4-0s from Kitson & Co. Variously numbered, because six of them were charged to revenue and three to capital., the new locomotives arrived during April–June 1888. This time 6ft 0½in coupled wheels were employed, cylinders were enhanced to 18in × 26in, and the firebox was lengthened to six feet. More importantly, balanced slide

Rebuild of Nos.1–3, the Class 'C' engines, was also spread over several years, 1897–1904. The end product, however, was much the same as far as these 6ft 1in engines were concerned. Mainly employed on Elgin–Keith–Aberdeen services, they drifted latterly into local and branch work. No.1 spent her last years at Kittybrewster, acting as spare engine and/or Inverurie pilot; then, in August 1925, still bearing her GNSR number, the locomotive was withdrawn. Her two sister engines, also classified D39 by the LNER, only lived a year or two longer. *(Author's Collection)*

This Elgin study, obtained on 27th August 1923, shows Class 'A' No.63 as rebuilt in October 1905. Smokebox wingplates have gone — and so too has its original Manson built-up chimney. First built, No.63, though tentatively allotted LNER No.6863, was also the first to go, in July 1924. The class became D44 under LNER auspices, and vanished by 1932. *(Author's Collection)*

Seen at Kittybrewster in 1926, former Class 'G' 4-4-0 No.6870, now LNER Class D48, had by this time also acquired a tender cab — a very useful amenity north of Aberdeen. One D48, No.6869, lingered on to 1934, but No.6870 went to the breakers long before that, in June 1928. *(Author's Collection)*

The prototype Class 'N' looks smart in LNER green livery at Kittybrewster, but still carries its GNSR number and Manson chimney. Wingplates have gone. No.5 was reboilered in April 1915, at which time working pressure was also raised from 140 to 165psi. Later given LNER No.6805, it outlived its sister engine by four years, by holding out to April 1936. The name *Kinmundy* it originally bore was that of the GNSR Chairman's residence. *(Author's Collection)*

Above:
The much larger bogie wheels of the Class 'Os' are self-evident in this Kittybrewster study of No.10 (Kitson & Co. Works No.3059). The swing link bogies these engines featured were almost the first in the country. Initially employed on main line passenger duties between Aberdeen and Elgin, the class 'O's were supplanted latterly by W. Pickersgill 4-4-0s, and tended thereafter to find work where they could, anywhere on the GNSR system. *(Author's Collection)*

Class 'O' No.10, now LNER Class D42 No.6810, still looked very smart when it was photographed in the mid-1930s. Rebuilt in May 1916, still in saturated form, the locomotive reappeared with a cast Johnson pattern chimney, and Manson's rather severe dome was softened in line. Ross pop safety valves were added later. The tender rails seen here raised coal capacity to 4½ tons, and the tender cab is a relic of branch working days. No.6810, meanwhile, served on until November 1939. *(Author's Collection)*

Seen here at Kittybrewster shed *circa* 1930, LNER Class D43 No.6812, the longest-lived GNSR Class 'P' engine, was shopped by R. Stephenson & Co. (Works No.2695) in saturated form in May 1890. Superheated in 1917, it again ran in saturated form from June 1932 until withdrawal 5½ years later. *(Author's Collection)*

---

contrived to hold four tons of coal and 3,000 gallons of water, a much greater capacity than any previous GNSR tenders. They were the first eight-wheeled tenders to be used in this country and, though rather ungainly in appearance, they were further developed on the Glasgow & South Western Railway when Manson took charge there in 1891. On the GNSR, however, eight-wheeled tenders were found to be something of a luxury for comparatively short-distance work and, removed about the time of Grouping, they were never used again on any class.

Subsequent reboilerings, before and after Grouping, brought differing histories to practically all six engines. The only two to remain saturated throughout their careers were No.13 (Class 'P') and no.76 (Class 'Q'). Even then, No.76 was withdrawn in February 1931, almost seven years before No.13 went to the breakers. The remaining four were all superheated at some time or other. 'P' Class Nos.12 and 14 (later LNER Class D43) were fitted with Robinson superheaters in 1917, but subsequent reboilering saw No.12 (by then LNER No.6812) revert to saturated form in June 1932, and the locomotive ran thus until withdrawal in January 1938. No.6814 was given a secondhand post–Grouping saturated boiler in January 1928, but was again superheated in March 1931 before withdrawal came in November 1936. The history of the Class 'Q' (later LNER Class D38) locomotive, however, was a mite less complicated. No.75, given a Robinson superheater in July 1917, retained it until the end came in January 1938. No.77, very much the odd man out, and the first Class 'Q' to be rebuilt, re-emerged from Inverurie

Works in October 1913 with a Schmidt superheater and clung to it right up to withdrawal in September 1937. At Grouping all six still possessed Westinghouse brake only, but No.6875, now LNER Class D38, and No.6812 were dual-fitted in 1926 and 1935 respectively.

So ended yet another phase in GNSR life, for on 1st September 1890, James Manson opted to return to familiar pastures by accepting appointment as Locomotive Superintendent to the Glasgow & South Western Railway. During his seven years at Kittybrewster he had, in addition to introducing some very useful locomotive innovations, earned the sincere respect of all who served under him. In the latter context his monumental contribution was the introduction of his automatic tablet exchange apparatus in 1886. Not only did this completely eliminate the physical hazards which had previously attended exchange by hand, but, typical of Manson's humanitarian philosophy, he refused to limit its benefits by patenting his invention.

The GNSR Board could hardly have made a better choice of successor when it appointed James Johnson whose father, the celebrated Samuel Waite Johnson, was at that time Locomotive Superintendent to the Midland Railway. The changeover happened to coincide with a period of GNSR prosperity — a period which ultimately concluded with removal to more spacious locomotive works at Inverurie at the turn of the century. Johnson, in the event, only served four years in GNSR employment; but the two locomotive classes he introduced were models of elegance and utility. The first consisted of nine neat 0-4-4 tanks. These served Aberdeen suburban purposes admirably. The other was a series of six Class 'S' 4-4-0s, numbered 78–83. Both types were supplied by Neilson & Co. of Glasgow in 1893.

Apart from its typical GNSR smokebox door, 'S' Class No.81, could easily have been mistaken for a Midland 4-4-0 as it prepared to leave Aberdeen Station on main line duty in the late 1890s. The locomotive was 'rebuilt' in February 1919, but re-emerged from Inverurie Works looking remarkably unchanged in appearance. *(Author's Collection)*

LNER Class D41 No.6883's slightly flattish dome cover reminds us that the locomotive entered traffic originally as GNSR 'S' class No.83 (Neilson & Co. Works No.4645/1893). In March 1940 it was one of two D41s which were transferred to Fife, to assist in rapidly generating NB Section goods traffic. Both locomotives returned home in 1943 and, renumbered 2230 in 1946, then 62230 in 1949, the one time Class 'S' duly perished in March 1952.
(Author's Collection)

The Class 'S' 4-4-0s were so elegant they might conceivably have emanated from Derby Works, as did Johnson himself. Their 6ft 1in coupled wheels, 18in × 26in cylinders, working pressure of 165psi and tractive effort of 16,184lb were all quite compatible with current GNSR practice; but detail alterations made in these 45 ton locomotives were arresting to a degree. Open-topped dome covers, for instance, came back into use, surmounted on this occasion by a single lock-up safety valve. A second safety valve was encased by a tall brass trumpet, Midland style, over the firebox, Westinghouse brake was provided, and a Johnson-type tender, again based quite closely on Midland Railway practice, accommodated 3,000 gallons of water and 3½ tons of coal. When later fitted with coal rails these tenders took 5 tons of coal. Interestingly, Johnson also discontinued use of the Clark smoke consuming apparatus which had been an almost common factor on the GNSR for decades.

A few years before Grouping all six Class 'S' engines lost their Johnson safety valves, and were given instead the usual Ramsbottom variety, cased and seated over the firebox. The original domes, however, remained for the time being. Then, in LNER days, came standard Ross pop valves and NBR pattern smokebox doors. During the late 1920s, vacuum ejectors were

also fitted to four of the class which had not so been treated two decades earlier. The purpose in fitting Nos.79 and 81 thus in GNSR days had been to enable them to work trains of Highland Railway stock, as required, during the years 1908 and 1914, when normally frosty relations between the two Companies thawed sufficiently to enable through trains to be run between Inverness and Aberdeen. The practice was never resumed, alas, after World War One. Came Grouping, and the six Class 'S' engines were merged with 26 slightly later Pickersgill Class 'T' 4-4-0s to form LNER Class D41.

Meanwhile, by the time James Johnson resigned his post and William Pickersgill, erstwhile Great Eastern Railway Locomotive Superintendent at Norwich, succeeded him in May 1894, the GNSR's need for more locomotives had grown even more acute.

The presence, *circa* 1914, of greenery and a top hat on the smokebox of 'T' Class No.110 suggests that the retirement of some GNSR official, possibly a stationmaster, was being celebrated. No.110 was duly 'retired' itself, as LNER No.2254, In January 1947. *(Author's Collection)*

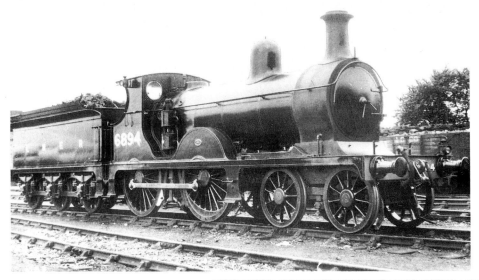

LNER Class D41 No.6894, formerly GNSR No.94, was one of three Class 'Ts' which were fitted with vacuum ejectors in the early 1900s. In 1928 No.6894 was also given a second Westinghouse pump for the transitional purpose of supplying compressed air to bridge riveting apparatus, and the locomotive was withdrawn, as BR No.62238, in August 1948.
(Author's Collection)

All 32 Class 'S' and 'T' locomotives reached Grouping safely enough. Only 22 entered BR stock, however, and No.62225, the pioneer Class 'S', was one of ten which were repainted in lined black livery. By early 1953 the last three D41s, Nos.62225 and 62241/2, could be found in Inverurie yard, patiently awaiting the breakers' attentions.
(Author's Collection)

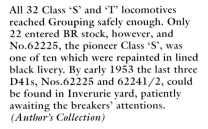

The opening of the Forth Bridge in 1890 had simply revitalised the whole of the Scottish eastern seaboard. Pickersgill, to his credit, did not hesitate, but ordered 26 more Johnson 4-4-0s from Neilson & Co. Built in 1895–96 (Works Nos.4877–90) and 1897–98 (Works Nos.5212–23), they were styled GNSR Class 'T' because of detail differences and were given running numbers which ranged between 19 and 112. Five of them were fitted with extended smokeboxes between 1928 and 1931 in an LNER effort to reduce coal consumption, but only two. Nos.6821 and 6902, were still so fitted when withdrawal came in September 1946 and August 1951 respectively. Two more, Nos.6823/4, retained Westinghouse brake only until the end. Likewise, Nos.101–12 always had fluted coupling rods, while the remainder ran with plain coupling rods. Steam heating apparatus was fitted to all 'S' and 'T' class engines between May 1912 and February 1917. In LNER and BR days, mobile tender cabs moved between four D41s as and when the locomotives undertook tender-first running on the windswept Lossiemouth branch. For a few months until January 1916, No.79 was even on loan to the Highland Railway and the association was further renewed after nationalisation, when D41s could be found working beyond their normal Boat of Garten destination to the ex-HR station at Aviemore. By then, however, the class was becoming rapidly redundant and extinction finally came in February 1953.

Certainly, the Class 'Ts', the bulk of which had been provided in time to cope with vastly improved GNSR services from 1897 onwards, served the Company with great distinction. Despite their 6ft 1in driving wheels, these free-running engines often touched 80mph as occasion arose. Yet they could be equally cheerfully employed working freight, handling local passenger trains, even shunting, as required. Therefore, in light of

their success, Pickersgill chose to recommend purchase of a further twelve in 1898. Demurring slightly, the GNSR Directors compromised on an order for ten and Neilson Reid & Co. duly delivered the first five, Nos.25, 26, and 113–115, in October 1899. Known as the 'V' Class, principal dimensions were as before. The main difference was that the Class 'V' engines were given square side-windowed cabs, with a raised ventilator on the roof. All five were saturated, and had unbalanced slide valves between the cylinders, which were, as usual, 18in × 26in. These engines were 1 ton heavier than the 'S' and 'T' classes.

Unfortunately, the volatile nature of GNSR finances was such that by 1900 the Company found itself unable to accept delivery of Neilson Reid's second batch of 4-4-0s. As luck would have it, Neilson were able to sell the five potential Class 'Vs' on to the newly formed South Eastern & Chatham Railway. The price was £3,300 apiece; thus the Aberdeen railway, having already been charged £2,975 for each engine, even got a rebate of £1,250 for the non-transaction! In the event, the SECR were so pleased with the performance of the Neilson Reid engines that they offered the GNSR £3,325 each for first five. The GNSR Board, though doubtless sorely tempted, kept its collective nerve and declined the offer...

Still disposed to persevere, particularly as the GNSR's new locomotive Works at Inverurie had come into operation over the turn of the century, Pickersgill, between 1903 and 1911, urged a ten year construction of eighteen more Class 'Vs'. His Directors eventually sanctioned eight; and they were shopped from Inverurie in two batches of four — one in 1901–10, the other in 1913–15. In keeping with the rest of the class, their distinctive GNSR type smokebox doors were replaced by NBR type doors in early LNER days. By then the Inverurie 'eight' had become Class D40 Nos.6827–29, 6831, and 6833–36.

No.115 (Neilson Reid Works No.5604/1899), the longest lived of a 'V' class which eventually totalled thirteen engines, illustrates the final neat appearance of the GNSR 4-4-0. Her standard tender, with its two coal rails, held five tons of coal and 3,000 gallons of water. Renumbered 6915, then 2264, by the LNER, and reclassified D40, the locomotive bore BR No.62264 when it finally surrendered in March 1957. *(Author's Collection)*

LNER D40 No.6828 has seen a change or two since it was shopped as Class 'V' No.28 from Inverurie Works in March 1913, and appears here as one of four D40s which carried tender cabs periodically for branch working. Its extended smokebox, some eleven inches longer than was normal with saturated engines, was a legacy of June 1930. Renumbered 2266 in 1946, the locomotive went to the wall in January 1947, exactly one year too soon to be taken into BR stock. *(Author's Collection)*

The five 4-4-0s sold on to the SECR were duly numbered 676–680 and were classified 'G'. Still undeniably GNSR in appearance. No.680 nevertheless looks quite at home in SECR livery. The last of the class was withdrawn in 1927. *(NRM)*

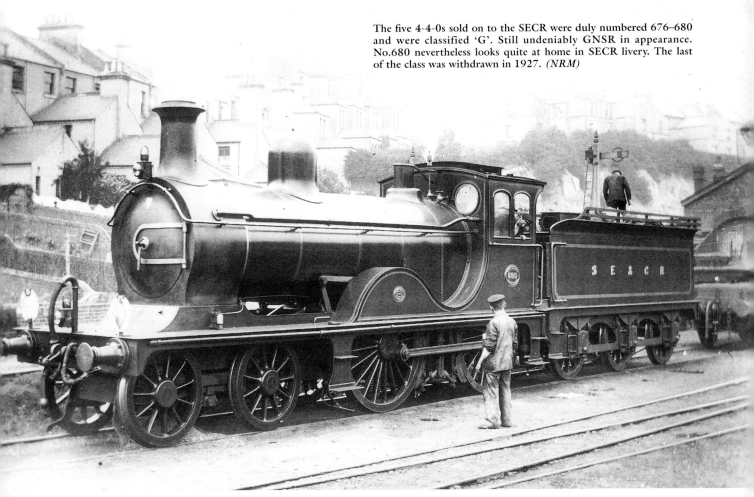

In this Works photograph 'F' Class No.54 (NB Locomotive Co. Works No.22566/1920) has not yet received its name, *Southesk*. A Kittybrewster engine for most of its life, it was the only one of its class which failed to enter BR stock, being withdrawn, still in LNER harness as No.2280, in January 1947. *(Author's Collection)*

Destined to become the most celebrated member of the D40 clan, 'F' Class No.49 (NB Locomotive Co. 22563/1920) played a unique role during the coal strike of 1921, when, alone amongst GNSR engines, it was fitted for oil fuel burning. Equipped thus from June to October 1921, *Gordon Highlander* was caught by the camera at Kittybrewster shed on 4th July. *(Author's Collection)*

More change followed for the GNSR shortly before World War One erupted. After serving twenty extremely constructive years at Kittybrewster and Inverurie, William Pickersgill was chosen, on 1st March 1914, to succeed J. F. McIntosh as Locomotive, Carriage & Wagon Superintendent on the Caledonian Railway. His successor at Inverurie, T. E. Heywood, came from the Taff Vale Railway and, instrumental in extending the use of superheating on the GNSR, he was to serve his new Company right up to Grouping. Subsequent service in the LNER's Northern Scottish Area, interspersed with three years at Gorton, took him to retirement in June 1942. He died in November 1953, still resident in Aberdeen.

The end of a long and weary war found the GNSR, like many other companies, desperately short of stock. Thus, eight more 4-4-0s were built to Heywood's requirements in 1920–21. Similar in most respects to the GNSR's Class 'V', these locomotives, however, were Robinson superheated and, as such, were classified 'F'. For the first time in 25 years, too, the practice of locomotive naming was revived, and all eight Class 'Fs' carried brass nameplates, with raised lettering. Nos.47–50, 52, and 54 were supplied by the North British Locomotive Co. (Works Nos.22561–66) in 1920, and the last pair, Nos.45–46, came

from Inverurie the following year. Tractive effort, as before, was 16,184lb. All eight locomotives were dual-fitted, and engine weight was 48 tons 13 cwts, 2¼ tons greater than that of their saturated sisters. The superheated engines were always readily recognisable by the large 'pepper pot' anti-vacuum valve they carried immediately below the chimney on the right hand side of the smokebox. Another original fitment on Heywood's engines appeared below handrail level in the form of a shut-off cock for the steam jet draught retarder. This apparatus, however, was removed shortly after Grouping.

Despite the fact that No.62277 *Gordon Highlander* only entered traffic in October 1920, the locomotive's black livery was replaced in July 1958 by a splendid coat of GNSR pre-Heywood green paint. As in the case of the NBR's *Glen Douglas*, full restoration was not effected; but *Gordon Highlander* was reconditioned sufficiently to be able to resume

One of two Class 'Fs' which were subscribed by Inverurie Works in 1921, and originally numbered 45, No.62273 *George Davidson* could still be found at Kittybrewster three decades later. Nameplates disappeared from six sister engines by 1954 in favour of painted lettering, after the fashion of the other Scottish Companies; but *George Davidson's* were still there when the locomotive was scrapped at Kilmarnock in January 1955. *(Author)*

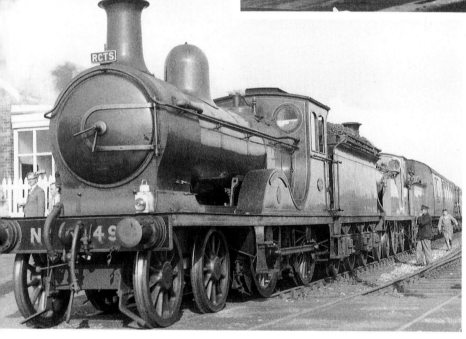

In a fitting climax to the RCTS ten day Scottish tour of June 1962 *Gordon Highlander* and ex-Caledonian single-wheeler No.123 join forces to haul the special train on its last stirring lap to Carlisle. *(Author)*

normal services on the Speyside sector. It later joined other pre-served Scottish engines at Dawsholm shed, and subsequently undertook quite extensive special workings over all Scottish metals. One such was an ambitious ten day tour of the Scottish Region, organised jointly by the Railway Correspondence & Travel Society and the Stephenson Locomotive Society in June 1962. Some of the 'preserved' Scottish locomotives were used at various stages. On the very first day, for instance, *Gordon Highlander* piloted ex-HR 'Jones Goods' No.103 between Perth and Inverness. Two days later, the ex-GNSR stalwart again piloted the tour train between Aviemore and Aberdeen. Then,

on 23rd June, the last day of the tour, *Gordon Highlander*, deputising perforce for the 'Jones Goods', joined the ex-Caledonian single-wheeler No.123 in handling the RCTS special for much of the way between Ayr and Carlisle. Much to the delight of all on board, a maximum speed of 65mph was recorded during the final sprint into Carlisle.

Eventually taken out of traffic in 1965, *Gordon Highlander* joined other Scottish veterans at the Glasgow Museum of Transport on 10th June 1966. And there, fittingly, it remains today as a stimulating reminder to youthful observers that Aberdeen, too, was once a highly independent railway centre.

Chapter 5
THE GLASGOW AND SOUTH WESTERN RAILWAY

IMAGINE A TRIANGULAR LINE drawn between Glasgow, Stranraer, and Carlisle, and you have a fairly clear concept of the territory traditionally served by this Scottish railway. The G&SWR was created by the fusion of two vigorous earlier concerns, the Glasgow, Dumfries & Carlisle Railway and the Glasgow, Paisley, Kilmarnock & Ayr Railway, and entered the fray quite modestly, on 28th October 1850, with a total route mileage of 171¾. Having also acquired 73 locomotives, plus three more on order, it numbered them, logically enough, 1 to 76. One third were four-coupled, the remainder were single-wheeled; and in due course all perished by 1873.

Initially, G&SWR engines were looked after at the GPK&AR's former workshops at Cook Street, Glasgow. Soon, however, these premises proved to be hopelessly cramped, and much more capacious new shops, sited conveniently by the junction of the main line and Troon branch, were opened at Kilmarnock in 1856. The G&SWR's main line, incidentally, terminated at Gretna Green, whence running powers over nine miles of Caledonian Railway track had to be exercised ere Carlisle was reached. As in the case of the North British Railway, G&SWR relations with the Caledonian were unfriendly in the extreme. Indeed, the Sou' West had to tolerate the same LNWR/CR blockade at Carlisle — until 1876, when the Midland Railway came to the rescue by facilitating through traffic to and from the South. Hardly surprisingly, animosity towards the CR remained a feature of G&SWR life right up to Grouping in 1923.

Meanwhile, Peter Robertson, formerly of the GPK&AR, graduated as the G&SWR's first Locomotive Superintendent in 1850. Under his aegis one single-wheeler and an 0-4-0 were built at Cook Street during 1851–52. More significantly, ten more 0-4-0s, added a year later by R. & W. Hawthorn, introduced the domeless boiler which was to feature so prominently in subsequent G&SWR locomotive history. The next chapter opened when Robertson resigned in January 1893, and a 33-year-old 'unknown' stepped into his place on 2nd May. His name was Patrick Stirling.

Thus soon the illustrious Stirling family entered the annals of British locomotive history. Ultimately, three members of the clan — Patrick, his brother James, and Patrick's second son, Matthew — created something of a record by putting in a total of 122 years as Locomotive Superintendents to five different Companies. Matthew had almost completed 38 years with his sole love, the Hull & Barnsley Railway, when absorption by the North Eastern Railway on 1st April 1922 hastened his retirement at the age of 65. In somewhat similar circumstances, James, fifteen years junior to Patrick, retired in his mid-sixties when his second Company, the South Eastern Railway, commenced joint operations with the London, Chatham & Dover Railway on 1st January 1899. Patrick, the family patriarch, was made of even sterner stuff. He soldiered on to the age of 75 with *his* second Company — until November 1895, when the Great Northern Railway Board had to *ask* him to retire! Poor Patrick, he died eleven days later. But, back to Scottish affairs. . .

A departmental works manager with R. & W. Hawthorn of Newcastle prior to his 1853 G&SWR appointment, Patrick Stirling had already spent sixteen quite varied years in locomotive and marine engineering. His basic lack of design experience, however, betrayed itself in the first Sou' West locomotives he introduced — four Neilson outside-cylindered 2-2-2s and four Hawthorn intermediate crankshaft 0-4-0s. Then came a serious attempt at express locomotive design, when twelve outside-cylinder 2-2-2s were shopped from Kilmarnock Works in 1857–60. These, and ten 0-4-2s, supplied by Hawthorn in 1858, were to be the last Patrick Stirling-designed engines to carry domed boilers. Within the next five years his well known round-topped cab also made its debut; while his lifelong partiality for single-wheelers, later to be expressed so eloquently at Doncaster, surfaced further in 1865, when the first of 11 elegant 7ft express 2-2-2s emerged from Kilmarnock Works. One remembers with wry affection Patrick's dictum that the sight of a coupled engine travelling at speed reminded him of a 'a laddie runnin' wi' his breeks doon!'. Ten months later he left Kilmarnock for Doncaster, where, on 1st October 1866, he succeeded Archibald Sturrock as Chief Locomotive Superintendent to the Great Northern Railway, Intriguingly, the G&SWR executive appointed his brother, James, presently Works Manager at Kilmarnock, as his successor.

There is no doubt that James Stirling, like his nephew, Matthew, was deeply influenced all thorough his professional life by the locomotive practices of his elder brother. Yet, as in the Stroudley/Drummond syndrome, he reserved the right to follow his own instincts as and when required. Thus, although James perpetuated employment of the domeless boiler, he had no hesitation in switching latterly from the traditional balance safety valves to the Ramsbottom variety. He also cut away the rather clumsy prototype Stirling cab side, to permit locomen to lean out. Inside cylinders, too, were a prerequisite of all James Stirling locomotives — just as 'singles' were taboo — and the steam reversing gear he introduced in 1874 proved to be a most practicable contribution to G&SWR's men's welfare. His first locomotives, fifteen 2-4-0s built at Kilmarnock in 1868–69, had an elegance about them which, rather surprisingly, he never again succeeded in recapturing. Quite a substantial series of minor four-coupled variations followed; then, no doubt inspired by the NBR's example, Stirling took a deep breath, and produced his first 4-4-0. The prototype engine, No.6, shopped from Kilmarnock Works in July 1873, was carefully tested before 21 more were built over the years 1874–1877.

Second only to Thomas Wheatley in introducing a British inside-cylindered 4-4-0, and with through Carlisle express traffic very much in mind, Stirling had applied great thought to his new design. Coupled wheels were stepped up to 7ft 1in and cylinders, 18in × 26in, employed a working pressure of 140psi. One might have thought that the provision of a fixed pivot bogie with a wheelbase of only 4ft 10in was a dubious gamble; but Stirling's 39 ton Class '6' 4-4-0s, in fact, handled heavy through express trains with great expediency once the Midland

No.11, a Kilmarnock Works product of July 1877 was the last-built of Stirling's Class '6' 4-4-0s, and was also the last of six which were somewhat prematurely withdrawn during 1894–96. The remaining sixteen locomotives, duplicate listed over the same period, were relegated to less exacting local duties until rebuild came their way, at the hands of James Manson, in 1899–1901. (Author's Collection)

Above:
Seen here in the late 1920s, the Class '119' prototype, now LMS No.14116, still looks the epitome of elegance as it leaves St. Enoch Station on local passenger duty. This locomotive was one of a minority which retained its original form right up to its withdrawal in December 1931. (Author's Collection)

The dramatically changed appearance of the rebuilt Class '119s' is illustrated in this view of No.14120, formerly G&WR No.126 (later 704), one of the first six shopped by Smellie in 1882. All traces of the Stirling influence have been eradicated above boiler level, and a capacious new cab bears the legend '2P', as opposed to the LMSR 1P classification given to seven which were never rebuilt. In the event No.14120 was one of three Class '119s' which survived until June 1934. (Author's Collection)

Railway reached Carlisle in 1876. The tight schedule the G&SWR imposed of 155 minutes over its heavily graded 115½ mile main line required an average speed of 44.7mph.

In light of the success of the Class '6s' it came as rather a blow to Kilmarnock when, less the twelve months after No.11 was built, James Stirling left G&SWR employment to take up duties as Locomotive Superintendent to the South Eastern Railway, with effect from 28 March 1878. Yet, significantly, the Stirling influence on G&SWR locomotive affairs was by no means ended; for his successor in office was Hugh Smellie, who had once served James Stirling as Works Manager at Kilmarnock, before moving on to the Maryport & Carlisle Railway. Further back still, Smellie (pronounced 'Smiley', by the way!) had entered an apprenticeship at the tender age of sixteen under Patrick Stirling at the G&SWR's 'new' Kilmarnock workshops.

Fitted rather startlingly with a removable smokebox extension, and one of five Hugh Smellie '153' Class 4-4-0s so equipped, No.89, a Kilmarnock Works product (Works No.222) of July 1889, was renumbered 463 in 1919. It was renumbered in LMS stock as 14155, and was withdrawn in 1930. (BR LMR)

It follows that he fully understood the implications of domeless boilers! Indeed, the latter feature, and many other Stirling trademarks, were faithfully embodied in Smellie's new G&SWR designs. He also succeeded in introducing a refinement of appearance which had hitherto been lacking in Sou' West locomotives.

Preoccupation with the matter of continuous brakes apart — whence the G&SWR followed the Midland Railway's example by switching to the vacuum brake in the main — Smellie's first locomotive adventure, a series of twelve 2-4-0s built at Kilmarnock in 1878–80, probably owed more to a paucity of suitable turntables on the G&SWR than to a distrust of leading bogies. Nevertheless, the difficulty of maintaining tight schedules on the Greenock road induced him, soon enough, to consider employing 4-4-0s. Kilmarnock Works obliged with the production of 24 Class '119' engines in 1882–85. With 6ft 1½in driving wheels and 18¼in × 26in cylinders these powerful engines set a new UK standard. The first half dozen performed excellently on the Greenock section; then, as the class increased in number, they could be found working expresses as far afield as Stranraer, once the turntable there had been lengthened. Held in great affection by G&SWR men, they were popularly known as the 'Wee Bogies'. Two were scrapped in 1914–15, but fifteen were rebuilt with X3 boiler and Whitelegg cab shortly before Grouping. Thus, 22 Class '119's in all survived to acquire LMSR numbers. By the mid-thirties, however, all had gone.

Came 1886, and Smellie embarked on the most ambitious and efficient design he ever produced — his quite beautiful Class '153' 4-4-0s. Built at Kilmarnock during 1886–89 for main line express work, and based on the '119' class, these twenty engines had coupled wheels of 6ft 9½in diameter and 2,500 gallon tenders. Their domeless boilers were made of Siemens steel and by dint of increasing the length of the firebox by three inches, an enhanced heating surface of 1,198sq ft was provided. Working pressure, too, was increased to 150psi. Four of the '153s', Nos.57, 67, 70 and 89 were the recipients of an experimental form of removable extended smokebox. This is believed to have been the first such application in the UK; but the accessory was removed from all by 1906. Under the 1919 renumbering scheme, when G&SWR locomotives were renumbered and grouped according to wheel arrangement, the nineteen surviving Class '153s' were allocated Nos.448 to 466. Under LMS auspices they were again renumbered 14138 to 14156.

On 1st September 1890 change again came the G&SWR's way, when Hugh Smellie, respected by all as an extremely practical railwayman, accepted the post of Locomotive Superintendent

with the Sou' West's arch-enemy, the Caledonian Railway. The latter, itself not averse to 'poaching', had just lost Dugald Drummond to Australia. It was as well, though, for posterity's sake that Smellie left behind him a legacy of free-steaming G&SWR locomotives and vastly enhanced facilities at Kilmarnock Works — for his career at St. Rollox was cut cruelly short. He died after only eight months in office. The G&SWR Board, meanwhile, had pinpointed yet another Kilmarnock-trained man as his successor. James Manson, in course of a varied locomotive and marine engineering career, had acted as Works Manager, under Smellie, over the years 1878–83, before leaving to take charge of Great North of Scotland Railway locomotive affairs. Now, Saltcoats born in 1846 and fresh from carrying out important reforms at Kittybrewster, Manson was returning to his native Ayrshire. He was to serve the G&SWR long and well before he finally retired in 1912. His long retirement (he died at Kilmarnock in June 1935, aged 89) must have been saddened by the cavalier treatment his locomotives subsequently received at the hands of R. H. Whitelegg and the LMS.

Manson's arrival at Kilmarnock certainly launched a new era as far as G&SWR locomotives were concerned. Well and truly his 'own man' after seven years' sound work in the North of Scotland, he was not of a mind to submit himself unquestioningly to Stirling tradition. Thus, he brought with him a new concept of tall domes, Ramsbottom safety valves over the firebox, and pleasingly shaped cabs. He did choose, however, to retain James Stirling's steam reversing gear and, initially at least, he adopted Smellie's neat six-wheeled tender. Pausing only to

Seen here in the early 1920s, Class '153' No.458 has long lost the extended smokebox it carried when it emerged as No.70 from Kilmarnock Works in February 1888. This locomotive handled the G&SWR's one and only Royal Train, when Queen Victoria travelled from Carlisle to Renfrew on 22nd August 1888 and, as a reward, it subsequently carried the Royal Arms on its cabside. Never rebuilt, it entered LMS stock as No.14151 — only to be scrapped in January 1926. *(Author's Collection)*

No.14143 was one of three Class '153' rebuilds which were fitted with Westinghouse brake by the LMS for the purpose of working the Lockerbie branch with ex-CR stock. Originally shopped at Kilmarnock in 1886 as No.154 (later No.466), the engine now weighs 46 tons 3 cwts and is classified LMS '1P'. The original 2,500 gallon tender, however, continued to serve the locomotive until withdrawal came in August 1932. This view was taken at St. Enoch Station. *(Author's Collection)*

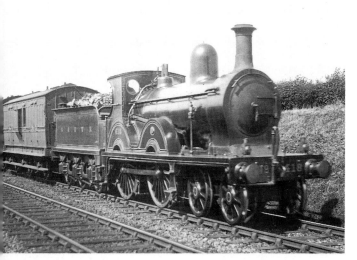

Manson Class '8' No.418 was shopped at Kilmarnock as No.78 in July 1893, and was one of six which carried an eight-wheeled tender from time to time. Working pressure of 150psi produced a tractive effort of 13,547lb and total engine and tender weight was 75 tons 1 cwt. Never rebuilt, No.418 survived, as LMS No.14165, until 1930. *(Author's Collection)*

tidy up an order, already placed, for 20 Smellie standard 0-6-0s, Manson promptly got into his stride by turning his attention towards designing a new G&SWR express engine. Using his GNSR 'Q' Class 4-4-0s as a model, the result was an attractive looking and highly capable locomotive; and, backing him to the hilt, Kilmarnock Works produced 57 Class '8' Manson 4-4-0s over the years 1892–1904. Closely equivalent to Smellie's '153s' both in dimensions and performance, but weighting two tons heavier at 45 tons, the new 4-4-0s, nevertheless, projected a more modern image. Two of Manson's eight-wheeled tenders were built for this class, and were used with the locomotives which handled 'The Diner' between Glasgow and Carlisle and *vice versa*, a 91 mile nonstop run each way.

Late in Manson's career, five Class '8' engines were rebuilt with larger boiler and higher cab. Then, in 1920, R. H. Whitelegg treated fifteen more to an even larger X1 boiler and a cab of his own design. On that occasion working pressure was raised to 170psi and total working weight increased to 49 tons 17 cwt. Although classified '2P' by the LMS, the Whitelegg rebuilds' performance remained rather disappointing.

Brushing aside the G&SWR's peculiar antipathy to tank locomotives, Manson next designed some very neat 0-4-4 tanks. Then, still troubled by the exacting demands of the Greenock route, his Locomotive Committee agreed to the construction of 25 new 4-4-0s. One of Manson's most successful designs, his Class '336' 4-4-0s were supplied by Dübs & Co. Ten were built in 1895 and the remainder followed in 1899. Quite akin in many ways to the Class '8's, they employed smaller (6ft 1½in) driving wheels, and worked on an increased pressure of 165psi. All were later altered to Whitelegg's motion design and six received X1 boilers in 1920–21. The 'Greenock Bogies', as they were affectionately known, were, of course, introduced at a time when Caley/Sou' West competition for Greenock traffic was at its fiercest. So keen, indeed, were the G&SWR to out-speed their rivals that at one stage some of their trains were even advertised as 'No Luggage'!

In April 1897, Manson conducted an experiment which resulted in the G&SWR beating the mighty London & North Western Railway by two months for the honour of shopping Britains first four-cylinder locomotive. The end product, G&SWR No.11, shopped from Kilmarnock Works, was, again, similar in many respects to his Class '8s' — except for those vital four cylinders, all of which took live steam. Their combined volume only slightly exceeded that of the Class '8s'; but working pressure was increased to 165psi and two sets of inside Stephenson valve gear drove four slide valves, while rocking-shafts were utilised to operate the outside valves.

Above:
The shape of Whitelegg's Class '8' rebuilds shows clearly in this photograph of No.14192. The pilot engine is ex-CR 'Dunalastair III' No.14340. As one might have expected, the Whitelegg rebuild perished in April 1931, fifteen years before the Caley 4-4-0 met its doom. (*Author's Collection*)

Seen here in early post-Grouping years, LMS No.14203, originally G&SWR No.336 (Dübs & Co. Works No.3239/1895), can afford to relax from more pressing duties as it couples up to a cattle truck and van. The locomotive retained its original shape to the end, which came, only too soon, in March 1927. (*Author's Collection*)

Notwithstanding this ingenious arrangement, valve setting soon posed problems once the engine was tried out on main line express work; and latterly it had to be conceded that overall economy was disappointingly inferior to that of the two-cylindered engines.

With two 14½in × 26in inside cylinders and two slightly smaller (12½in × 24in) outside cylinders, No.11's 6ft 9½in coupled wheels yielded a tractive effort of 15,860lb. Subsequent performance on Carlisle express work was, however, rudely interrupted on 19th January 1898, when collision with a derailed goods train at Gretna Green inflicted heavy damage. Duly repaired, No.11 resumed rather subdued normal duty. They with the advent, in 1903, of Manson's new 4-6-0s on main line work, No.11 was transferred to Hurlford (Kilmarnock) shed. In November 1915 came 'renewal', in the form of rebuild with a larger (4ft 9¼in) boiler. This consequently increased the weight of the engine to 50 tons 17 cwt, but little improvement seems to have effected.

Renumbered 394 in 1919, a third and final phase came the way of Manson's experimental locomotive in December 1922, when it was again rebuilt, this time more extensively, by R. H. Whitelegg. New cylinders — inside (2) 14in × 26in, outside (2) 14in × 24in — were fitted. The locomotive now carried two piston valves only, and a new 5ft 4½in boiler increased total heating surface to 1,802sq ft. Tractive effort had also been stepped up to 18,390lb. at a cost of 10½ extra tons in locomotive weight. Duly equipped with Robinson superheater, Drummond-type steam

The effect of an X1 boiler and Whitelegg's 1920 attentions show clearly as rebuilt '336' Class No.14213, originally G&SWR Nos.346 and 360, and Dübs-built in 1899, backs on to its train at St. Enoch Station in April 1931. Nothing about the engine's appearance suggests that it was, in fact, involved in an accident here on 31st July 1925. In the event, No.14213 proved to be the second longest lived of its class, and was not withdrawn until September 1932. (*Author's Collection*)

Britain's first four-cylinder locomotive, James Manson's 4-4-0 No.11, built in 1897, ran 140,000 miles in the first three years of its existence. Results, however, were disappointing, and 4-6-0s took over main line work in 1903. *(LMS official)*

Clad in LMSR lined black livery, No.14509 *Lord Glenarthur*, R. H. Whitelegg's rebuild of Manson's four-cylinder 4-4-0, looked very handsome at Corkerhill shed in November 1933, exactly twelve months before Derby's distaste for non-standard types ordained its withdrawal. *(Author's Collection)*

reverser, a secondhand tender, enlarged to accommodate five tons of coal and 3,260 gallons of water, and, most unusually for the G&SWR, given a name, *Lord Glenarthur*, the strangely composite 4-4-0 was allocated to Ayr shed. Classified '3P' by the LMS in due course, and renumbered 14509, it performed worthily on Ayr–Glasgow expresses, until Derby-built Compounds and 2P 4-4-0s arrived on the scene.

In marked contrast to his four-cylinder adventure, Manson next paid neat tribute to James Stirling by 'renewing' all sixteen survivors of the latter's Class '6' 4-4-0s. Fitted with rebuilt, rather than new, boilers, given a Manson cab and chimney, but still remaining domeless in the main, the little locomotives, warmly regarded by Sou' West men as the 'Aul Bogies', were shopped from Kilmarnock Works in 1899–1901. Though all lived to pass into LMS ownership as Nos.14228–243, and were classified '1P', none survived beyond 1930.

Three years later another Manson 4-4-0 design, his '240' class, arrived on the scene to enliven G&SWR life. Still mindful of past virtues, Mason had simply added a larger (4ft 9¼in) boiler and a higher cab to his original Class '8' concept. This, coupled with an increased working pressure of 170psi, produced an engine which was compatible in size and power with the

Caledonian Railway's much vaunted 'Dunalastairs'. Fifteen of these new Manson 4-4-0s were accordingly constructed at Kilmarnock Works over the years 1904–06. Intriguingly, the two eight-wheeled tenders which had previously been associated with the '8' class engines were now transferred to '240' class locomotives for selective use as and when members of that species handled special fitted freight trains which were now operating between Glasgow and Carlisle with only one midway stop for water. Five '240s', Nos.240–24, 244, and 252, shared this benefice over the years.

The year 1907 saw James Manson's last 4-4-0 design, his Class '18s', introduce important modifications to what was fundamentally a Class '240' layout, in that the deep square firebox of the latter now gave way to a much longer shallow box. It would appear that Manson had taken cognizance of experiments at Crewe which had clearly demonstrated the economic advantages of a shallow firebox. The long firebox of the Class '18s', however, sloped up over the the rear axle; which meant that the frames had to be longer and the cab set further back. Safety valves, as a consequence, were mounted unusually far forward on the firebox, and the reversing rod was obliged to curve gracefully over the leading splasher. Again, capuchoned chimneys

James Manson's 'renewals' of Stirling's Class '6' 4-4-0s were held in great affection by G&SWR men as the 'Aul Bogies'. Numbered 193 when it emerged from Kilmarnock Works in July 1899 (Works No.322) and renumbered 471 in 1919, this engaging specimen was withdrawn as LMS No.14230 in December 1925. *(NRM)*

were fitted on all twelve Class '18' 4-4-0s which emerged from Kilmarnock between the years 1907 and 1909, and on three more which followed in 1911–12. New flat-sided 2,900 gallon tenders also made their debut on this class. During the summer of 1908, though, two class '18s', Nos.18 and 26, were lent Manson's 'special' eight-wheeled tenders to enable them to work non-stop expresses between Carlisle and Glasgow. One other deviation from the norm, No.27, spent most of the years 1913–19 running with a Weir feed pump and water heater. But, all in all, the Class '18s' proved to be efficient machines. Their only shortcoming was that incommensurate rear overhang which made them rough riders. Fortunately, G&SWR locomen were a tough breed.

The NB Loco. Co. supplied the last two of James Manson's elegant 4-6-0s in July 1911. Then came retirement, on 28th November that year; and, one month later, the loss of this gifted, and highly respected, locomotive engineer was strangely highlighted when Peter Drummond was appointed as his successor. The shock came not from Drummond's personality — for he was a much more equably disposed man than his brother Dugald — but from the 'big engine' philosophy he was likely to superimpose on G&SWR locomotive policy. Indeed, fresh from the Highland Railway, where his 'Castle' 4-6-0s had scored an undoubted success, both at home and abroad, Drummond soon showed his hand early in 1913 by instructing the NB Loco. Co. to build fifteen huge 0-6-0 tender engines. Nicknamed 'The

A neat capunchoned chimney endowed the Class '240s' with a jaunty air which had hitherto been absent from James Manson designs; witness No.264 as it saunters along with a Carlisle stopping train. Alone of its class, this locomotive was fitted with Westinghouse pump and train pipes. Later renumbered LMS 14264, its active life came to an end in 1930. *(Author's Collection)*

Conversely, Class '240' No.14258 confirms the well known fact that the shape of a chimney can have a profound effect on a locomotive's general appearance, as, *sans capuchon*, it pauses at Dumfries Station with a 'stopping passenger' from Glasgow (St. Enoch). The year is 1931, and the locomotive's rather gaunt appearance suggests Caledonian Railway pedigree rather than G&SWR. More to the point, No.14258 vanished later that year. *(Author's Collection)*

No.14248, formerly G&SWR Nos.242 and 381, was carrying one of Manson's unique eight-wheeled tenders when it was caught by the camera at Corkerhill shed shortly before being scrapped in 1932. *(Author's Collection)*

No.14377's flat-sided 2,900 gallon tender is well in evidence as the former G&SWR Class '18' locomotive prepares to leave St. Enoch Station on 30th July 1931. It is bearing (unusually) the pre-1928 LMS *goods* engine livery of plain black. Considering that many of the class had already been withdrawn in the late 1920s, this engine, and two others, did rather well to survive until October 1932. *(H. C. Casserley)*

Pumpers' because of the feed pumps and steam drier Drummond insisted on installing, they were loathed by G&SWR men.

A few months later, still perpetuating these much maligned Drummond family fetishes, came Peter Drummond's 'version' of Smellie's immortal 'Wee Bogies' — six ponderous 4-4-0s, Nos.131–136. Again supplied by the NB Loco. Co., these engines, weighing nearly 62 tons, were clearly based on Dugald Drummond's contemporary D15 Class London & South Western Railway 4-4-0s. Even the latter's unusual features of placing Walschaerts valve gear inside, and driving piston valves on top of the cylinders, were faithfully reproduced. One can well imagine Sou' West men's misgivings in 1913 as these 6ft monsters began to appear in their midst — particularly as Peter

Drummond had also chosen, quite unaccountably, to switch their driving position from the right to the left hand side of the footplate!

Despite provision of a useful 3,800 gallon tender, G&SWR footplate men's scepticism anent No.131 and her five sisters proved to be not unfounded. Not only were the '131s' sluggish in hill climbing, but a favourite discipline Sou' West men had long practised, of picking up lost time by rollicking down hill, proved to be quite invidious on these machines; they rolled too badly in such circumstances. So troublesome, too, were the Drummond 'accessories' that, in 1917, all six locomotives were brought back to Ayr, whence R. H. Whitelegg, Drummond's successor, removed both steam drier and feed pumps, and substituted injectors.

Built by NB Loco. Co. (Works No.20128) in June 1913 as No.131, Peter Drummond's prototype 4-4-0 was renumbered 331 in 1919. The locomotive is seen here leaving Ayr in grand style, circa 1920, on a fitted express goods train. *(NRM)*

After twelve months' experience with the '131s', even Drummond was forced to concede the value of superheating. Thus, his next 4-4-0s, very similar in general respects to the '131s', carried both Schmidt superheater and double-acting Weir feed-water heating equipment. The latter was mounted on the side plating. This time, all six of his new 'improved' '137' Class, Nos.137–140 and 151/2, were built at Kilmarnock and were delivered in 1915. Though the weight of these locomotives had now soared to a UK record of 64 tons, at least right hand drive had been restored on them. Performance, too, proved to be highly satisfactory. When handled by competent men, the '137s' climbed like stags, and their fuel and water consumption was quite a revelation. Considerably cheered by this intelligence, Drummond had two '137s' allocated to Carlisle shed. The remaining quartet were posted to Ayr and Stranraer, where they readily proved their worth.

Alas, life is not always logical. Impressed by the '137s' performance in the West of Scotland, the G&SWR management took it upon itself to have all six locomotives stationed at Carlisle. The object was to employ them on main line express work. Unfortunately, Carlisle men, deeply prejudiced by earlier experience in handling Drummond's notorious 'Pumpers', failed to respond to Authority's promptings and instructions. The result was that unenthusiastic and inexpert use of the '137's' novel equipment produced such low grade performances that, latterly, these potentially fine locomotives were relegated to less important duties. R. H. Whitelegg later removed the feed-water heating equipment, but to no avail; and the '137s' finished their days on west of Scotland coastal services.

We know now that Peter Drummond had every intention of introducing a very large four-cylindered 4-6-0 to G&SWR metals; something, possibly, akin to his brother Dugald's monstrous L&SWR 'Paddleboxes'. Mercifully, perhaps, the project never got further than the drawing board; for, on 29th June 1918, Peter Drummond died in harness at the age of 67.

In 1923 the '137' Class prototype engine, seen here as LMS No.14516, was fitted with a Robinson-superheated boiler similar to that of *Lord Glenarthur*, and reversing gear was moved to the right hand side. Despite these administrations, the locomotive perished in the mid-1930s in common with the rest of the class. *(Author's Collection)*

Surprisingly, for a railway which not only had little time for tank engines, but tended to retreat too easily as electric tramways bit deeply into its short-haul suburban passenger traffic, the G&SWR Board decided that Drummond's successor should be R. H. Whitelegg, one time Locomotive Superintendent of the London, Tilbury & Southern Railway. The latter was, of course, the traditional home of suburban passenger tanks. Such, however, were the economic consequences

In the light of the Class '137s' undoubted superiority over the '131s', the LMSR fitted five of the latter with superheaters between 1923 and 1931. Seen here at Hurlford shed in the mid-1930s, No.14515, formerly '131' Class No.136, had already been given 'pop' safety valves as far back as the 1920s. When it was built in 1913, No.136 was experimentally fitted with a domed firegrate. *(Author's Collection)*

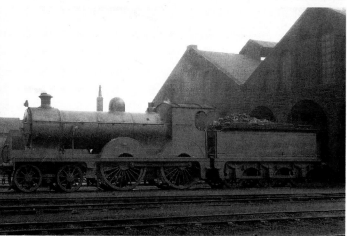

No.14270, née 485, shopped in July 1921 as the G&SWR's final word in 4-4-0s, was one of the last three locomotives to be shopped at Kilmarnock Works. Typical of post-Grouping years, the Sou' Western locomotive, having reached Carlisle, now seeks hospitality at the Caledonian Railway's old Kingmoor shed. Equally typically, its short life ended in December 1933. *(Author's Collection)*

It must have come as something of a relief to Whitelegg when slightly improved economic conditions in 1921 enabled the resumption of new locomotive construction to be made, albeit on a modest scale. Kilmarnock Works responded cautiously by 'replacing' two 0-6-0s and 4-4-0. The original engines have never been identified, and the 4-4-0, No.485, with its 6ft 9½in driving wheels, X1 boiler, and 18¼in × 26in cylinders, proved to be identical with earlier Whitelegg rebuilds of Manson Class '8s'. Finally, early in 1922, came Whitelegg's last astonishing contribution to G&SWR locomotive stock — his six giant 4-6-4Ts. But that is another story . . .!

The effect of Grouping on G&SWR affairs was both swift and disastrous. R. H. Whitelegg left Kilmarnock on 1st March 1923 to become General Manager of Beyer Peacock & Co., Manchester. Meanwhile, pending the introduction of standard LMSR types, locomotives of the Caledonian Railway, easily the largest of the three companies which now constituted the LMS Northern Division (Scotland), began to enjoy a distinct preference. The figures speak for themselves. Ten years after Grouping, the CR, it was found, had lost 137 engines, precisely 12.7% of its total stock. Elsewhere, the Highland Railway fared badly enough with a loss of 63 locomotives (36.4%); but this nowhere approached the G&SWR's haemorrhage, which amounted to a cool 79.4% of the 582 locomotives it had subscribed in 1923! The residue shrank even further to fourteen by 1939, and only one G&SWR engine, a North British-built 0-6-2T, survived to enter BR stock on 1st January 1948; even then, it did not last long enough to carry its allotted number, 56905.

As for Glasgow & South Western 4-4-0s, memories were by now mistier still — for the last to tread metals, Drummond '131' Class No.14513, went in December 1937.

of World War One, that the immediate task which faced Whitelegg was that of rehabilitating the G&SWR's sadly run down stock. This process involved rebuilding old, rather than designing new, locomotives. Hoping, therefore, to resuscitate the best features of existing Manson and Drummond engines, Whitelegg laid comprehensive plans to introduce a range of new unsuperheated boilers. Construction of four distinct classes of boiler was swiftly put in hand; though, in the event, only three types, X1, 2, and 4, were ever applied to sundry 0-6-0 and 4-4-0 classes. Sadly, overall results were disappointing. Many of Whitelegg's unsuperheated rebuilds lacked steaming capacity and, inevitably, coal consumption shot up. The alterations he made to Manson valve gear proved equally unrewarding and, indeed, the only crumb of comfort to come G&SWR locomen's way arrived in 1919, when ten 0-6-2 tank engines, previously ordered by Drummond from the NB Locomotive Co., were modified, before completion, to incorporate right-hand drive.

Chapter 6
THE HIGHLAND RAILWAY

THE GREAT NORTH OF SCOTLAND, by opening its link between Kittybrewster and Huntly in September 1854, was indubitably the first railway concern to penetrate the Highland region of Scotland. The crippling cost, however, of the long and arduous Parliamentary campaign it had to wage to achieve that distinction so inhibited implementation of its intention to reach Inverness that a thirteen mile westward extension to Keith, opened on 10th October 1856, with coach connection by road to Inverness, proved to be as far as GNSR ambitions were allowed to advance, in that direction at least. Meanwhile, well aware of the GNSR's impotency, a newly formed rival concern, the Inverness & Nairn Railway, thrusting eastward in an attempt to fill the vacuum, opened for public service on 5th November 1855.

Next, on 18th August 1858, and with financial assistance from the GNSR, the 40 mile gap between Nairn and Keith was closed by yet another Company, the Inverness & Aberdeen Junction Railway. At long last through travel between Inverness and Aberdeen had become a reality and to clinch matters, the I&AJR duly absorbed the Inverness & Nairn Railway on 17th May 1861. Four years later, on 1st February 1865, the I&AJR amalgamated with the Inverness & Perth Junction Railway, which up until then had been worked by the Scottish North Eastern Railway, to form the Highland Railway. Between them, the two concerns were able to muster 242 route miles of track. All but a $6\frac{3}{4}$ mile stretch between Inverness and Dalcross was single line. In later years, however, subsequent amalgamations of lines north of Inverness added a further $264\frac{1}{2}$ miles to the HR's route mileage.

For four years prior to 1865, locomotive affairs on both Highland Railway constituents had been managed by William Barclay. Considering that Barclay was a nephew of Alexander Allan, the well known inventor of straight link valve gear and Locomotive Superintendent of the Scottish Central Railway until that august concern merged with the Caledonian Railway in 1865, it came as no surprise that the Highland Railway's initial intake of 55 locomotives consisted almost entirely of 'Crewe' type singles and modestly powered 2-4-0s. Though supplied by various Makers, all sported inclined outside cylinders supported by double frames, leading wheels with underslung springs, and domeless boilers with safety valves on the barrel and above the firebox. Hawthorns of Leith, Neilsons, and Sharp Stewart had provided the lot. In the absence of rail communication with Central Scotland most had been delivered by sea to Lossiemouth, whence they found their way to home metals by courtesy of the Morayshire Railway.

The railway fraternity had no way of knowing it at the time, but the year 1865 was to be a particularly historic one, in that it brought into conjunction at Inverness three men whose names were later to ring famously in locomotive annals. The process commenced on 31st May 1865, when William Barclay, caught

neglecting his duties, was forced to resign by the newly formed Highland Railway Board. Pending subsequent deliberations, Barclay's principal assistant, a young man called David Jones filled the vacancy as Acting Locomotive, Carriage & Wagon Superintendent. And here, if you please, was an intriguing situation. Manchester-born in 1834, Jones had left school at the tender age of 13 to enter a lengthy apprenticeship at Longsight, Manchester. He completed it at Crewe under the great John Ramsbottom, who seems to have recognised his considerable potential. On 15th November 1855, a fortnight after leaving Crewe, Jones then set off for Inverness, where he obtained employment on the Inverness & Nairn Railway. Two and a half years later, Barclay, spotting Jones' talent, appointed him as his principal assistant. It follows, then, that Jones must have harboured pardonable personal ambitions when the HR chose to dispense with Barclay's services.

Alas, the Highland Railway Board, in its wisdom, chose to appoint William Stroudley as its new Locomotive Superintendent. One might add that the latter, operating until then as Manager of the Edinburgh & Glasgow Railway's Cowlairs Works at the princely salary of £200 a year, was only too glad to accept a £300 increase in annual salary *and* escape from the rather overbearing presence of S. W. Johnson — in one fell swoop. So, swallowing his disappointment, David Jones had to content himself with soldiering on at Inverness as Locomotive Running Superintendent. Meanwhile, the third member of the trinity mentioned a moment ago was an even younger man who was about to serve Stroudley and the Highland Railway as Works Manager at Inverness. His name was Dugald Drummond. . .

One can only presume that financial stringency on the Highland Railway conditioned Stroudley's comparatively inauspicious debut as a Locomotive Superintendent. For the most part he was confined to the chore of rebuilding older locomotives which had been handed down by the I&AJR. Yet, significantly, Stroudley's sole individual contribution to HR locomotive development, No.56 *Balnain*, a small 0-6-0 tank he had built at Lochgorm in February 1869, was a clear forerunner of the immortal 'Terriers' he was to introduce at Brighton three years later. Equally typical of Stroudley was the 'Improved Engine Green' livery he pioneered at Inverness in lieu of the dark green which the HR had inherited from the I&AJR. Within less than a decade, Stroudley's striking new livery was adopted by the North British and London, Brighton & South Coast Railways. Even the Dutch Central Railway copied it later on.

Fortunately for the HR, David Jones' wait was not intolerable. His opportunity finally came in February 1870, when Stroudley defected to the LB&SCR following the resignation of J. C. Craven, and Jones was appointed Locomotive Superintendent at Inverness. Capital funds still being at a low ebb on the Highland Railway, Jones had little option but to

Typically Crewe type in design, Inverness &
Aberdeen Junction Railway No.11 was designed
primarily for goods traffic, and was supplied by
Hawthorns of Leith (Works No.209) in October
1859. The locomotive originally bore the name
Stafford, but this was removed in 1864. Cylinders
were 16in × 22in, coupled wheels were 5ft, and the
engine weighed 28½ tons in working order. Its
four-wheeled tender added a further 28 tons.
(Author's Collection)

HR No.7, a Hawthorn 2-4-0 built in 1858, is seen here after
rebuild by David Jones in May 1875. Provision of an Adams bogie
and an increase in cylinder dimensions to 17in × 24in have
advanced working weight to 32½ tons, and opportunity has been
taken to add a six-wheeled tender. The name *Dingwall* was applied
later. Meanwhile, although the familiar Crewe-type framing and
boiler fittings have been faithfully retained, the provision of a Jones
louvred chimney and new-style cab offers clear indication of a new
era in HR locomotive design. Duplicated listed in 1898, No.7A
served for one more year before being withdrawn in May 1899.
(Author's Collection)

emulate his predecessor by continuing the process of reconstituting more rugged engines from some of the old I&AJR types. Thus, by and large, single-wheelers were rebuilt as 2-4-0s. In this context, however, an interesting and thoroughly significant diversion occurred in 1873 and 1875, when two old Hawthorn 2-4-0s, HR Nos.10 and 7, were rebuilt as 4-4-0s, expressly for work on the Dingwall & Skye Railway. The latter concern, operated from inception by the Highland Railway, had soon discovered that acute curvature and severe gradients taxed 2-4-0 locomotives beyond their capacity. 1875, incidentally, was also the year in which Dugald Drummond, who had quit HR employment in 1870 to follow Stroudley to Brighton, returned to his native pastures as Locomotive Superintendent to the North British Railway. Both Drummond and Jones were soon to reveal how deeply they had been influenced by their individual associations with William Stroudley.

It is more than a trite truism to say that David Jones' long and faithful service as Locomotive Superintendent at Inverness played a crucial role in the advancement of Highland Railway affairs. Yet, they were remarkably undramatic years. Always an immaculate man where both dress and railway disciplines were concerned, Jones' grave personal demeanour and the simple, yet purposeful, nature of the locomotives he designed simply earned total respect from all who served with him. The crux of the matter was that David Jones felt equally at home in the drawing office, the workshop, or on the footplate. He never let his men down, and they were happy to repay the compliment. While he was content to follow the Crewe line in the general layout of his early 4-4-0s, he did not hesitate, for instance, to introduce his famous louvred chimney. This apparently simple device lifted exhaust well clear of cab windows, particularly when an engine was drifting downhill, and proved to be of great practical value to Highland enginemen. So, too, were the roomy cabs Jones introduced. The elegance of their rounded corners and square fronts must surely have been an echo of Stroudley influence?

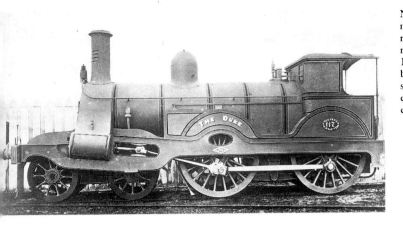

No.67 (Dübs & Co. Works No.721/1874) gave the 'Duke' class its name. Renamed *Cromartie* in January 1877, this locomotive was rebuilt with a new 150psi boiler in December 1897, when, for some reason, the total heating surface was reduced from 1,228sq ft to 1,151sq ft. In 1913 *Cromartie* was the beneficiary of a secondhand boiler from No.74, one of seven 'Dukes' which were additionally subscribed by Lochgorm Works in 1876–88. Finally Duplicate listed in 1918 as No.67A, a further change in number to 70A coincided with the locomotive's withdrawal in 1923. *(Dübs & Co.)*

No.4 *Ardross*, the first of the seven Lochgorm 'Dukes', entered traffic in May 1876, and was reboiled in May 1895 with a working pressure of 150psi, again with reduced total heating surface. The other six 'Dukes' were not shopped from Lochgorm Works until 1883–88, and the last, No.84, carried a larger 2,250 gallon tender. *Ardross*, renumbered 31 in 1899 and renamed *Auchtertyre* two years later, was Duplicate listed as No.31A in 1911, and went to the breakers in 1913. Four 'Dukes' contrived to hang on until 1923, but none ever bore an LMS number. *(Author's Collection)*

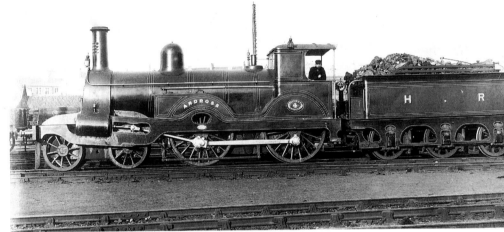

Perth General Station provided this dramatic, yet typical, view in pre-Grouping days as two 'Duke' Class 4-4-0s leave on an Inverness express. The train engine, No.74 *Beaufort*, shopped from Lochgorm Works in September 1885, later lost its name, but otherwise remained serenely unaltered until it was withdrawn in 1913. (LMS official)

'Skye Bogie' No.88, a Lochgorm Works product of April 1895, relaxes in its native element at Kyle of Lochalsh. Fitted with a Drummond chimney around 1920, it was later allocated LMS number 14281; but was still bearing its old Highland number when it was withdrawn in 1926. *(LMS official)*

Again, the distinctive yellow livery introduced by Stroudley during his comparatively brief stay at Inverness was retained without qualm on Highland Railway locomotives until 1885, when Jones elected to employ bright green. But, even then, the finished livery of a Jones engine, with its elaborate lining and panelling, remained as lush as anything ever turned out at Brighton.

One of Jones' earliest individual designs for the HR saw ten outside-cylindered 'Duke' Class 4-4-0s turned out by Dübs & Co. between June and August 1874. Working to a pressure of 140psi (later increased to 150psi) these engines entered traffic with 6ft 3½in driving wheels and 3ft 9½in leading wheels. Cylinders were 18in × 24in and, with a boiler 10ft 9½in long, the 'Dukes' weighed 41 tons in working order. Traditional Crewe-type fore end framing was retained. So, too, was Allan link motion; but provision of brass slide valves and a dome on the second ring of the boiler were evidence of things to come. Later to become an ardent advocate of the automatic vacuum brake, Jones fitted his 'Dukes' at the outset with counter pressure brakes. After subsequent tests, however, on two 'Dukes' with Westinghouse and vacuum brake he adopted the latter for the entire class. The 'Duke' tenders, a shade on the small side, held 1,800 gallons, and weighed 30 tons apiece. The locomotives carried HR Nos.60–69.

Meanwhile, Jones, encouraged by the proven success of his two 2-4-0 Skye & Dingwall conversions of 1873-75, went on to design a custom-built 4-4-0 for that difficult section. As a result, No.70, his celebrated 'Skye Bogie', was shopped by Lochgorm Works in May 1882. Cylinders, frames, and motion were similar to those of the 'Dukes', but as the 'Skye Bogie' was intended to work as a mixed traffic locomotive, and for that reason was never named, driving wheels on this occasion were reduced to 5ft 3in and leading wheels to 3ft 3in. Working pressure of 150psi was employed, and No.70 outweighed the 'Dukes' by one ton. The

really surprising feature was that a full ten years elapsed ere the 'Skye Bogie' ranks were augmented by the construction of eight more at Lochgorm Works between 1892 and 1901. Numbered 85–88, 5–7, and 48, the newcomers also remained unnamed.

In the event, only four new 'Skye Bogies', Nos.85–88, contrived to enter traffic before David Jones retired on grounds of ill health in October 1896. As four more had been scheduled for construction at Lochgorm, however, these were duly completed during 1897–1901 by Peter Drummond, Jones' successor. Drummond chimneys were fitted to this quartet, and compensating levers between the coupled wheels were dispensed with. Apart from No.85, which was sold for scrap in August 1923, the class worked into the latter half of the 1920s, and Nos.70 and 7, latterly bearing LMSR Nos.14277 and 14284, were the last to perish, in June 1930.

'Skye Bogie' No.14284, formerly HR No.7, is tenderless in this Inverness view, but the locomotive looks quite resplendent in immediate post-Grouping LMS crimson livery. The Drummond chimney alters Jones' original perspective somewhat, though the LMS emblem on the cabside and neat overall lining adds distinction. Note, too, the typical Jones arrangement of placing the safety valves astride the firebox. *(Author's Collection)*

Curiously, Jones' next 4-4-0s came from the Clyde Locomotive Co. Ltd's works at Springburn, Glasgow, a concern which had been newly founded by W. M. Neilson, the former owner of the Hyde Park Locomotive Works. Clyde Locomotive's first order, in fact, came early in 1886 in the form of a commission to construct eight 6ft 3in 'Bruce' Class 4-4-0s for Highland Railway main line service. Duly shopped between May and December 1886, these locomotives differed from the 'Dukes' by employing shorter boilers and longer fireboxes. Boiler pressure was 160psi and each engine and 2,250 gallon tender weighed 43 and 31½ tons respectively. Unusually, the tenders had both inside and outside bearings, and vacuum plus counter-pressure brake operated on both engine and tender. No.76 *Bruce* was the first to be built, though it did not enter traffic until December 1886; for the HR proudly displayed the locomotive at the Edinburgh Exhibition of Science, Industry and Art that year. It certainly made an interesting comparison with NBR 4-4-0 No.592 and the Caley single-wheeler No.123. Two years later, after building only fourteen locomotives, the Clyde Locomotive Co.'s Springburn Works were sold to Sharp Stewart & Co. Happily, they were to blossom, still in Glasgow, as Sharp Stewart's Atlas Works.

W. M. Neilson's hope that future orders from some of his former Hyde Park Locomotive Works customers might follow him to the Clyde Locomotive Company proved to be sadly unfounded. Hyde Park continued trading under its old title of Neilson & Co., and it was from there that the Highland Railway ordered its next batch of main line 4-4-0s. These were twelve 'Strath' class locomotives, HR Nos.89–100, and all were delivered in 1892. By now Hyde Park Works were supplying locomotives on a worldwide scale. The 'Straths', however, though they emerged from a different stable, retained a distinct similarity in appearance to the earlier Clyde Locomotive engines. Jones, though, had increased the boiler diameter by four inches; thus the Neilson locomotives required a slightly shorter chimney. They also weighed two tons heavier, at 45 tons, but the tender weight remained constant at 31½ tons. The most important factor was that the tractive effort of 14,100lb offered by the 'Bruce' class had now been stepped up considerably to 16,786lb.

The bright apple green livery and crimson underframes which Jones adopted around 1885 show up well in this portrait of No.93 *Strathnairn*. In 1916, this locomotive received a new steel firebox at the hands of the North British Locomotive Co., a 1903 amalgam of Neilson Reid, Dübs & Co. and Sharp Stewart. But, sadly, like four other 'Straths', No.93A *Strathnairn*, was sold for scrap in 1923.
(Author's Collection)

No.96 *Glenbrium*, one of six 'Straths' which survived to be allotted LMS running numbers, acquired No.14275. Seen here at Inverness in the late 1920s, its Jones chimney has shrunk even further, due to the fact that a new steel boiler was fitted by Hawthorns in 1920. The dome, too, is wider and deeper and the engine now carries Ross pop safety valves. The end duly came for No.14275 and the other remaining 'Straths' in 1930. *(Author's Collection)*

The year 1894 must have stamped itself on David Jones' memory in more ways than one — for not only did his famous 'Large Goods', the first 4-6-0s to run in Britain, emerge from Sharp Stewart's Atlas Works that year, but it was in course of trails with the prototype engine that Jones met with the scalding accident, on 7th September, which nearly cost him his left leg. Certainly, the consquences were later to hasten his retirement, at the age of 62, in 1896. Yet, only six years earlier, this was the man who had been offered, and chose to decline, the post of Locomotive Superintendent at Brighton following William Stroudley's sudden demise in Paris. How different the course of London, Brighton & South Coast locomotive development might have been! Meanwhile, the 'Jones Goods' 4-6-0s, with their completely radical departure from established locomotive practice, both on the Highland and elsewhere, took the railway world by storm. Mercifully, the prototype, No.103, has been preserved for posterity.

Less than two years after his 'Large Goods' triumph came David Jones' last design, his equally impressive 'Loch' 4-4-0s.

Once again, as with the 4-6-0s, Crewe-style framing was abandoned in favour of inside frames. The well tried and trusted Allan link motion was, however, retained, and, in all, fifteen 'Lochs', HR Nos.119–133, were supplied by Dübs & Co. between July and September 1896. Cylinders on this occasion were 19in × 24in, and, in contrast to previous Jones 4-4-0s, the boiler diameter had been increased to 4ft 4⅞in. Yet, despite their quite modest proportions, the 'Lochs' packed such a powerful punch that they handled HR express passenger traffic as to the manner born for the next twenty years. Their tractive effort of

Although the advent of Peter Drummon's 'Castle' Class 4-6-0s in 1900 saw the 'Loch's' monopoly over HR express traffic challenged, the smaller engines remained great favourites well into the 1920s. In this view No.14384 *Loch Laggan*, freshly rebuilt by Hawthorn Leslie in the early 1920s, and now looking immaculate in LMS crimson, leads a 'Castle' through Luncarty station at the head of a Down Inverness express. The 'Loch' carried on for another fifteen years before being scrapped in September 1938. *(Author's Collection)*

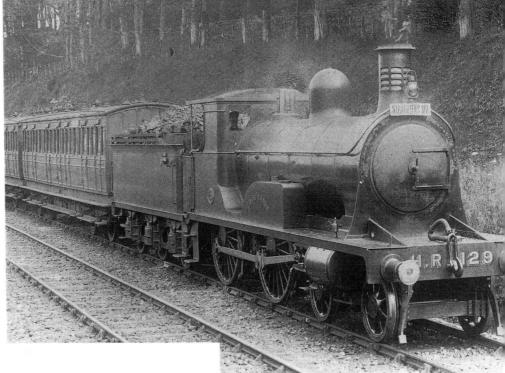

No.127 *Loch Garry* and No.129 *Loch Maree* were the only two Dübs-built 'Lochs' to end their careers exactly as they were built. All others were either rebuilt before Grouping, or were fitted with CR-type N31 boilers under LMS auspices and lasted much longer. In this view, No.129 (withdrawn as LMS No.14389 in 1931) is seen in HR days hauling a Strathpeffer Spa train near Dingwall. (*LMS official*)

The final phase. Devoid of smokebox wingplates and clad in LMS black livery, No.14379 *Loch Insh*, when photographed at Inverness in the mid-1930s, still looked impressive enough to command respect as David Jones' last design for the Railway he served with such distinction. (*Author's Collection*)

17,070lb even exceeded that of their Caledonian Railway contemporaries, the 'Dunalastairs', by nearly 2,000lb. The working pressure of the 'Lochs' was higher, at 175psi but driving and leading wheels were smaller, at 6ft 3½in and 3ft 3in respectively. Conversely, the weight of a 'Loch' in working order was 49 tons, two tons greater than McIntosh's locomotive. Rather surprisingly, though, the 'Lochs' six-wheeled tender held only 3,000 gallons of water, as opposed to the 'Dunalastairs' 3,735 gallons. The clue to this anomaly lay in the automatic tablet exchange apparatus which could be seen on all 'Loch' cabsides. Long fast runs were simply not a practicable proposition on Highland Railway metals.

The first-built 'Loch', No.119 *Loch Insh*, probably had the most charismatic career of all fifteen. Distinction came as early as September 1896, when it hauled a special train conveying the Duke of York, later King George V, from Perth to Grantown, and for some time after sported the Prince of Wales' insignia on its leading splasher. Later records reveal that this engine had a Drummond chimney by 1920. In 1925, by which time a new

LMS number, 14379, had been allotted, *Loch Insh*, like several others, was given an N51 type ex-Caledonian Railway boiler. The resultant increase of two inches in the boiler diameter required the provision of a shorter Pickersgill chimney. Next, in August 1944, the name *Loch Insh* was removed — only to be restored again in 1946! By mid-1947 No.14379 was one of only two surviving 'Lochs', and, though allotted BR No.54379, the locomotive, withdrawn in March 1948, did not live long enough to enjoy its new guise. Neither, for that matter, did sister engine, No.54385, though it hung on until April 1950.

David Jones' enforced retirement at the end of October 1896 was inevitably regarded by the Highland Railway directorate as a sad loss. Still mentally alert, Jones, reluctant to abandon activity in the railway field, carried on for a few years as a consultant. He even designed a number of locomotives for Colonial railways. But his health remained poor, and when, in the early 1900s, a motor accident brought injury to his right leg he never really recovered. He died in his home at Hampstead, aged 73, on 2nd December 1906.

A product of Lochgorm Works in 1899, No.10 *Ben Slioch* is seen here a few years later alongside that very establishment. It was one of ten 'Bens' which were fitted with vacuum brake only. Handsome white lining and the presence of the full legend 'The Highland Railway' on the tender, two Drummond innovations, suggest that the photograph was taken around 1903. Note, too, the eight-wheeled tender which came from a Drummond 0-6-0 of slightly later origin. No.10 managed to live to acquire LMS No.14406, and worked on until July 1947. *(Author's Collection)*

This companion study of London & South Western Railway C8 Class No.296, a product of Nine Elms Works in 1898, illustrates the close affinity many of Peter Drummond's locomotive designs had with those of his brother Dugald. No.296 and *Ben Slioch* might conceivably have been constructed from the same drawings! While it is generally conceded, however, that Drummond locomotives were long lived, No.296's career came to an end in November 1935, whereas *Ben Slioch*, bred in hardier circumstances, did not bow the knee until July 1947. *(Author's Collection)*

Peter Drummond, the man chosen to succeed Jones as Locomotive, Carriage & Wagon Superintendent at Inverness, was, like his older brother, Dugald, something of a rolling stone. But the stones rolled together; for, born in 1850 at Polmont, Stirlingshire, right in the heart of Edinburgh & Glasgow territory, and apprenticed as a lad to a Glasgow engineering firm, Forrest & Barr, Peter Drummond gained his first job at Brighton, where Dugald was also working under William Stroudley. Four years later, in 1875, Peter followed his brother to North British Railway employment at Cowlairs. Then, in 1882, both men made the short move to the rival Caledonian Railway establishment at St. Rollox. Duly appointed Assistant Locomotive Engineer and Works Manager, Peter not only reorganised St. Rollox Works, but superintended production of McIntosh's famous 'Dunalastair' 4-4-0s. Hence, by the time Drummond arrived at Inverness he already possessed quite a pedigree.

Running true to family tradition, Peter Drummond immediately set to work reorganising Lochgorm Works. Recognising the peculiarities of Highland Railway working, he also designed a variety of snowploughs. These were so successful in practice that other railways copied them. Next, emulating brother Dugald in all but the fire and brimstone that the older Drummond habitually breathed (!), Peter went on to introduce his own quiet revolution in HR locomotive affairs, by building three types with inside cylinders — 4-4-0s, 0-6-0s (the HR's

first), and 0-6-4 tanks. Nevertheless, modest as well as astute, he did not hesitate to employ an original, but unconsummated, outside-cylindered 4-6-0 design of David Jones when his celebrated 'Castles' made their debut in 1900. The following year he reclassified HR engines by alphabetical letter. The 'Castles' took pride of place at 'A', but it is interesting to note that Jones' 'Lochs' came next at 'B', ahead of Drummond's own HR 4-4-0s, the 'Bens', which were classified 'C': fair acknowledgment that the 'Loch' was the larger engine of the two.

The first eight of Drummond's new inside-cylindered 4-4-0s, later to be affectionately known to HR men as the 'Wee Bens', were a product of Dübs & Co. (Works Nos.3685–92/1898–99). Nine more came from Lochgorm Works in 1899–1901, and the North British Locomotive Co. was commissioned to build a last three (Works Nos.17398–400) in 1906. Cylinders were 18¼in × 26in, and the boiler was wider, though a shade shorter, than that of the 'Lochs'. Working pressure of 175psi remained unchanged, but possession of 6ft driving wheels, as opposed to the 'Loch's' 6ft 3½in, gave the 'Bens' a slight advantage in tractive effort, at 17,890lb. The engines in working order weighed 46 tons 4 cwt. Stephenson link motion was now employed, as was a new type double-slide regulator, and safety valves were placed on top of the dome. The seventeen 'Bens' built by Dübs & Co. and Lochgorm were not, however, uniform in detail. Nos.2, 11–17, for instance, were dual brake fitted with Westinghouse and vacuum; the others had vacuum

brake only. Again, six-wheeled 3,000 gallon Drummond tenders were standard equipment at the outset, but a handful of the 'Bens' latterly acquired double-bogied 3,200 gallon tenders, 'borrowed' from a 1900 series of Drummond 0-6-0s. Meanwhile, all but two of the 'Bens' received ex-CR N34 boilers during the late 1920s. Interestingly, the Westinghouse brake carried by eight of the 'Bens' came in particularly useful in the Spring of 1908, when, inspired by a more amicable relationship which had evolved between the HR and the GNSR, principal trains between Aberdeen and Inverness were worked by one engine throughout. The arrangement, alas, ended when World War One erupted — and was never revived.

Of all the 'Bens', No.2 *Ben Alder* (Dübs & Co. Works No.3686/1898) surely led the most chequered existence. Rebuilt by Hawthorn Leslie just before Grouping, it was given an ex-CR N34 boiler six years later. The latter was similar to that carried by CR 'Jumbo' 0-6-0s. Although ten 'Wee Bens' entered BR stock in 1948, No.54398 *Ben Alder*, one of only three destined to carry its BR number, outlived the lot by remaining in service, latterly in the Wick/Thurso sector, until February 1953. For months the locomotive then lay behind Lochgorm Works; and all indications were that it was going to be preserved. By mid-1954, however, ominous patches of rust begin to appear on the smokebox and chimney and in August that year, the 'Ben' was moved to a more sheltered spot inside the GNSR's former shed at Boat of Garten. Two years later the shed itself was in a parlous state, and *Ben Alder* was moved outside. Time passed, and after some attention at St Rollox Works the locomotive was found new lodgings at Dawholm. Next, still untouched as far as preservation was concerned, it moved on to Parkhead shed. One year later found it in the encouraging company of five other 'preserved' Scottish engines at Kipps shed. Unfortunately, appearances in this case flattered to deceive. The 'Famous Five' duly found refuge in Glasgow Transport Museum in June 1966 — but *Ben Alder*, the last of the 'Wee Bens', simply disappeared quietly from sight. Apparently, because of its replacement Caley' boiler, it was not considered 'original' enough to be worth saving. .

Long before this sad saga came to an end, so, too, did *new* locomotive construction at Lochgorm Works. The last of four HR 0-4-4Ts entered service in February 1906, and from thence Lochgorm reverted solely to rebuilding and repair work. The

Works themselves were eventually closed by BR on 18th July 1959. The turn of the century also witnessed a major upheaval in the Scottish locomotive building industry, when Neilson Reid & Co., Dübs Co. and Sharp Stewart & Co. merged in 1903, to form the North British Locomotive Co., the largest locomotive factory in Europe. The three constituent Companies had already built 15,437 locomotives between them and with their three Works — Hyde Park, Queens Park and Atlas — retained in full production, the NB Locomotive Co. was able to construct 11,318 more steam locomotives before going into liquidation in 1962. The Highland Railway had already contributed its mite by ordering three 'Bens' in 1906 and, two years later, the firm was again instructed to build an interesting and rather deceptive version of HR 4-4-0 in the form of six 'Big Bens'. Larger, and heavier by six tons, the latter worked to a pressure of 180psi, but yielded no greater tractive effort, at 17,880lb. One still wonders why Peter Drummond thought it necessary to introduce this additional class.

Presumably in recognition of services rendered, the Highland Railway Board elevated Peter Drummond, in 1906, to the status of Chief Mechanical Engineer. At the same time F. G. Smith, who had joined the HR in 1903 as Works Manager, was appointed as Drummond's assistant. Cooler counsel prevailed in

The first four 'Big Bens' (NB Locomotive Works Nos.18269–72/1908) were given 3185 gallon six-wheeled tenders. The two built in 1909, Nos.60 and 62, received 3,600 gallon double-bogied tenders, as per this Works photograph of No.60 *Ben Bhreac Mhor*. This engine was also one of four, Nos.60–63, which were dual fitted. In 1924 it lost its Westinghouse brake and acquired LMS No.14421. First to be withdrawn, it was taken out of service in October 1932. *(Author's Collection)*

December 1911, however, when Drummond resigned to take up appointment with the G&SWR; for when Smith was given Drummond's job two months later he assumed office under the old title of Locomotive, Carriage & Wagon Superintendent. His salary, a disgrace at £500 year, was exactly that which Stroudley had received half a century earlier! Nor was Smith's subsequent career with the Highland Railway much happier. In 1915, after an altercation with the HR's Civil Engineer over six large 'River' 4-6-0s he had been rash enough to order without prior consultation, Smith was arraigned before the HR Board on 24th September. The Board demanded his immediate resignation. Smith duly obliged, returned to Newcastle and gave railways a wide berth from thereon. Ironically, the six 'Rivers', sold to the Caledonian Railway, at a profit, and later classified '4P' by the LMS, could be found working most efficiently on ex-HR main line metals throughout the 1930s.

During his rather turbulent three year career with the Highland Railway Frederick Smith contrived, nevertheless, to effect quite drastic changes in the external appearance of HR locomotives. The dark livery which Drummond had adopted was changed by Smith to a lighter unlined green, cabside number plates were removed and the running number was resited much higher up in large gilt letters. A small aluminium number plate with raised numerals also found a place on the smokebox door.

Christopher Cumming, Smith's successor at Inverness as from 7th October 1915, came directly from NBR employment at Burntisland, and faced the unenviable task of coping with an unprecedented surge of wartime traffic over Highland Railway metals. Admiralty bases at Invergordon and Kyle required enormous railway service. Thurso, too, became a focal point for all transport requirements of Scapa Flow, the Home Fleet's offshore base. In 1918, the pressure of American troop supplies being landed at Kyle was so intense that public railway service there was limited to one passenger train each way per day. Goods traffic from Glasgow went by sea. In light of this upheaval, Cumming's starting salary of £550 a year, with £600 promised after six months, was, once more, an enlightening example of Highland Railway parsimony. Wisely perhaps, he relied on trusted precedent for his initial locomotive contribution. thus, the NB Locomotive Co. supplied three more (dual fitted) 'Lochs', Nos.70–72, in 1916, and three 'Castle' 4-6-0s the following year. That same year, however, Cumming, employing a design reputedly left behind by Smith, commissioned

Two of the original 'Big'Bens' later had their six-wheeled tenders replaced by 3,200 gallon bogie tenders taken from HR 'Barney' 0-6-0s. Then, over the years 1924–27, the whole class was rebuilt with superheater and extended smokebox. Working pressure was now reduced to 175psi and the 'Big Bens' weighed heavier still, at 53¾ tons. No.14417, originally HR No.61, seen here on local duty in the far North, reminds us of how closely these engines resembled Dugald Drummond's contemporary L12 Class L&SWR 4-4-0s. In this instance, though, the L12s were still working long after *Ben na Caillach* went to the breakers in 1936. *(Author's Collection)*

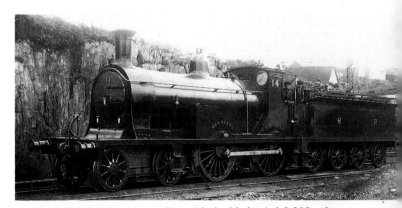

'Wee Ben' No. *Ben Dearg*, complete with double-bogied 3,200 gallon tender, illustrates the Smith livery changes as it awaits its next duty at Kyle of Lochalsh shed. Rebuilt in 1928, *Ben Dearg* duly entered BR stock, but was withdrawn in December 1949 still bearing its LMS number, 14410. *(Author's Collection)*

This Works photograph of HR No.73 *Snaigow* (Works No.3172/1917) conveys much of the power and beauty of Cumming's radical 4-4-0s. F. G. Smith's style of presenting the running number no longer obtains, but the lamp placed high on the cabside remains a typical feature of Highland (and Caledonian) Railway practice. *(Author's Collection)*

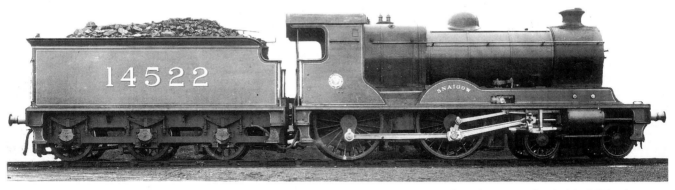

Opposite side view of *Snaigow*, now liveried in LMS crimson as No.14522. Later fitted with a Caledonian Railway chimney. *Snaigow* outlived its sister engine by twelve months, and was taken out of service in April 1936. *(BR LMR)*

Hawthorn Leslie & Co. to build two very large 4-4-0s, Nos.73 and 73. Destined to be the last HR locomotives of that wheel arrangement, they were extremely handsome in appearance, and were given the names *Snaigow* and *Durn*.

Cumming's new 4-4-0s posed a quite remarkable combination of 6ft 3in coupled wheels, 20in × 26in cylinders, 160psi working pressure, outside Walschaerts valve gear, Robinson superheater, Belpaire firebox, and inside admission valves. Each engine weighed 55 tons, and its 3,500 gallon tender added a further 43½ tons. Their initial tractive effort was even further expanded to 20,627lb once boiler pressure was later raised to 175psi. Suffice it to say that subsequent employment of these big 4-4-0s on far north HR service thoroughly justified their later LMS 3P power classification. Unfortunately, the post-grouping LMS policy of standardisation ensured that the two locomotives did not enjoy long lives. *Durn* went in April 1935 and exactly one year later, *Snaigow*, after suffering the indignity of being fitted with a Caledonian chimney in 1934, followed suit.

Despite heavy odds, Cumming's career with the Highland Railway finished in a blaze of glory with his excellent 'Clan Goods' and 'Clan' passenger 4-6-0s. All were supplied, again by Hawthorn Leslie, between 1918 and 1921. Then, alas, poor health accelerated Cumming's retirement in 1922 and his short-term successor, D. C. Urie, hastily recruited from Midland Great Western Railway service in Ireland, held the fort until Grouping

was effected at the end of the year. Even during that brief spell, however, Urie contrived to effect useful improvements in Peter Drummond's 'Big Bens'. He was rewarded in January 1923 by being appointed Assistant CME to William Pickersgill on the new Northern Division of the LMS.

It still seems rather a pity, though, that *Ben Alder* was not spared to join the select ranks of preserved Scottish locomotives. It would have looked perfectly at home on today's Strathspey Railway.

Chapter 7
POST GROUPING IMMIGRANTS, LNER AND LMS

As far as Scotland was concerned, the impact of Grouping on 1st January 1923 found the LNER and the LMS faced with a common problem — that of providing a new source of express passenger locomotives. On the LNER, the management of the North British Railway, its largest Scottish constituent.had cannily refrained from building further 4-4-0s and 4-4-2s after 1920 once rumours of Grouping reached its ears. Further north, Great North of Scotland locomotive stock had been kept in good order, but age and comparative frailty were beginning to take their toll. The LMS, for its part, chose to exacerbate a somewhat similar situation on its Glasgow & South Western Railway section by imposing a ruthless policy of extinguishing small non-standard classes, goods and passenger alike. Fortunately, the fact that Caledonian Railway stock consisted in the main of large robustly-built classes enabled locomotives of that sturdy concern to take up the slack elsewhere — for the time being, at least.

Thus it was the LNER, securely commanded by Nigel Gresley, and blessedly free from the Crewe/Horwich/Derby inhibitions which plagued the early years of LMS corporate existence, which made the first move. Gresley was a particularly engaging figure in that he tempered his considerable engineering skill with a healthy respect for other men's locomotives. He might conceivably have rushed production of a new four-coupled design he had in mind. Instead, he allowed his regard for J. G. Robinson's highly successful 'Improved Director' Great Central 4-4-0s to prompt an immediate solution to NB Section problems. Accordingly, two independent contractors, Kitson & Co. and Armstrong Whitworth, were instructed in December 1923 to build a dozen each of Robinson's tried and trusted 'Directors'. The orders were executed in the remarkably short space of five months, Eastfield men were duly despatched to Gorton and Gateshead to collect the finished products and by the end of November 1924, the 24 'Directors', garbed in green and judiciously distributed amongst the main NBR sheds, were ready to open their colourful chapter in Scottish railway history. They were given LNER Nos.6378–401.

Because of detail differences, Robinson had classified his original 'Directors', built in 1913, '11E', and his later batch of 'Improved Directors' '11F'. The LNER maintained the distinction by classifying them 'D10' and 'D11' respectively. The latter designation, however, soon had to be altered to 'D11/1' to distinguish them from the 'Scottish Directors', which were then styled 'D11/2'. Mechanically, the latter were facsimiles of the GCR engines, but the less generous nature of the NBR loading gauge called for a smaller flowerpot chimney (1ft 0in as opposed to 1ft 3in), a flattened dome, and a lower cab roof. These features apart, a single Gresley anti-vacuum valve behind the chimney, the employment of inside admission valves, a shorter pattern of Ross pop safety-valves, the absence of brass beading round the splashers and, latterly, the fitting of drop grates, were the only other hallmarks of the 'Scottish Directors'. Cylinders, as before, were 20in × 26in, coupled wheels were 6ft 9in, boiler pressure was 180psi and tractive effort remained at a modest, but useful, 19,644lb. The absence of water pick-up gear in their otherwise standard Robinson 4,000 gallon tenders merely acknowledged the fact that the NBR never had occasion to require water troughs.

Greeted with the caution which Scottish locomen customarily extended to 'foreign' engines, the new 4-4-0s certainly caused quite a stir at their various shed locations. Initial vexations were not hard to come by. Right-hand drive, to start with, was completely alien to NBR tradition, and meant that experienced drivers had to relearn their roads. Firemen, too, were obliged to alter their long-standing technique; for although firing could be conveniently accomplished with both hands on the 'D11/2s', their sloping grates required a shorter throw of coal — and that through a smaller, and higher, door. Again, drivers and firemen found common cause for grievance in the absence of a door between cab and tender, and the swirling dust which consequently pervaded the cab once speed was attained. Nevertheless, respect for their new charges grew amongst the men as the 'Scottish Directors' began to prove their worth throughout the length and breadth of Central Scotland; and within a year quite a number of ex-NBR drivers were prepared to concede that they were 'braw engines, if a wee thing big in the wheel'. No doubt the qualification was inspired by the 'Directors' well known inability to get off the mark quite as smartly as the smaller-wheeled NBR 4-4-0s when faced with Cowlairs Bank! Whatever, the process of general acceptance was shrewdly advanced in 1925–26, when the LNER, in an inspired moment, elected to name the big 4-4-0s after Sir Water Scott characters. After that, what Scottish driver could possibly fail to be proud of handling locomotives which bore names like *The Fiery Cross, Wizard of the Moor*, and *Luckie Mucklebackit*! During the naming process the majority of the 'Scottish Directors' lost the GCR-type sheet metal valance which partially concealed their driving wheels. Seven of them, however, carried both name and valance for a further nine months or more.

Equipped, unusually for Scotland, with steam brake for engine and tender and vacuum brake for train braking, the 'Scottish Directors' soon made themselves thoroughly at home on the various Glasgow–Edinburgh–Perth–Dundee–Aberdeen circuits. They appeared to handle express and lesser traffic with equal expedition; and both Eastfield and Haymarket sheds took especial pride in working the 'Queen of Scots' Pullman when that train was extended to Glasgow in 1928. But only very occasionally did one spot a 'Director' at Carlisle or Newcastle. Two of them, though, spent brief periods much further south — when No.6399 *Allan-Bane*, sent to Stratford in November 1926, ran abortive trials on the Colchester and Cambridge lines and No.6401 *James Fitzjames* stood in at Neville Hill in 1943 while rebuilt 'Hunt' No.365 was tried out on Scottish metals. Dundee 'Directors', meanwhile, worked regularly to Edinburgh and Aberdeen, either single-handedly or in tandem with ex-NBR types, depending on the load.

Liveried in green, D11/2 No.6400 *Roderick Dhu* (Armstrong Whitworth Works No.615/1924) was still carrying both name and valance when it was photographed at Leuchars Junction on 11th August 1925. The name was added in April that year, but the valance was not removed until June 1926. *(Stirling Everard)*

Black livery, however, relieved only by a single red line, became the order of the day after the economies of 1928; *vide* this portrait of No.6401 *James Fitzjames*, taken in June 1930 as it left Falkirk (High) station at the head of a Glasgow–Edinburgh express. Note the GCR pattern oval-headed buffers which remained with most 'Directors' for the whole of their working lives. *(A. R. Martin)*

Dundee (Tay Bridge) shed, August 1936, and No.6378 *Baillie MacWheeble*, the first-built Kitson 'Scottish Director' (Works No.5379/1924) poses alongside ex-NBR No.9896 *Dandie Dinmont* before undertaking a return working to Edinburgh. The distinctive narrowing of the forward portion of the footplate from 8ft 9in to 8ft 0in shows clearly in this study. So, too, does the small tender lettering which Cowlairs frequently employed at that time.

Rather sadly, after having won over the hearts of the men who manned them, the primacy of the 'Scottish Directors' over Edinburgh–Glasgow express work was challenged sooner than one might have expected — when a first batch of Gresley's new 'Shire' 4-4-0s arrived on the Central Scottish scene in the Spring of 1928. One year later an influx of eight more 'Shires' settled the issue, and the 'Directors', though still based primarily on Edinburgh and Glasgow sheds, had to be content with a variety of less prestigious duties. The Fife and Dundee areas began to see much more of them. The subsequent introduction of 'Pacifics' and 'V2s' on the Aberdeen main line, however, had little effect on the 'Directors' general utility value, and all 24 'D11/2s' survived World War II to enter BR stock intact as a class. Two years earlier, Cowlairs Works, acting swiftly on an LNER decision to restore express passenger livery, performed wonders in turning out sixteen green 'Scottish Directors'. Then, in 1948, while the Railway Executive were deliberating the question of post-War liveries, Cowlairs again stole a march by taking in four of the green 'Directors'. They re-emerged bearing their new BR numbers on the cabside and 'BRITISH RAIL-WAYS' in full on the tender. The pity was that it was all in vain, in light of BR's eventual decision to bestow black livery on the 'Directors' and their like.

The final threat to *all* LNER 4-4-0s in Scotland came with the introduction of Edward Thompson's 6ft 2in 'B1' 4-6-0s. 410 were built from 1942 onwards and by 1952, the presence of 70 of them at various sheds throughout Scotland began to toll a really ominous bell for 'Scotts', 'Glens', 'Directors' and 'Shires' alike. The run down was remorseless. Starting in September 1958 with the withdrawal of Nos.62679 and 62683, the 'Scottish Director' ranks were progressively thinned, until only fourteen remained by the end of 1959 — and all but one of these were languishing in store at various Scottish shed locations. Curiously, this static state of affairs persisted until May 1961, when No.62671 *Baillie MacWheeble* was summoned to the breakers. Twelve more were scrapped that year, and the last active 'Director', No.62685 *Malcolm Graeme*, only just outlived its less fortunate sisters by holding out at Haymarket shed until January 1962. One must add, though, that it had spent the last

The original GNR 'D1' 4-4-0 No.57, a May 1911 product of Doncaster Works (Works No.1302) spent most of its English working life around Grantham, before being allocated to St. Margaret's shed, Edinburgh in 1925. Thornton and Carlisle sheds later accommodated the engine, and it was withdrawn as BR No.62208 from Hawick shed in July 1950. *(Author's Collection)*

months of its 'active' life on stationary boiler duties at the Caledonian Hotel, Edinburgh.

Less than twelve months after the 'Directors' were introduced in Scotland, Gresley made a second move by sending all fifteen ex-GNR Class D1 4-4-0s to that beleaguered Area. Ivatt's final passenger class and the only 4-4-0s turned out new at Doncaster with superheaters, these 1911 vintage locomotives, now numbered 3051–65, had long been displaced from prime GNR main line work by Ivatt 'Atlantics' and Gresley 'Pacifics'. It seemed to Gresley that their $18\frac{1}{2}$in × 26in cylinders, 6ft 8in coupled wheels, 170psi boiler pressure, and 16,074lb tractive effort might be put to good use further North on local passenger, branch line, and piloting duties. As before, the Scottish loading gauge presented problems, but Doncaster soon resolved these by fitting a 1ft $11\frac{1}{4}$in chimney, and lowering the dome and whistle stand. Thus, the D1's original maximum height above rail of 13ft $3\frac{3}{4}$in was reduced to 12ft 11in. The Schmidt type superheaters remained.

Class D1 No.3053 illustrates the final Cowlairs positioning of the Westinghouse pump. This locomotive lost its Westinghouse equipment in May 1939, by which time it was stationed at Norwich. It was eventually withdrawn in March 1946. *(Author's Collection)*

Early days. In this Leuchars Junction scene, dated 11th August 1925, D1 No.3064, a Haymarket engine, is piloting ex-NBR 'Atlantic' No.9509 on a heavy northbound express. Curiously, *Duke of Rothesay*, built by the NB Loco. Co. (Works No.22689) in June 1921, was withdrawn in February 1937, while the D1, a Doncaster product of 1911, lasted until February 1950, before being withdrawn as BR No.62215. *(Stirling Everard)*

The initial Scottish distribution saw Haymarket shed receive six D1s. Eastfield, Ladybank, and Carlisle were given two each and single locomotives went to St Margaret's, Dunfermline, and Hawick. Wherever they went, however, their main function never rose above local passenger work, main line piloting and other lesser duties. Between 1925 and 1927 all attended Cowlairs Works, whence they were converted from vacuum brake to Westinghouse, albeit the vacuum ejector was retained for alternative train braking. The correct positioning of the Westinghouse air pump, however, took some time to resolve. The first three converts had their pumps sited high on the right-hand side of the smokebox. This soon brought complaints from drivers that their view was being obstructed. Ergo, seven more D1s which were converted between July 1926 and April 1927 had the pump fitted high on the left-hand side instead. Alas, this modification displeased firemen, whose job it was to oil the pump — and, in a final compromise, the Westinghouse pump on the last five was moved lower down on the left-hand side. Engines treated earlier were re-adjusted in due course.

In truth, graver issues were at stake; for, right from the outset, the 'D1s' met with nothing but hostility at all Scottish sheds. Not only were they dismissed as GNR 'cast offs', or 'Ponies', but a second contemptuous nickname which came their way, 'Tambourinies', said all that needed to be said anent their GN-style cabs, which NB locomen, long accustomed to more sheltered accommodation, swore were not only flimsy, but

extremely uncomfortable and draughty. Add to that the 'D1s' right-hand drive, pull-out regulator handle, screw reversing gear, indifferent steaming ability, and unfailing capacity for rough riding, and it hardly needed NB firemen's problems in coping with a strange GN-type firedoor to cap a state of complete disenchantment, Significantly, the normal proud Scottish Area practices of regular manning and rostering were never extended to the 'D1s'. The acute dislike of the class, in fact, even spread as far afield as Gateshead. There, quite often, once a 'D1' had piloted a 'Pacific' on a southbound express as far as Newcastle, the NE shed, well aware of Haymarket drivers' distaste for a repeat performance, sent the 'D1' back light, all of 124 miles, to Edinburgh

It follows that the wretched reception the D1s received in Scotland had a considerable bearing on their subsequent history. Erratic performance, low grade employment, inferior maintenance — all chased each other in something of a vicious spiral. In Fife, apart from main line piloting duties by Dunfermline shed's sole representative, the D1s led very menial lives indeed. Haymarket shed's complement fare only marginally better by being employed on local passenger work as well as main line piloting. The Hawick and Carlisle D1s never rose above local passenger duties. There was no brooking the fact: the Scottish D1 experiment had misfired badly. Matters came to a head at a meeting of the Mechanical Engineers on 25th November 1930, when decision was made to exchange four D1s for four

No.2754 *Rutlandshire*, one of eight 'D49/1s' added by Darlington
Works in 1929, poses at Eastfield shed early in its long Scottish
Area career. Last of that batch to go, the 'Shire' was withdrawn as
BR No.62729 in May 1961. *(Author's Collection)*

Southern Area D3 4-4-0s. What effect such a transfer might
have had in Scotland will never be known; for, as it happened,
although seven D1s were duly transferred south by 1932, the
seven D3s sent in exchange went not to Scotland — but to the
North Eastern Area! The seven repatriated D1s were stored
awhile at Doncaster, and their Westinghouse brake equipment
subsequently found employment for them in East Anglia.

By 1939 four D1s could still be found at Haymarket shed;
though most of them spent lengthy periods of inactivity from
time to time. Even those, however, had to be dragged into
action once war broke out. They made heavy weather of assisting 'Pacifics' on heavy East Coast night trains. The remaining
Scottish D1s were allocated, two each, to Hawick and Carlisle
sheds, where they, too, were kept fully employed on wartime
duties. The years 1942–45 saw further change, when six of the
Scottish D1s were altered from Westinghouse to steam brake.
The vacuum ejector, however, was retained for train braking.
Significantly, the two which escaped this modification, Nos.3051
and 3061, were early post-war withdrawals, in January 1946 and
July 1947 respectively. Hawick D1 No.3065 was also taken out
of service in September 1947 and this left five Scottish D1s, duly
renumbered by the LNER in 1946, available to enter British
Railways' service. Thinly spread over five different sheds, their
various locations were: Dunfermline No.2205, Hawick
No.2208, Haymarket No.2214, Perth No.2215 and Stirling
No.2209. The Dunfermline engine was first to go, when withdrawals resumed in November 1948. Haymarket lost No.2214 a

year later, No.62215 left Perth for the last time in February
1950, No.62208 (Hawick) followed in July that year and,
almost simultaneously, the last of the English 'D1s' vanished
from Colwick shed. Then came the final demise of the class,
when No.2209 (formerly LNER No.3058), unloved and
unmourned, was called in from Stirling shed. Archetypical of the
species, it had spent the last years of its life very much in 'foreign' parts — assisting heavy north-bound expresses over the ex-
LMS heavily graded main line to Kinbuck!

Meanwhile, in the mid-1920s Gresley had cleared the decks
for fast, heavy Anglo-Scottish East Coast passenger traffic by
putting 52 of his celebrated class 'A1' 'Pacifics' to work. The last
of these, No.2562 *Isinglass*, was shopped from Doncaster in July
1925. Unfortunately, the use of these magnificent engines on
the ex-NBR main lines to Aberdeen and Carlisle was forbidden
at the time and Gresley was obliged, therefore, to turn his mind
towards providing a suitably powerful engine to assist NB
'Atlantics' on these difficult routes. Within a year or two a similar predicament would arise on the North Eastern Area as older
NER types were progressively phased out. Darlington Works was
duly instructed to develop a three-cylinder Gresley 4-4-0 design
and the prototype, No.234 *Yorkshire*, entered traffic in October

Shopped from Darlington Works in August 1928 as the last of six 'D49/3s', No.329 *Inverness-shire* is seen here shortly after being posted, new, to Perth shed. Two years later it left Perth for the last time. It was eventually withdrawn, as BR No.62725, in 'D49/1' form in November 1958. *(Stirling Everard)*

The Scottish activities of 'D49/2' No.336 *Buckinghamshire* were rarely photographed. In this view, however, the locomotive is seen leaving Polmont Station in August 1930 after having made its scheduled stop on the 10.14am ex-Glasgow to Edinburgh express. Note the ex-NBR stock. *(A. R. Martin)*

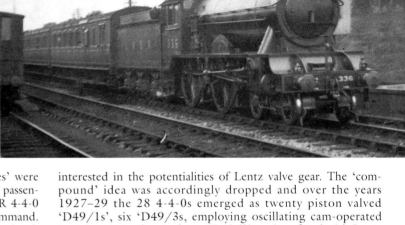

1927. Within seven months a further nineteen 'Shires' were turned out. Apart from being the first LNER-designed passenger locomotive, the class was also to be the last LNER 4-4-0 gambit before six-coupled express engines assumed command. Many variations on the original 'Shire' theme still lay ahead, however,

With Darlington Works given a fairly free hand in determining their design, the first twenty piston-valved 'Shires', classified as 'D49/1', were an interesting blend of Darlington and Doncaster practice. The boiler was the same as that which had been fitted, a year earlier, to the J39 0-6-0 goods engines and, quite contrary to Doncaster practice, all three 17in × 26in cylinders and the steam chest were embodied in one casting. Inside steam pipes were duly employed. Coupled wheels, at 6ft 8in, conformed to Doncaster passenger engine habit but bogie wheels on the 'D49s' followed NER standards by being smaller and more widely spaced Group Standard tenders, with stepped-out tops and fuel capacities of 7½ tons and 4,200 gallons were provided for all. So, too, was water pick-up apparatus — even for the fifteen 'Shires' which were destined for Scotland. Left-hand drive also applied, as did NER-type steam reversing gear. Westinghouse brake pumps were initially fitted but within a year or two, a change was made to steam brake for the engine, with vacuum ejector for the train brakes. Boiler pressure was 180psi and tractive effort 21,556lb.

Darlington's original instructions, issued in April 1926, postulated the construction of 28 'D49s': thirteen for the North Eastern Area and fifteen for Scotland. Of them, 26 were to be piston-valved (Part 1), and the remaining Part 2 pair were to be 'compounds'. Within months, however, Gresley became deeply interested in the potentialities of Lentz valve gear. The 'compound' idea was accordingly dropped and over the years 1927–29 the 28 4-4-0s emerged as twenty piston valved 'D49/1s', six 'D49/3s, employing oscillating cam-operated Lentz poppet valves and two 'D49/2' engines fitted with Lentz rotary cam valve gear. In the event, the Running Department reacted so favourably to the 'D49/2' version that rotary cam gear was again employed when 40 'Hunts' were added to the Class between 1932 and 1935. In the meantime, eight more 'D49/1s' were built for Scottish use in 1929. Six of them, however, bore English Shire names. This batch was given straight-sided tenders; while other important detail differences included the provision of screw reverse gear (instead of steam) and steam brake in lieu of Westinghouse.

On the face of it the impact of the six Lentz oscillating cam-valve operated 'D49/3' engines on Scotland was minimal in that only one of the species, No.329, ever served the Scottish Area. Yet that very locomotive played an important role during the rather convoluted development of the class. Posted when new to Perth in the Autumn of 1928, the 4,500 miles which *Inverness-shire* ran during its initial six weeks, fully supported contemporary English contentious that the centre cylinder valve gear, despite sundry tinkering, left much to be desired. Close inspection of a 268 ton working to Edinburgh confirmed matters, and early in June 1929, No.329 entered Darlington Works; whence standard Gresley 2 to 1 levers were fitted to the offending valve gear. This produced such an improvement in performance that the other five 'D49/3s' were altered similarly over the next fourteen months.

As it happened, Darlington returned No.329 swiftly enough

to Perth; but within a matter of weeks the men there were again expressing dissatisfaction with the new valve setting. Gresley, ever alert to Scottish locomen's opinions, promptly had the locomotive returned to Darlington — and took up the Scottish slack in intriguing fashion by despatching No.336 *Buckinghamshire*.one of the LNER's two 'D49/2s', to Scotland on a temporary trial and observation basis. No.329, meanwhile, after examination at Darlington, was tested for the next twelve months on sundry express jobs based on York and, in October 1930, just on the 50,000 mile mark, the central cylinder valve gear failed once more. As a consequence, the cut-off in full gear of all six 'D49/3s' was reduced from 65% to 62%, and the engines were placed on less strenuous duties. During the year 1938, as and when new cylinders were required, poppet valves and oscillating cams were removed, and all six re-emerged as conventional piston-valved 'D49/1s'.

Buckinghamshire's 'loan' to the Scottish Area lasted longer than expected. Posted to Eastfield shed in November 1929, the 'D49/2' handled Glasgow–Edinburgh express traffic in the main — and no doubt yielded Gresley much valuable, and highly practical, information in the process. Latterly, No.336 moved on to Perth shed; then, in March 1931, having completed its Scottish sojourn, it rejoined sister engine No.352 at York. The following year, when serious production of 'Hunt' class 'D49/2s' got under way at Darlington, both pioneer 'D49/2s' dropped their 'Shire' names, and became No.336 *The Quorn* and 352 *The Meynell*. Of the two, the one-time *Buckinghamshire* lived the longer by three years, being withdrawn as BR No.62727 in January 1961.

By and large, the 'D49/1s' served the LNER's Scottish Area well. They handled express traffic most expeditiously on all main lines between Aberdeen and Carlisle — until an influx of 'Pacifics' and 'V2s' in the mid-1930s ended their period of supremacy. During the 1939–45 War they even coped with a deal of goods work; but, of course, three-cylindered 4-4-0s were hardly designed to be at ease on such humble duties. In any case, the freight loads allocated to them were no greater than those normally handled by ex-NBR class J35 0-6-0s. The most vexing problem of all, however, was their unfailing unpopularity with many Scottish locomen. Not only were the 'Shires' capacious cabs as draughty as those of their predecessors, the 'Directors', but the rough ride the 'D49s' offered, quite analogous to that of the ill-starred 'D1s', caused many older drivers to revert voluntarily, and prematurely, to shunting duties. One final grudge lay in most ex-NBR men's conviction that the 'Shires'

had been deliberately introduced to replace the NBR 'Atlantics'. Gresley constantly refuted such intention — but the rapid demise of the much loved NB 'Whippets' only rubbed salt into the wounds . . .

By mid-1929, when production of 'D49/1s' terminated with a final batch of eight, the Scottish Area's allocation of 'D49s' stood at 23. Distributed over five main sheds, all were piston valved except for 'D49/3' No.329 *Inverness-shire*. Eastfield shed had the lion's share with seven, St. Margaret's and Dundee had six each, and Perth and Haymarket had equal shares in the remaining four. Little change obtained until June 1943, when Haymarket received two more 'D49/1s', English 'Shires' Nos.253 and 320, to compensate for the withdrawal of two long-term resident ex-North Eastern 'Atlantics'. Thus, with No.329 having already reverted to 'D49/1' form in 1938, a total of 25 Scottish Area 'D49/1s' entered BR stock in 1948. At this juncture Haymarket topped the league with eight, Carlisle and Thornton had five each, Dundee had three and St. Margaret's and Perth had two each. Some time later, the two Perth engines were transferred to Stirling, whence, interestingly, they emulated the feat of the last 'D1', by working a former LMSR service, this time between Stirling, Larbert, and Edinburgh (Princes Street). The North Eastern Area's complement of 'D49s', meanwhile, consisted of the remaining nine 'D49/1s'. 41 'D49/2s', and *The Morpeth*, Edward Thompson's solitary class 'D' rebuild of August 1942. Surprisingly, the latter locomotive was destined to be withdrawn in November 1952, almost five years before inroads commenced in the 'D49' ranks.

As it happened, the dubious distinction of providing the first 'D49' withdrawal fell to Thornton shed, when it lost No.62713 *Aberdeenshire* in September 1957. Subsequent Scottish Area withdrawals then swelled to eight and six in 1958 and 1959 respectively, before dropping to two in January 1960. Twelve months later No.62717 *Banffshire* was taken out of service.

All three locomotives seen here at Larbert in July 1935 were products of the early 1920s, and were taken out of service in the 1950s. Ex-CR No.14497 (left) was built by the NB Loco. Co. to William Pickersgill's order in November 1922, Compound No.1126, the pilot engine on the Glasgow–Aberdeen express, left Horwich Works in December 1925 and, behind it, Class '60' 4-6-0 No.14630, the locomotive associated with the Preston–Carlisle trials of 1925, was a St. Rollox Works product of July that year. Surprisingly, the Caledonian 4-4-0 outlived the others, by lasting to October 1959. *(Author's Collection)*

Seen here at its home shed, Corkerhill (Glasgow) in August 1936, No.1080 was one of a first batch of 40 LMS Compounds which were shopped from Derby in 1924 with low pressure cylinders increased to 21¾in diameter and high pressure cylinder to 19¾in. Evidence of right-hand drive is also apparent.

Freshly delivered by the NB Loco. Co., No.1141 (Works No.23235/1925) proudly demonstrates its crimson lake LMS passenger engine livery in Kingmoor shed yard. 1925 was also the year when Compounds were turned out with left hand drive. Sister engine No.1136 lies behind. (*W. G. Tilling*)

Four more Scottish 'D49/1s' followed suit in March/April 1961, and in May that year the last two in traffic, Nos.62711 *Dumbartonshire* and 62729 *Rutlandshire*, both went to the breakers.

Theoretically, the last 'D49/1' to be withdrawn was No.61712 *Morayshire*. Though not officially written off by BR until July 1961, it had, however, already spent four months as a stationary boiler, raising steam for the Slateford Laundry in Edinburgh. This state of affairs continued until January 1962, whence it was rescued and stored, first at Dalry Road shed until September 1963, then at Dawsholm shed until July 1964. The reason for *Morayshire's* protracted farewell only became clear when news broke that the locomotive had, in fact, been purchased privately by an enthusiast, Ian N. Fraser by name. Duly restored, externally at least, at Inverurie Works in 1964, the locomotive was presented to the Royal Scottish Museum, Edinburgh in 1966. But here, happily, the story does not end; for, some years later, the Scottish Railway Preservation Society, entering into a fortuitous loan agreement with the Museum, undertook to restore the 'D49/1' to full working order. One needs hardly add that much hard work was put in at the Society's Springfield Yard Depot before *Morayshire* finally re-emerged in 1975, resplendent in green livery, and proudly carrying its old LNER number, 246, for all to see.

The benefits of unified command which served the LNER so well were sadly lacking, initially at least, on the LMS; for during the latter's formative years Crewe, Derby, and Horwich each strove mightily for locomotive precedence. Indeed, the only new passenger tender locomotives introduced by the LMS in 1923 were 21 Hughes L&YR type four-cylinder 4-6-0s. Any conclusion one might have drawn from this, however, that the likelihood of new LMS 4-4-0 construction was slight proved to be very wide of the mark, particularly once dynamometer car trails between a superheated ex-Midland Compound, an ex-Midland '999' class 4-4-0, and an ex-LNWR 'Prince of Wales' 4-6-0 began on the Settle–Carlisle line towards the end of that year. The Midland Railway had never doubted the prowess of its 4-4-0s Compounds since they were first introduced as far back as 1902. In keeping with Company policy, however, it had always observed a marked reluctance to 'overload' them. Thus, Midland Compounds running non-stop between Leeds and Carlisle had always been confined to loads of 230–260 tons. In light of this, one can well imagine Derby's gratification when, during the 1923 trials, No.1008 made light of climbing to Ais Gill with 355 tons behind its tender. Not only that — but its coal consumption was distinctly superior to that of the LNWR 'Prince'!

In any case, Derby, it seemed, had already made up its mind to perpetuate the Compound design; for twenty new engines, Nos.1045-64, built under Works Order No.5938, entered LMS service between February and July 1924. Compared with the superheated rebuilds of the original Johnson locomotives, their coupled wheels were three inches smaller at 6ft 9in, and both high and low pressure cylinders had been stepped up by ¾in.

That year, without pausing for breath, Derby turned out a further batch, Nos.1065–84. Significantly, these were given shorter chimneys to conform with the restrictions of Scottish loading gauge, and Ross pop safety valves were fitted in lieu of the previous Ramsbottom valve arrangement. Two of them, Nos.1065 and 1066, took part in a new series of trials between Leeds and Carlisle. This time, intriguingly, a St. Rollox-built Caledonian Railway Pickersgill 4-4-0, No.124 (later LMS No.14466) competed — and was thoroughly trounced by the Compounds. A Pickersgill class '60' 4-6-0, No.14630, did rather better in a further series of trials which were conducted between Preston and Carlisle in the spring of 1925; but the performance of No.1065 again showed clearly that in terms of 350 ton loads and light coal consumption the 4-4-0 Compound had no equal. From that moment the question of seconding increasing numbers of LMS Compounds to the Scottish Area was never in doubt. By the summer of 1925 no fewer than twenty could be found at Kingmoor shed, Carlisle. They handled most northbound express passenger traffic on both the old Caledonian and G&SWR routes.

During 1925 production of LMS Compounds really got into its stride. Derby shopped 30 that year, and Horwich 20. Meanwhile, the NB Locomotive Company's Queens Park Works and the Vulcan Foundry's Newton-le-Willows establishment added 25 each. Commencing with No.1085, the first of the 1925 Derby complement, however, cylinders reverted to the original Midland Railway 1902 diameters of 19in (high pressure) and 21in (low pressure), and a permanent change from right to left-hand driving position was also instituted. The latter was an important concession to long-standing practice on the LNWR, L&YR, Caledonian, and Highland Railways. 6ft 9in coupled wheels, though, still remained the order of the day.

In 1927 Vulcan Foundry subscribed another 50 Compounds and 25 of them, Nos.900–24, were immediately allocated to the LMS Northern Division. Polmadie shed received the first ten, and the remainder were spread amongst eight other Scottish sheds, ranging from Corkerhill to Ferryhill, Aberdeen. The other 25 went to the Midland Division. Then, in September 1932 — quite remarkably, in light of the fact that 'Royal Scot' and 'Baby Scot' 4-6-0s were by now firmly in the main line saddle — Derby shopped a final batch of five Compounds, Nos.935–39. Easily the most numerous 4-4-0 Class in the country, 45 Midland 7ft Compounds (Nos.1000–44) and 195 of the LMS 6ft 9in version (Nos.1045–1199 and 900–39) could now be found operating all over the LMS system.

For a brief spell during the summer of 1927, when the prestigious 10.00am 'Royal Scot' express began to stop at Carnforth and Symington only, a pair of Polmadie Compounds revelled in working both the Up and Down train between Glasgow and Carnforth. Unfortunately, their pleasure was abruptly terminated in September that year, when the 'Royal Scot' began to stop at Carlisle only, and 4-6-0s took charge. Still, morale was suitably restored seven months later, when, in the Spring of 1928, Compound No.1054 entered the record books by accomplishing a feat which had never before, and has never since, been equalled by a British 4-4-0.

The background was typical of the times, for by now competition for Anglo–Scottish traffic was ultra-keen between the LMS and the LNER. Thus, when the latter company announced, with a pardonable flourish of publicity, that, as from May 1928, it intended to run the 10.00am 'Flying Scotsman' non-stop between King's Cross and Edinburgh, the LMS, instead of rocking on its heels, quietly responded by running *its* Down 'Royal Scot' in *two* non-stop portions from Euston on 27th April — the Friday *before* the great LNER event was due to take place!

Derby-built in November 1928, No.607 is seen here at Ayr in August 1931. It was one of the Ardrossan shed 'faithfuls', and was ultimately withdrawn from store at Hurlford in July 1959. Like many other Scottish 2Ps it retained its Midland-type chimney to the bitter end. *(A. R. Martin)*

No.563, the first of Fowler's LMS Class '2P' 4-4-0s and seen here in works grey finish, was shopped from Derby Works in March 1928. Steam brakes on the bogies and by-pass valves, features seen quite clearly in this official Works photograph, were later removed during the Stanier régime, and the locomotive itself was withdrawn in May 1962. *(LMS official)*

Even the most avid LNER supporter had to admit it was a masterstroke; albeit the LMS had no immediate intention of perpetuating such a service. Preparations at Euston were thorough, none the less. Both trains were manned by volunteer three-man crews and, to ensure adequate coal capacity, the two locomotives concerned were fitted with long wheelbase Deeley tenders. These, borrowed from Midland simple 4-4-0s, were specially modified to carry nine tons of coal. Scotland, therefore, witnessed two remarkable events that evening; when 'Royal Scot' 4-6-0 No.6113 *Cameronian* arrived at Glasgow (Central) with one non-stop portion — and Compound No.1054, with six bogies behind her, drew into Edinburgh (Princes Street) Station with the other — exactly one minute late after running 399.7 miles non-stop in 8 hours 11 minutes! The Compound's coal consumption of 6¼ tons that day yielded a heartening figure of 35lb per mile, and great was the LMS rejoicing!

But such a figure, of course, was very much a product of No.1054 working under optimum conditions — ie operating full compound practically continuously over a long distance. Shorter haul main line work, and stopping passenger duties which, by their very nature, demanded a higher proportion of simple working, produced rather different results. In 1927, for instance, it was estimated that Compounds in general were averaging 44lb per mile. A year later, the figure rose to just over 47lb and once Stanier 4-6-0s arrived on the scene in 1934 to relegate the Compounds to a variety of lesser tasks, the latter's coal consumption soared over the 50lb mark. Unwilling to face the cost of completely rebuilding locomotives which now seemed doomed to serve their days out on secondary express

duties at best, LMS management, guided shrewdly by W. A. Stanier, opted to restock with a succession of fine six-coupled modern types. These combined much of GWR practice with the best features of existing LMSR designs.

Provided the LMS Compounds were allowed to run with a wide open regulator, and were not flogged — conditions with which Midland Railway drivers were already well familiar — they were undoubtedly efficient machines. Western Division men, however, weaned on an LNWR tradition of hard driving, heavy trains, and tight schedules, adopted a generally hostile attitude to their new crimson charges. Conversely, up in the Central Division, a batch of fifteen Compounds, Nos.1185–99, shopped by Vulcan Foundry in 1927, were warmly received by ex-L&YR men. North of the Border there was never any doubt.

Drivers on the G&SWR section, in particular, with their inborn love of fast running, took the Compounds very much to heart, and ere long one heard of loads approaching 400 tons being handled with consummate ease. Caledonian men, too, soon developed the knack of getting the best out of the unfamiliar. Thus, by 1928 no fewer than 49 of these popular engines could be found amongst the various LMS Scottish sheds. The Caledonian section had 31, the G&SWR section fifteen, and three others were free to operate as required. Certainly, by 1930 it was no uncommon experience for one to travel behind Compounds all the way from St. Pancras to St. Enoch, or Carlisle to Aberdeen for that matter. In later years the majority of the English Compounds acquired Stanier chimneys. Two sizes were used, allowing clearances of 13ft 3in and 12ft 10¾in. But, aesthetically speaking, neither had anything like the dignity of the short Fowler chimney. The latter remained a firm favourite in Scotland and, thanks to St. Rollox Work's perseverance in the matter, many Scottish Compounds were still proudly carrying their original chimneys when they went to the breakers in the late 1950s.

The increase in freight traffic which was generated by the outbreak of war in 1939 at least enabled the Compounds to recover a certain proportion of long lost express passenger work. The honeymoon did not last long, however, for six years later, once production of Stanier 'Black Five' 4-6-0s was vigorously resumed and new Fairburn 2-6-4Ts began to assume a wide variety of passenger traffic duties, more and more Compounds began to be laid up, both in England and Scotland. The number of Compounds in the Scottish Region reached a peak of 62 by

Class 2P No.40663 looked spruce enough on 14th June 1960 as it headed an ambitious RCTS/SLS Scottish Rail Tour through Forres Station. The two restored Caledonian coaches immediately behind the engine were a nostalgic feature of the Tour. So, too, was the MR-type chimney the locomotive still carried. Derby works had no compunction in fitting Stanier chimneys as 2Ps passed through its Shops. St. Rollox works, however, had an aesthetic preference for the original chimney, and did its best to perpetuate it. Certainly No.40663 carried the adornment until the end came in September 1961. *(Steamchest)*

Conversely, the scene at Kittybrewster in April 1961 was only too typical of that year. Class 2P Nos.40650 (left) and 40648 were Crewe products of September 1931, and No.40663 emanated from Derby three months later. All three were finally pensioned off by BR in September 1961.
(Steamchest)

1953. Alas, most were in store; and resolution of this sad situation began in earnest in December that year, when No.41171, a Dumfries engine, and five other Scottish Compounds were officially withdrawn. The disagreeable task of demolishing the remaining 56 went to Kilmarnock Works; and in May 1958, Scotland bade farewell to its last surviving Compound, when a work-weary No.40920 made its final exit from Stranraer shed.

The English story was only marginally less gloomy. There, the sole remaining 'active' Compound, No.40907, worked a last Sheffield–Derby 'slow' on 21st August 1960, before proceeding to Doncaster(!) a month later for cutting up. Eleven months later, the Birmingham area released the last of its stored English Compounds, and No.41168 quit Monument Lane. The more thankful we must be, therefore, that the prototype Midland Compound, No.1000, though withdrawn as long ago as July 1951, was eventually restored in full Midland red livery by Derby. Happily, now in the safe-keeping of the National Railway Museum, it is still capable of making odd forays at the head of steam specials, though at the time of writing (1994), its boiler certificate is well-expired!

One more LMS class falls to be considered in this review of post-Grouping Scottish 4-4-0s and, almost inevitably, it too was Midland in origin. I refer, of course, to the 138 Class '2P' engines which were turned out during the years 1928–32. Derby built 98 of them (Nos.563–635, and 661–85) between March 1928 and April 1932, and Crewe, getting off to a later start, supplied 40 (Nos.636–60, and 686–700) between August 1931 and December 1932. Quite a history, in fact, lay behind their introduction.

As is well known, Samuel Waite Johnson, the Midland Railway's distinguished Locomotive Superintendent during the period 1873–1903, complemented the work of his essentially practical predecessor, Matthew Kirtley, by introducing a marked element of grace and beauty into MR locomotive design. He also elevated the practice of economic running to a fine art; and, as a consequence, Midland engines were never worked to full capacity. Indeed, Johnson set the seal of the Midland Railway's traditional 'small engine' policy when he introduced his three-cylinder Smith type Compound 4-4-0 in January 1902. His successor, R. M. Deeley, took matters a stage further by developing the Midland Compound into a powerful and efficient machine. Deeley's additional pioneering work in enhancing other Johnson 4-4-0 and 0-6-0 designs might, in fact, easily have led to bigger and better things on the Midland — had not personal antipathy between Cecil W. Paget, the MR's newly appointed General Superintendent, and Deeley culminated in the latter's bitter resignation, at the age of 54, in 1909. It was a great pity; for Deeley had already drawn up plans for a 4-6-0 and 0-8-0, and there can be no doubt that implementation of these projects would have placed the Midland Railway much more in line with other major British companies As it was, Henry Fowler, the man appointed to succeed Deeley, though a man of many parts (he was at once a metallurgist, a scientist, and an acknowledged expert on locomotive boilers and fireboxes) was no thrusting locomotive designer. Hence, during his years as Chief Mechanical Engineer to the Midland Railway Fowler was content to build superheated versions of already established Johnson and Deeley designs.

Seen here at Ayr on 30th May 1959, 2P No.40670 worked on through the decimation which so reduced 2P ranks over the next three years. Derby-built in January 1932, it was the last of its class by the time withdrawal came in December 1962. *(Author's Collection)*

Came Grouping in 1923, and Fowler, now Sir Henry by virtue of meritorious wartime service in munitions and aircraft production, was appointed Deputy CME to the LMSR, under the more senior leadership of George Hughes. Lamentably, acrimonious personal relationships again intervened. Hughes retired in September 1925, just before his 60th birthday, CME headquarters were transferred from Horwich to Derby and Fowler took over. He quickly got into his stride by reorganising Derby Works repair shops in typically efficient and economic fashion. Fowler's failure, however, to exercise strict control over traditional hostilities which seethed within the LMS CME department meant that his locomotive contribution tended to remain as parochial as ever. Midland 'thinking' had become paramount by now. Thus, when, in the mid-1920s, an acute shortage of passenger locomotives in Scotland, particularly in the G&SWR section, called for urgent fresh thinking in the way of a suitable utility design, Derby thought automatically in terms of a 4-4-0. At first an outside cylinder version of the MR '2P' was considered. Such a scenario might well have provided an LMS equivalent of Gresley's 'Shires'. Unfortunately, the idea was rejected, and the best Fowler was able to conjure up was a revamped version of his two-cylinder Midland Railway '483' Class 4-4-0s of 1912. Even the latter, though profuse in number, had been 'renewals' of an earlier Johnson type.

Still, Fowler's new black-liveried inside-cylinder Class '2P' 4-4-0s did make *some* concession to modernity. The '483' front end had been improved, and an increased boiler pressure of 180psi enabled cylinder diameter to be reduced from 20½in to 19in. These factors, plus a reduction in coupled wheel diameter of 3½ inches to 6ft 9in, combined to offer a quite reasonable tractive effort of 17,730lb — albeit one nearly 5,000lbs short of the Compounds. The piston valves were placed under the '2P's' cylinders, and had outside admission. Double exhaust valves

were fitted to most and Ross pop safety valves appeared on all. Fortunately for Fowler, many of the '2Ps' went to the G&SWR section, where they soon gained a measure of popularity with men who had learned to adjust themselves over the years to a variety of locomotive types. Further South, Fowler's '2Ps' also featured prominently on Somerset & Dorset Joint Railway express passenger traffic — until the arrival of Stanier Class '5s' in 1938 tolled the inevitable bell. Three '2Ps', in fact, numbered 44–46, had been built in 1928 specifically for S&DJR use; but when the locomotives on that line were absorbed by the LMS in 1930 they were regrouped as Nos.633–35, to fit in with the parent Class '2P' number sequence. Significantly, their S&DJR classification of '3P 2G' was promptly reduced to '2P' by the LMS.

The new Class 2Ps duly multiplied in typical Midland fashion and soon began to show up in Scotland. Several were observed working from Glasgow Central and St. Enoch Stations in the latter part of 1928 and by the turn of the year, a handful of Corkerhill 2Ps were handling slow trains between St. Enoch and Carlisle. Later in 1929 five 2Ps were allocated to Dumfries shed and Stirling received two. Meanwhile, Derby's marked antipathy to non-standard locomotive classes was playing havoc with ex-GSWR engines; and in 1937 the last remaining Sou' West 4-4-0s, four Peter Drummond locomotives built as recently as 1913–15, vanished from human ken. Two years earlier the sole survivor of Smellie's 44 4-4-0s had gone to the breakers, while Manson's numerous 4-4-0s fared even worse — as did his elegant 4-6-0s — for none saw service beyond October 1934. Hence, in this melancholy catalogue lies the reason why Derby's new 4-4-0s soon flooded into ex-GSWR territory.

1934, as it happened, was a sad year in other respects, for it witnessed the premature withdrawal of two Scottish Class 2P 4-4-0s. The circumstances were sombre to a degree. At 5.38pm on Thursday 6th September 1934, in broad daylight and at the height of evening traffic, No.639 (Crewe/Aug 1931), having left St. Enoch Station on a local passenger train to Kilmarnock, was crossing from the Up Main to the Up Fast Canal line when it collided head on with No.591 (Derby/Sept 1928). The latter was heading the 5.12pm Down local passenger train from

Paisley. The accident occurred on the diamond crossing at Port Eglinton Junction, near Cumberland Street Station and the impact of the combined 500 ton trains was later estimated at 45–50mph. Whatever, six passengers, the driver of the Kilmarnock train and the firemen of both trains lost their lives, while 31 passengers were injured. Subsequent enquiry reached the inescapable conclusion that the driver of the Paisley train had failed to observe, much less obey, home signals; and Driver Kerr was duly charged with 'culpable homicide' at Glasgow Sheriff Court in July 1935. Mercifully, the Jury, however, returned a unanimous verdict of 'not guilty', and Kerr was acquitted. The two 2Ps, meanwhile, had been so badly damaged that they were judged to be beyond repair.

The influx of Class 2Ps into the Scottish Area continued apace, and reached its apogee in mid-1950, by which time no fewer than 75 of these popular 4-4-0s were stationed in the North. The shed allocations tell their own tales:

Corkerhill (67A)	15
Hurlford (67B)	24
Ayr (67C)	10
Ardrossan (67D)	12 *
Kingmoor (68A)	3
Dumfries (68B)	3
Stranraer (68C)	4
Kittybrewster (61A)	3
Carstairs (64D)	1
Total	**75**

*Interestingly, eleven of Ardrossan's 2Ps, Derby-built in 1928–29 and 1932, were sent there when new, and remained faithful *en bloc* to Ardrossan shed until early 1959, when three of them were transferred to Hurlford.

The year 1954 appeared to hold ominous overtones for Scottish 2Ps; for between 23rd March and 5th June, five Stanier Class 5 4-6-0s were variously employed on a series of Dynamometer Car tests over the ex-GSWR line from Carlisle to Hurlford and back. One notes that several Class 2Ps were also repaired at Cowlairs Works that year and, in November, the tip of a potential iceberg loomed on the horizon in the form of the first *calculated* 2P withdrawal, when No.662, one of Hurlford shed's 'faithfuls', was, rather unexpectedly, taken out of service. Yet, the years rolled on and, apart from a solitary English 2P withdrawal (No.676) in August 1957, the ranks held firm.

The truce, however, was an uneasy one and the guillotine duly descended in 1959, when 43 Class 2P 4-4-0s were withdrawn of which 23 were Scottish. A total of ten casualties the following year offered a brief respite. Then the real holocaust came in 1961, when 66 more 2Ps, many of them already stored, were officially withdrawn; this time, 39 were Scottish Area engines. As the year opened normal northern wintry conditions merely accentuated the gloomy situation which now obtained anent Class 2Ps at the various ex-GSWR strongholds. Fourteen lay in store at Hurlford and the remaining six which were still in use vanished by October 1961. Corkerhill, meanwhile, offered an equally desolate scene, for there a lengthy row of unserviceable 2Ps awaited final disposal. No.620, the only Corkerhill 2P still working, was taken out of circulation in October that year. Further south, Stranraer shed had three 'dead' 2Ps in store, and two more joined them in the Autumn. Two survivors, Nos.40638 and 40664, contrived somehow to work on until May and July 1962 respectively. At the other end of the Scottish spectrum, on ex-GNSR territory, an area where quite a few 2Ps found employment in later life, three were laid up at Kittybrewster and two more lay desolate beside the ruins of the old Highland shed at Keith.

1962 was a fateful year for steam all over Britain, as erosion began to bite amongst the ranks of even quite modern express locomotives. The Class 2Ps were no exception. Fourteen of them still existed, both North and South, in January 1962, but as it transpired, none were to live to welcome 1963. A dozen or so, remnants of 1961 withdrawals, still mouldered in dumps at Kilmarnock Works, Ardrossan, and Hurlford and as the year progressed, two more were laid up at the latter site. Indeed, by October 1962, Hurlford's line of 25 sundry locomotives offered painful testimony to the almost indecent retreat of steam. The following month saw England's last 2P, No.60694, withdrawn from Bourneville shed. The Scottish picture was little brighter; for by April 1962, only two Class 2Ps remained active. No.40638 worked on locally at Stranraer for one more month before withdrawal came, leaving No.40670, the sole survivor, to pursue its passenger pilot duties at Dumfries. Alas, even that modest task came to an end in September, when No.40670 was placed in store at Dumfries Goods Yard — and had to suffer the additional humiliation of seeing its pilot duties taken over by an ex-Caledonian 3F 0-6-0. Three months later, in December 1962, No.40670 was officially withdrawn, and the Class 2P 4-4-0, so proudly introduced by Derby in March 1928, became yet another extinct species.

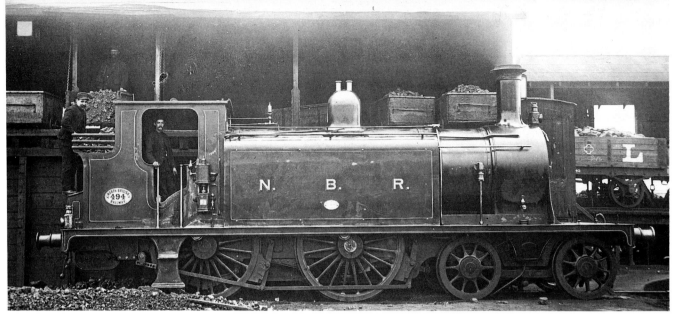

The attentions of Matthew Holmes were self-evident when NBR Class 'P' 4-4-0 tank No.494 was photographed at Eastfield at the turn of the century. The locomotive still relies on Westinghouse brake for both engine and train. Alone of its class, however, it was dual-fitted just before Grouping, and finished its days at Stirling before withdrawal came in March 1926. *(Author's Collection)*

Chapter 8
SCOTTISH 4-4-0 TANKS

IN THE BRITISH ISLES, as elsewhere, the 4-4-0 tank always was an endearing object. Nimble to a degree and industrious as the day was long, the type, notwithstanding its severe limitation in bunker capacity, found early favour with London railways which specialised in handling intensive, and comparatively short-haul, suburban passenger services. In this context the names of the Metropolitan and North London Railways spring readily to mind; and, indeed, it was from the latter that Scotland acquired its *oldest* 4-4-0 tanks. The story goes back to 1886, when the Girvan & Portpatrick Junction Railway, hitherto worked by the Glasgow & South Western, came under the control of a new contractor called William T. Wheatley.

Wheatley! The very name evokes plangent Scottish railway memories: for, a decade or so earlier, this same man had managed the NBR's Carriage & Wagon Department at Cowlairs at a time when his older brother, Thomas, was acting as Locomotive Superintendent. All went well — until an official investigation into alleged Cowlairs financial irregularities persuaded both men to submit their resignations in October 1874. Never at a loss, the two brothers then drifted off in the direction of Wigtownshire, and calmly resumed independent railway careers.

Thomas Wheatley's subsequent activities do not concern us here. The fact, though, that William bought three second hand Slaughter Gruning 4-4-0 tanks from the North London Railway in 1886 does; for he promptly introduced the 1861 veterans to his new employers, the Girvan & Portpatrick Junction Railway. Duly numbered G&PJR 1–3, the little tanks had 5ft 3in driving wheels, 3ft 2in leading wheels, and, with $15\frac{1}{2}$in × 22in cylinders working to a boiler pressure of 120psi, each engine weighed 37 tons. Twelve months later, the G&PJR was taken over by the Ayrshire & Wigtownshire Railway, and under these new auspices Nos.2 and 3 worked on until 1891. No.1 managed to hang on to 1892. Earlier that year, however, the A&WR was itself absorbed by the Glasgow & South Western, and the three ex-North London 4-4-0Ts, never taken into parent stock, went to the breakers in 1893.

In the meantime, Scotland's *first* 4-4-0 tanks had already arrived on the scene — in April/May 1879, when Neilson & Co. implemented a Dugald Drummond design by shopping three new Class 'P' tanks for the North British Railway. The NB classification 'P' had, oddly enough, already been accorded to six Stroudley-like 0-4-2 tanks which Drummond had introduced in 1877 for the purpose of handling fast business trains between Glasgow and Helensburgh. Unfortunately, excessive weight over the trailing wheels brought problems, and these were never truly resolved until 1881–82, when all six, working in Fife by then, were rebuilt as 0-4-4 tanks.

Faced afresh in 1879 with the task of drawing up a new design for the NBR's important Clyde Coast work, Drummond boldly opted on this occasion to follow Thomas Wheatley's example, rather than Stroudley's, by introducing a leading bogie in his second Class 'P' tanks. The new Neilson 4-4-0Ts were certainly a handsome sight, for their 3ft 6in leading wheels were complemented by coupled wheels six feet in diameter, the largest seen for many years on any British tank locomotive. Their 17in × 26in cylinders, too, employed the longest stroke yet used on an NBR passenger tank and a later increase in boiler pressure from 140 to 150psi ultimately yielded a tractive effort of 13,305lbs. Yet, traces of the Stroudley influence still lingered: witness the round edges borne by their side tanks and the local place names, No.494 *Craigendoran*, 495 *Roseneath*, and 496 *Helensburgh*, Drummond's new tanks received. Water and coal capacities of 950 gallons and $1\frac{1}{2}$ tons were compatible with those of Stroudley's celebrated 'D' Class 0-4-2 tanks. Fortunately for

Although No.1391, formerly NBR No.495 *Roseneath*, ended its LNER career as Class D50 No.10391 on local branch service at Polmont, it went to Dundee long before Grouping, and is seen here shunting at Anstruther in the early 1920s. Note the large bunker which W. P. Reid provided in June 1905. *(Stirling Everard)*

In typical Drummond fashion, the name 'R' Class No.103 carried when it emerged from Cowlairs Works in June 1881 indicated the locality it was about to serve. Exhibited at Newcastle on 9th June that year as part of the Stephenson Centenary celebrations, the locomotive was eventually withdrawn as LNER Class D51 No.10427 in March 1928. *(Author's Collection)*

'R' Class No.294 bore the name *Clydebank* when it left Cowlairs Works in June 1882, but had long lost its NBR identity by the time it was photographed at Kittybrewster in 1927 as LNER No.10461. The fore and aft cowcatchers seen here were obligatory for any locomotive which worked the Fraserburgh–St. Combs branch. The 50-year-old was still at Kittybrewster when its last call came in October 1932. *(Author's Collection)*

all concerned, Drummond's Class 'P' 4-4-0Ts addressed their allotted task with equal relish, and took to fast Clyde Coast service like ducks to water.

Came 1882, and Matthew Holmes, Drummond's successor, was content initially to pursue and develop traditional NBR Drummond locomotive design. The Stroudley/Drummond practice, however, of lavishing local place names on engines, then altering them as regional circumstances dictated, must have seemed both parochial and wasteful to Holmes, for he lost little time in disposing of NBR locomotive names. Ramsbottom safety-valves, too, were eliminated in favour of the Holmes lock-up variety and the familiar Drummond tallow cups on the smokebox front soon gave way to an improved type which was situated on the smokebox waist. Duly subjected to these changes, Drummond's Class 'P' 4-4-0Ts were also given an extra footstep to facilitate access to the motion, and the addition of coal rails to

their bunkers raised total capacity to nearer two tons. Then, in 1905, Holmes' successor, W. P. Reid, took matters a stage further by reboilering all three locomotives. He even enlarged their bunkers by removing the toolbox at the rear. Thus, in their final state, Drummond's 4-4-0 tanks weighed 47 tons 4 cwt and carried 2½ tons of coal. In 1919, long after they had been displaced from their original Clyde Coast duties by an influx of NBR 4-4-2Ts, the three Class 'P' tanks were placed on the Duplicate List. They still contrived to enter LNER stock as Nos.10390–92; but life was short, for the last of the gallant trio went in March 1926.

One year after the Class 'Ps' were launched came Drummond's fourth and last NB passenger tank design. The contrast could not have been greater; for the six Class 'R' 4-4-0 tanks which Cowlairs shopped in the Autumn of 1880 must surely rank as the daintiest ever to tread Scottish metals.

Weighing a mere 37¼ tons, these fleet-footed little engines were in many ways a four-coupled version of Drummond's earlier 0-6-0 passenger tanks. They combined 5ft driving wheels with 2ft 6in solid bogie wheels - hence their latterday nickname 'Dundee Rollers' — but, while boiler pressure remained at 140psi, cylinders were now 16in × 22in. Surprisingly for such dainty morsels, the resultant tractive effort was 11,170lbs. Cowlairs added further yearly instalments right up to February 1883 and Holmes had six more built in 1884. This brought the class total to 30. In due course Holmes alterations were effected on the first two dozen whence, of course, the Drummond locomotive names, ranging in this instance from *Morpeth* to *Montrose*, vanished. Later still, between July 1908 and December 1910, Reid equipped all 30 with new boilers. This time, however, the rear toolboxes remained untouched and the little tanks, latterly LNER Class D51, soldiered on with their Holmes-induced coal capacity of 1 ton 13 cwt. The sidetanks held 950 gallons.

Drummond's spruce little 4-4-0 tanks were a success wherever they were sent. As fast as Cowlairs turned them out they found employment on almost every branch line the NBR owned, as well as on busy suburban passenger trains around Edinburgh and Glasgow. Yet, all through their long hard-working lives only five were ever dual-fitted. Meanwhile, everywhere they went they tended to become much-loved fixtures. No.79, for instance, sent new to the Galashiels–Selkirk branch in October 1884, spent its entire working life there, until it was taken out of service, as LNER No.10469, in January 1927. More than half of the D51s perished in the 1920s, particularly as larger NBR tanks began to dominate the Glasgow suburban scene; but those centred on Edinburgh seemed to enjoy a rather more sheltered existence. St. Margaret's shed, which always had the largest complement, still had eight of them in the year 1930, with all but one still actively engaged on local branch service. Further convincing evidence of the D51s' utility value emerged in 1926–32, when four of them were transferred to the LNER's GNS Section to handle Fraserburgh–St. Combs Branch trains. One of them, No.10462, was the last D51 to be withdrawn, in August 1933.

The next Scottish Company to embrace the 4-4-0 tank was the Highland Railway; in 1885–87, when three 'Crewe'-framed Jones 2-4-0Ts, Nos.58 *Burghead*, 59 *Highlander*, and 17 *Aberfeldy*, built less than a decade earlier, were called back into Lochgorm Works. Originally intended for shunting duties, the 2-4-0Ts had, in fact, soon found more congenial employment on the Burghead and Aberfeldy branches, and experience there had obviously convinced Jones that the provision of a leading bogie would add much desired flexibility to their rigid frames. Rebuilt accordingly as 4-4-0 tanks, all three re-entered service

with 4ft 9½in driving wheels, 2ft 7½in leading wheels, 16in × 24in cylinders, and a working weight of 37 tons 12 cwt. Tank and bunker capacities remained unchanged at 700 gallons and 1¼ tons. So, too, for the time being, did their names. The country branch duties to which they reverted did not, however, last long and by 1900, Nos.58 and 59, both rendered nameless, were operating as station pilots at Inverness. *Aberfeldy*, renumbered 50 about then and given larger 850 gallon tanks, still appeared from time to time on the Aberfeldy branch until about 1910, when it, too, became a station pilot — at Perth General. By 1919, *Aberfeldy* had lost its name and all three 4-4-0Ts were carrying (Peter) Drummond flares to their louvred Jones chimneys. Duly absorbed by the LMS, with no great enthusiasm, as 'Unclassified' tanks Nos.15010–012, they continued to function as station pilots until the last of them, No.15010, formerly HR No.59, was withdrawn in November 1932.

The Highland Railway's final indulgence in the type came in 1892, when two 4-4-0 tanks were obtained from Dübs & Co. of Glasgow. Circumstances were unusual. Five of these small tanks had been ordered by the Uruguay Eastern Railway, but had never been delivered because of economic difficulties in that country. Dübs & Co. had approached such British railways as might be interested in buying them and once Jones had made a careful inspection of two which had been completed, his Locomotive Committee agreed to accept both on a year's trial. A price of £1,500 per locomotive was mooted and with cowcatchers and American style headlamps duly removed, but still retaining their tall shapely chimneys, the two Dübs tanks arrived at Inverness late in September 1892. They were given HR numbers 101 and 102.

David Jones' judgment proved to be sound. Within months the Dübs tanks were performing so admirably on the Burghead branch, where a busy extension to Hopeman had just been added, that the Highland Railway management, always alert to a 'bargain', hastened to order three more. The latter (Dübs Works Nos.3077–79), completed this time to HR specification with Jones louvreless chimneys, were initially allocated HR Nos.11, 14, and 15. They were later renumbered 51, 54, and 52. Equipped as before with 5ft 3in driving wheels, 3ft 0in leading wheels, and a boiler pressure of 140psi, albeit a shade heavier at 42½ tons because tank capacity had been stepped up to 900 gallons, they were strategically employed on various HR branch lines. Despite the fact that Highland locomen had been long accustomed to left-hand drive, the right-hand drive of the Dübs tanks did not inhibit their ready acceptance as 'The American Tanks'. Soon familiarity overcame geographical accuracy, and they acquired the nickname 'Yankee Tanks'. . .

The only major change affecting the class came in Peter Drummond's time, in 1906, when No.102, taken into

Seen here as delivered to the Highland Railway in 1892, 'American Tank' No.101 (Dübs Works No.2778) never strayed far from Burghead shed during its first 25 years of working life. Its crew appear to be not displeased with the arrangement. *(Author's Collection)*

The final appearance of No.15014, formerly HR No.102, offered little clue that it started life in 1891 as a 'Yankee Tank'. The brass plate on the frame, however, reminds us that the locomotive was rebuilt at Lochgorm Works in 1906. *(Author's Collection)*

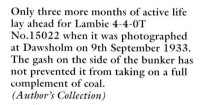

Only three more months of active life lay ahead for Lambie 4-4-0T No.15022 when it was photographed at Dawsholm on 9th September 1933. The gash on the side of the bunker has not prevented it from taking on a full complement of coal. *(Author's Collection)*

Lochgorm, was given a slightly larger and higher pitched new boiler. On that occasion the engine was altered to left-hand drive, and tank capacity was increased from 700 to 900 gallons. Coal capacity remained at 1½ tons. After that, it only required its large dome to be surmounted by lock-up safety valves and a Drummond chimney to be added to completely alter the locomotive's external appearnce. The 754,221 miles it subsequently ran, however, before bowing the knee in November 1934, bear

ample testament to the thoroughness of Lochgorm's handiwork. Years later, in 1919, No.101 was given a new boiler almost identical to the original. It therefore retained its authentic Dübs profile. Then, four years later, all five Dübs tanks were grouped by the LMSR, again as 'Unclassified' tanks, under Nos.15013–17. Their fates varied. The three 1893 engines were all withdrawn during the 1920s, while the two 'originals', probably because of their newer boilers, lasted to 1934.

No.15025, the last survivor of its class, is seen here in its final LMS livery in the distinct form employed on this class: black with pre-1928 insignia, St. Rollox having been advised to 'use up old transfers' on non-standard engines! *(Author's Collection)*

Scotland's last 4-4-0 tanks, the heaviest and most powerful of all, arrived on the scene during that extraordinary decade when Glasgow's harassed and rapidly increasing rail commuters were offered the relief of *three* underground systems. The NBR opened the batting in 1886, when the Glasgow City & District Railway, employing a shrewd mid-City link at Queen Street (Low Level), made journeys to and from the Clyde coast much easier for Glaswegians. The only snag was that its 1¾ mile underground section, which had been burrowed through rock, shale and sand at an enormous cost of £334,000 per mile, thoroughly rivalled London Inner Circle pre-electrification days with its foul smoke-laden atmosphere. Holmes, in his solitary venture into tank locomotive design, provided twelve 0-4-4Ts to plumb the Stygian depths.

A similar project by the Caledonian Railway, the Glasgow Central Railway, opened in August 1896, also connected main line metals with coastal interests which lay north of the Clyde

Again, construction of the central portion, which ran directly below the city, consumed enormous engineering energy; but at least the locomotives operating thereon consumed *some* of their own smoke, for John Lambie, that most practical of locomotive engineers, fitted condensers to the twelve St. Rollox-built 4-4-0Ts, Nos.1–12, which he provided for Glasgow's new subterranean line. Three of them had Gresham & Craven steam sanding; the others relied on gravity. Westinghouse brake was fitted to all and with their 5ft driving wheels, 3ft 2in leading wheels, and 17in × 24in cylinders working to a pressure of 150psi, Lambie's gallant 50¼ ton tanks, capable of generating a tractive effort of 14,739lbs, held the fort until reinforcements arrived in the shape of ten 0-4-4 tanks. The 4-4-0 tanks, classified '1P' by the LMSR, ended their days on rather less strenuous country branch work, and No.15025 outlived its sisters by lasting until June 1938. Steam continued to function, but the Glasgow Central Low Level Line was abandoned on 5th October 1964.

The third member of the Glasgow underground trinity, Glasgow Corporation, wisely drew its own conclusions from the foul atmosphere of its two predecessors when it opened its famous Subway in 1897 — and employed cable-haulage!

Chapter 9
SPREADING THE GOSPEL: SOUTH OF THE THAMES

WE HAVE ALREADY MENTIONED the significant 'Caledonian' excursion into Belgium, but the story of The Scottish 4-4-0 would hardly be complete were consideration not given to the closing Southern English careers of two men mentioned earlier in these pages — James Stirling and Dugald Drummond. Both took their Scottish convictions south with them — and experienced varying fortunes.

Stirling, the older man by five years, at least restored some semblance of stability to South Eastern Railway locomotives affairs once his appointment as Locomotive Superintendent, at an annual salary of £1,200, was ratified on 28th March 1878. His almost immediate reaction on taking up duties at Ashford was that the provision of new and more powerful locomotives for both passenger and goods services was an urgent priority where the SER was concerned. Time was precious and with a view to hastening a solution to the problem, Stirling based his maiden passenger design unhesitatingly on the inside-cylindered 4-4-0s he had introduced on the G&SWR a few years earlier. Vexed, too, by the SER's haphazard way of classifying its locomotives, Stirling also immediately imposed a simple form of lettered classification. Letters A to R were ultimately employed; and it follows that the twelve SER 4-4-0s he pioneered between September 1879 and December 1881 were styled Class 'A'. Built at Ashford Works, they cost £1,940 each. As with his Kilmarnock 4-4-0s, the Class 'As' employed 18in × 26in cylinders and a working pressure of 140psi. Bogie wheels were one inch larger at 3ft 8in, but, in view of their intended employment on the steeply graded Tonbridge–Hastings line, coupled-wheels on the SER engines were reduced to 6ft 0½in. Stirling's own design of bogie and steam reversing gear were duly incorporated. So, too, were the traditional Stirling family rounded cab and domeless boiler. The tender, which carried three tons of coal and

2,100 gallons of water, had inside frames and bearings, with springs above the running plate, and on all but four Class 'As', sandboxes were attached to the leading splashers. The running plate, meanwhile, was exceptionally deep skirted — another legacy from Stirling's Class '6' Sou' West 4-4-0s.

All twelve were sent new to Bricklayers Arms and for the next eight years or so they handled semi-fast traffic; though not with any great distinction, for their boilers were temperamental. Between 1881 and 1883, however, SER management, bent on competing more vigorously with the LC&DR, implemented many improvements in the way of signalling and rolling stock. A consequent requirement for more powerful engines was met when Stirling shopped the first of his new Class 'F' 4-4-0s in December 1883. By October 1891 Ashford Works had contrived to build over 40 of the new species and, with many more in the pipeline, the employment of Class 'As' on boat trains came to an end. A resultant redistribution saw one remain at Strood, and three at Ashford — but the remaining eight were transferred to Maidstone to handle less demanding London services. Footplate men soon dubbed them 'Maidstones' or 'Dartford Bogies'. All, too, were reboilered between 1889 and 1894; hence a 200sq ft reduction in heating surface to 923½sq ft improved steaming to a marked degree.

Fusion of a sort between the SER and its arch rival, the London Chatham & Dover Railway, came on 31st December 1898 and in due course, all twelve Class 'As' were treated to the new attractive SE&CR Brunswick green livery. Within a decade, however, the writing appeared on the wall. Two, Nos.160 and 166, were withdrawn in June 1907. Nine of the remainder were duplicate listed soon after, and the odd man out, No.179, already reboilered twice, went to the breakers in October 1908. The duplicate listed Class 'As' fared little better, with five with-

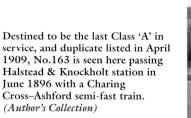

Destined to be the last Class 'A' in service, and duplicate listed in April 1909, No.163 is seen here passing Halstead & Knockholt station in June 1896 with a Charing Cross–Ashford semi-fast train. *(Author's Collection)*

drawn in 1908. Three of the Maidstone engines, Nos.19, 36, and 159 continued to work London slows for a few more months in 1909 and in May that year, No.175 left Redhill on its last mission — that of supplying steam for the repair shops at Bricklayer's Arms while the latter's stationary boiler was away for repair. Curiously, although its purpose was served by August, the locomotive was not taken away from Bricklayer's Arms for scrapping until July 1910. Meanwhile, the last Class 'A' in service, No.163, was employed by Ashford shed on Appledore — New Romney duties until it, too, was laid aside on 30th June 1909. Typical of a gallant, if short-lived class, it finished up with a very creditable mileage of 831,947.

Once again, Stirling's Class 'F' 4-4-0s mirrored Kilmarnock practice. As with his 'A' Class, 18in × 26in cylinders were employed in the first four, built at Ashford in 1883–84; but three more, completed in 1884, were tried out with 19in diameter cylinders. The experiment was a success, and from thereon the 19in format was adopted as standard. In similar fashion the initial working pressure of 150psi was raised to 160psi from 1889. Tenders, meanwhile, were akin to those fitted to the Class 'A' engines; but an extra water capacity of 500 gallons, plus the 7ft coupled wheels of the locomotives themselves, offered considerable encouragement to footplate men who were currently struggling to maintain schedules with boat trains of rapidly increasing weight. South Eastern men responded by taking the new 4-4-0s very much to heart — and, latterly, the Class 'Fs' earned the affectionate nickname 'Jumbos' from staff and travellers alike.

An even earlier source of pride came the SER's way in 1889 when, shortly after completion in February that year, Class 'F' No.240 was elaborately prepared at Ashford paint shop, and christened *Onward*, for show at the Paris Exhibition, together with other British locomotives. Greatly impressed by the British exhibits, the management of the Paris, Lyons & Mediterranean Railway sought, and obtained, permission to organise a series of competitive trials between *Onward*, an LB&SCR 0-4-2 No.189 *Edward Blount*, and PLM 4-4-0s. In matters of both speed and fuel consumption the South Eastern 4-4-0 fared quite creditably. Once returned to Dover on 30th January 1890, however, No.240 was given standard black livery at Ashford Works. It re-entered traffic on 16th March nameless, but the Gold Medal it earned at Paris was commemorated on plaques which were attached to the driving splashers.

The fact that 88 Class 'Fs' were built at Ashford works in a series of annual instalments over the years 1883–1898 at prices varying from £1,700 to £2,110 must have afforded James Stirling great satisfaction. The latter, though, must have been tempered somewhat at a Board Meeting on 29th July 1897, when a member of the Locomotive Committee was imprudent enough to enquire into the real *overall* cost of building a Class 'F'. What overheads, he wondered, might, however inadvertently, have been overlooked in the compilation of Stirling's figures? Stirling, nonplussed for the moment, was, nevertheless, obliged to pursue the query and subsequent frantic calculations at Ashford eventually produced a sobering figure of £2,680. Bearing in mind that private manufacturers were currently quoting a similar figure for a final batch of 'O' Class goods 0-6-0s, the SER Board firmly resolved that Ashford Works should in future concentrate solely on routine locomotive maintenance, and that a new class of express engine Stirling had in mind should be built by Neilson, Reid & Co. of Glasgow.

One year later, Stirling avenged this slight in his own quiet way. Ten more Class 'Fs' had already been authorised for construction in 1898, but only four, in fact, were ever completed. The remaining six were cancelled in midstream — and Stirling, smarting from constant Locomotive Committee reminders that more powerful engines were required, quietly utilised the frames and other salient parts of the unfinished six when nine of his new 'B' Class 4-4-0s were built at Ashford between October 1898 and July 1899. In accordance with the SER Board's 1897 dictum, twenty had already been supplied by Neilson Reid & Co. (Works Nos.5325–44) during July–September at an agreed price of £3,230 each. The cost of the Ashford-built quota emerged, rather pointedly, at £2,775.

Stirling's sleight of hand, however, could not conceal the fact that, despite carrying larger boilers, fireboxes and tenders, his new 4-4-0s were really a revamped version of his Class 'Fs' with 19in × 26in cylinders still the order of the day. So, too, were 7ft coupled wheels and a working pressure of 160psi. Externally, the main differences lay in the 'square' cab which now graced the Class 'Bs' and the repositioning of tender springs below the running plate. The latter refinement enabled water capacity to be raised to 3,000 gallons. As before, Ramsbottom safety valves occupied their traditional Stirling family position atop the boiler, albeit now decorated with burnished brass caps and seatings. A striking change of livery to Prussian green, however, coupled

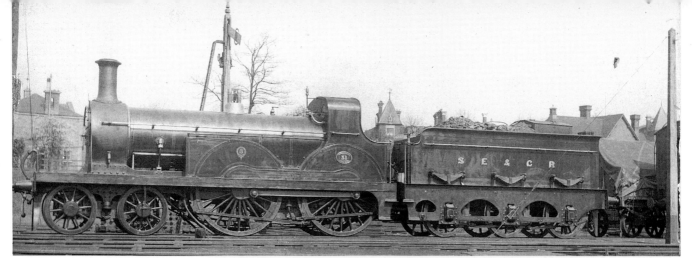

SER Class 'F' No.31, built at Ashford Works in September 1894, appears to have altered little ten years later, except for the 'SE&CR' inscription on her tender. Despite that, the SER coat of arms continues to adorn the leading splasher. Rebuilt in December 1906 under Wainwright auspices, No.1031 even contrived to enter British Railways stock before bowing to the inevitable in May 1948. *(Author's Collection)*

with the appearance of the Company's coat of arms on both tender and leading splasher did much to enhance these handsome locomotives in South Eastern eyes. While this apparently high note supplemented Stirling's retirement from office on 1st January 1899, in retrospect one must doubt his wisdom in pursuing standardisation so stubbornly at a time when expansion and ever-increasing loads were being imposed on the SER and other major Companies. As it happened, Stirling continued to reside at Ashford and, unlike his older brother Patrick, enjoyed an active retirement before dying, at the age of 81, on 12th January 1917.

Uneasy labour relations were a distinct factor in British industrial life as the nineteenth century neared its end and possibly that consideration helped persuade the two erstwhile rival Companies, the SER and the London, Chatham & Dover Railway, to pool their resources in an effort to minimise wasteful duplication of resources. Ergo, the South Eastern & Chatham Railway Companies Joint Management Committee was formed on 1st August 1899, once the appropriate Act of Parliament was passed. Joint working had, in fact, already commenced earlier that year, and Harry S. Wainwright, previously employed by the SER as Carriage & Wagon Superintendent, had already been appointed Locomotive Superintendent to the new Company, the South Eastern & Chatham Railway, on 27th September 1898 at a salary of £1,250 per annum. Being the larger of the two constituents, the SER, one might add, with its 459 locomotives and 382 route miles, contributed a good two-thirds of the total stock and mileage which came SE&CR's way. The unusual factor in this 'Amalgamation' was that both Companies agreed to maintain their separate identities. Indeed, the incomplete task of fusing the two systems dragged on until the Southern Railway was created on 1st January 1923.

Conversely, No.458, one of twenty 'B' Class engines delivered to the SER in 1898 by Neilson Reid & Co., was the only one of that batch which was never rebuilt. A lively and versatile performer, it is seen here at Bricklayer's Arms on 22nd May 1920. The livery is now deep glossy black and a plate on the cabside indicates 'SE&CR' ownership. The locomotive lived on to acquire Southern Railway green livery in March 1925, but perished as No.A458 in December 1931 with a total mileage of 804,427. *(The late J. N. Maskelyne)*

One of twelve 'F' Class 4-4-0s which were built in 1897, No.A222 was still serving the Southern Railway when it was captured leaving Dover Marine in the late 1920s. A Ramsgate engine, it was by that time sharing light duties to Ashford, Dover and Faversham with six other survivors. In due course it and four others were withdrawn in March 1930. *(Author's Collection)*

Shopped from Ashford Works in December 1895, and rebuilt in June 1907, 'F1' Class No.110 displays its short smokebox as it steps out briskly for Dover, via Chatham. After entering SR stock as No.A110, it finished up as No.1110 at Hither Green and was withdrawn from there in July 1946. *(Author's Collection)*

The last surviving 'F1', No.1231, seen here at Ashford awaiting the breakers, accumulated a total mileage of 1,506,944 before it embarked on its final journey from Reading to Ashford Works on 12th March 1949. Preservation in original Stirling form was considered, but the idea had to be abandoned as an impossible task. *(Steamchest)*

Sadly, one must record that ambitions which were fired by the 1899 amalgamation fell far short of realisation. Within a year or two, major shareholders began to wax increasingly restless — and sundry committees which were formed urged replacement of many of the aged and quite inadequate locomotives their new Company had inherited. The SE&CR's Locomotive Committee, only too well aware of the problem, called for the necessary finance to support such action. This, of course, was not forthcoming and, in lieu, the Committee was instructed to examine its stock closely, with a view to implementing a long term programme of reboilering or rebuilding the best of its locomotives. The Class 'Fs' were selected as candidates for such treatment and between 1903 and 1916, 75 of them were rebuilt to 'F1' specification. Later, when one of the rebuilds, No.20, had to be laid aside after an accident in November 1919, another Class 'F' was rebuilt to keep the 'F1' ranks intact. The remaining twelve Class 'Fs' retained all their Stirling characteristics, and entered SR stock as such. Withdrawals, however, commenced in October 1924, and the 1,042,197 mileage of the last survivor, No.A172, came to an end in December 1930.

Rebuilding to Class 'F1' consisted of providing new 18in × 26in cylinders, increasing working pressure to 170psi and stepping up the total heating surface to 1,124sq ft. The appearance of the locomotive was also enhanced by the provision of domed boilers and 'square' cabs. Initially, most of the rebuilds carried short smokeboxes and brass dome covers, but from 1915 onwards, extended smokeboxes and painted dome covers were adopted as standard SE&CR practice. Well accepted by men of both Sections, they handled secondary passenger services with great expedition and all except the ill-fated No.20 duly entered Southern Railway stock. Between the years 1923 and 1927 their dark wartime SE&CR livery was replaced by Maunsell green and

the prefix 'A' was added to their running numbers. Subsequent withdrawals between 1925 and 1932, however, reduced the class to 63 and the expansion of electrification on all three Sections saw only 22 'F1s' left in service by January 1939. Only nine, however, survived to enter British Railways stock, and the last went in March 1949.

During the first ten years of their working life Stirling's 'B' Class 4-4-0s, meanwhile, served the SE&CR with great distinction. Driven by regular crews, and well-groomed by shed staffs, they handled top link services as to the manner born. Yet strangely, once Wainwright's 'D' and 'E' Class 4-4-0s took over and the Class 'Bs' were relegated to secondary tasks, their performance and coal consumption began to deteriorate. Wainwright considered the problem, and came to the conclusion that 4ft 7in boilers and 19in cylinders were over extravagant for minor duties. Reboilering was imminent in any case, and this offered him the opportunity to rebuild the Class 'Bs', using the 4ft 3in domed boiler, 18in cylinders and 170psi working pressure which had so benefited the 'F1s'. As a result, the 25 'B1' Class engines which emerged from Ashford Works over the years 1910–1916, and two more which followed in the mid-1920s, were not only virtually identical with the 'F1s', but shared their popularity and aptitude for all categories of secondary passenger duty. Nos.34 and 458, never rebuilt, still managed to function from Bricklayer's Arms shed on a variety of Southern Railway activities before being withdrawn in December 1930 and 1931 respectively. James Stirling would have been gratified to know that the last of his 'Scottish' 4-4-0s ran 804,427 miles before surrendering.

The 25 'B1s' which entered Southern Railway stock soon acquired green livery and the prefix A before their running numbers. So, too, did the two late rebuilds, Nos.13 and 441. By the

Part of Bricklayer's Arms' allocation throughout World War I and beyond, together with the three other remaining 'B' Class 4-4-0s, No.13, painted SE&CR austerity grey, demonstrates the Maunsell top feed apparatus it inherited from sister engine No.34 in October 1920. This special boiler was finally abandoned in May 1923, and No.13, rebuilt to 'B1' specification in February 1926, survived to enter British Railways stock as No.1013 before being scrapped in September 1948. *(Author's Collection)*

A Battersea engine at the time, 'B1' Class No.1443 spent a number of years in the late 1930s on Victoria–Brighton passenger service. Built by Neilson, Reid & Co. (works No.5328) in 1898, and rebuilt at Ashford in 1913, No.1443 was finally withdrawn from Reading as the last surviving 'B1' in 1951. *(Author's Collection)*

early 1930s, however, the prefix had been eliminated on most while running numbers were increased by 1000. An acute shortage of passenger locomotives on the Eastern Section had also eased by then and this enabled eight 'B1s' to be withdrawn between 1933 and 1936. Thanks to the exigencies of World War II, however, the remaining nineteen 'B1s', despite increasing decrepitude, were obliged to soldier on longer than might have been expected. Nos.1441 and 1446, repaired as Ashford in December 1940, were even loaned to the LMS, as were nine 'F1s' eleven months later and, operating from Burton, worked many a 'foreign' duty before returning to the SR fold in January 1945. Subsequent developments saw three more 'B1s' taken out of service in 1947. British Railways, therefore, acquired sixteen 'B1s' in January 1948; though, by now, practically all had completed their million miles. Many, indeed, were already in store, and it came as no surprise that further sporadic withdrawals left only one survivor, No.1443, by mid-1950. Steamed very occasionally from its base at Reading, even No.1443 had to yield to the inevitable by the time it completed 1,320,917 miles and, having reached the venerable age of 52, it was broken up at Ashford Works in March 1951.

All through the course of British railway history Scottish engineers, by and large, have tended to exercise their own brands of independence. None, however, ever approached the stubbornness and insistence on discipline which so characterised Dugald Drummond's career with the London & South Western Railway once he took up office as Mechanical Engineer on 1st August 1895. One might add that a change of title, ten years later, to the more elevated status of Chief Mechanical Engineer did not deflect him in the slightest. The fact was that his immediate predecessor, William Adams, a genial, music-loving man, apart from providing his Company with adequate stocks of sim-

ple, robustly constructed main line locomotives, had also created a distinctly relaxed atmosphere at Nine Elms. It follows that the arrival of Drummond, with all his fire-eating propensities, triggered off something of a volcanic eruption at that admittedly somewhat complacent establishment. Typical of the man, Drummond countered an almost immediate welter of resignations and sackings by importing an equivalent number of fellow Scots. One of them, R. W. Urie, recruited in 1897 as Works Manager, was later to succeed Drummond as the LSWR's last CME.

Pausing only to confound his Nine Elms Locomotive Committee by out-shopping 25 distinctly Caledonian-type M7 0-4-4 tanks at a peculiarly low price of £1,400 each — and overseeing provision by Dübs & Co. of 30 '700' Class 0-6-0 goods engines at a more conventional price of £2,695 — Drummond, an inveterate disbeliever in superheaters and compound expansion, next shook all and sundry when his first large LSWR express locomotive emerged from Nine Elms in August 1897. It was a remarkable maiden effort, for although No.720, duly classified 'T7', bore some resemblance to his traditional Scottish 4-4-0s, it was, in fact, a 'double-single', with four high pressure cylinders driving two pairs of *uncoupled* wheels. With the bit firmly in his teeth, Drummond further intrigued the railway world by incorporating firebox water tubes, and in an oblique compliment to his one-time guide and mentor, William Stroudley, he had the locomotive painted Brighton yellow. Total costs were estimated at £2,815.

Initial trials soon convinced Drummond that he had erred in matching No.720's comparatively modest boiler with $16\frac{1}{2}$in × 26in cylinders. Thus, four 15in cylinders were substituted, at a cost of £234, before the 'double-single' entered general service. Even so, the desired working pressure of 170psi was rarely

Even after reboilering, as seen here, in 1904, 'T7' Class No.720 remained highly unpopular with LSWR men. Yet, remarkably, the locomotive survived to enter Southern Railway stock, and was not withdrawn until April 1927. The last two of Drummond's kindred 'E10' 4-2-2-0s accompanied it on that solemn occasion. *(Author's Collection)*

Above:
LSWR 'C8' Class 4-4-0 No.297, a Nine Elms product of November 1898, was transferred with three others to Exmouth Junction midway through 1900, and worked Salisbury semi-fast traffic for the next four years. After acquiring a new 4,000 gallon tender in September 1904, it continued to function in the West Country until withdrawal came in May 1936. *(Author's Collection)*

With sandboxes detached from the leading splasher, a resisted below the platform in latter day fashion, Class 'C8' No.298, the last of the species, quietly awaits breaking up at Eastleigh Works early in 1938. *(Author's Collection)*

reached, despite the provision of top class coal and a hand-picked crew. Hot boxes and other defects became almost endemic over the next five years and required frequent, sometimes lengthy, recourse to Nine Elms works. Four new 14in cylinders were fitted in 1902, but within months No.720 was back in store in unserviceable condition. Mileage to date was only 73,651.

Far from abandoning the project, as many a lesser man might have done, Drummond had the locomotive rebuilt early in 1904 with a larger five foot boiler, shorter chimney and heavier Joy gear valve rod. Relatively intermittent activity, however, saw only a further 79,419 miles completed by the time general repair at Nine Elms was again required in September 1912.

Subsequent test runs then revealed an interesting truth — that, as with five Class 'E10' 'double-singles' which had been additionally shopped from Nine Elms in 1901, the uneven wheel slip which had so plagued the species for years was caused by the fact that the two inside cylinders were, in practice, providing two-thirds of the total tractive effort. They, of course, were driven by Stephenson valve gear, as opposed to the outer pair which employed Joy's system.

'T9' Class No.731 was built by Dübs & Co. (Works No.3774) in January 1900, and was initially stationed at Salisbury. Two years later it acquired a double bogie 4,000 gallon tender and by the time this photograph was taken, firebox water tubes had been removed. The locomotive's war-time livery, however, is still in immaculate condition. *(Author's Collection)*

Driver and fireman pose proudly at Exmouth Junction with 'T9' No.336, a wide-cabbed Nine Elms product of September 1901. Duly superheated in the mid-1920s, the locomotive also lost its eight-wheeled tender to 'L11' No.167 in July 1925 and acquired a six-wheeled one from '700' Class 0-6-0 No.697, prior to entering Eastern Section traffic. Thirty years later it earned BR lined black livery before being withdrawn, as No.30336, in February 1953. *(Steamchest)*

So intriguing was the problem of No.720 that Robert Urie, Drummond's successor in November 1912, even aspired to fit Stephenson valve gear to the locomotive's outside cylinders. Alas, wartime shortages precluded such an interesting development and all six 4-2-2-0s were left to plod on. Once peace was restored, however, and passenger services picked up, the 'E10s' were deployed on a variety of main line slows. All five passed into Southern Railway ownership and the last to be withdrawn, No.373, perished in April 1927 with a reasonably respectable mileage of 487,548. No.720, by comparison, spent a good deal of its post-war time in splendid isolation at the back of Nine Elms shed. Yet, despite the desultory nature of the duties it ultimately performed, it acquired green livery and a new non-water tube firebox at Eastleigh Works in May 1925. Its subsequent lease of life, however, was short; for only 23,476 more miles were completed ere the last call came from that establishment in April 1927. That made 577,207 miles in all. During the breaking up process, No.720's boiler was carefully salvaged, nevertheless, and found its way eventually to Clapham Junction, there to heat carriages. Four boilers from the 'E10s' were put to similar good use.

Fortunately for all concerned at Nine Elms, Drummond did not neglect the more conventional aspects of passenger locomotive construction while his 'double-single' saga was pursuing its hair-raising course. In 1898, for instance, ten 'C8' Class inside cylinder 4-4-0s, each carrying a 4ft 5in boiler identical to those already fitted to his 'M7' and '700' Class engines, entered service at a cost of £1,875 each. Trim little locomotives, the 'C8s', with their 18½in × 26in cylinders, 6ft 7in coupled wheels, and 175psi working pressure, were yet another manifestation of Drummond's earlier Scottish days. Their general appearance

Built at Nine Elms Works in 1900, 'T9' No.E287 looked vastly different by the time it was photographed at Eastleigh a quarter of a century later. The presence of a snifting valve high on the smokebox indicates that a Maunsell superheater has been fitted; and a prominent capuchon on the stove pipe chimney adds to the locomotive's impressive appearance. Still in sprightly form by the late 1950s, No.30287 was eventually withdrawn in August 1961 with a cumulative mileage of 1,927,593. *(H. Gordon Tidey)*

offered no illusions to anyone who was at all familiar with North British and Caledonian Railway affairs. Within four years of leaving Nine Elms, however, it became apparent that the water capacity of the 'C8's' tender was inadequate. Thus, the fitting of new 4,000 gallon double bogie tenders between February 1903 and May 1907 offered a very welcome additional 500 gallons. The old tenders were judiciously distributed amongst 'K10' and 'L11' Class 4-4-0s which were currently being built at Nine Elms.

Rather curiously, the whole class found itself reassembled at Nine Elms shed by 1910. The official intention, it seems, was to use the engines on a variety of secondary services in and around the Capital. Unfortunately the 'C8s', never adept at handling stopping passenger trains, were unable, somehow, to earn the esteem which LSWR men happily accorded to other Drummond 4-4-0s. Somewhat neglected as a consequence, three of them at least found refuge at Basingstoke shed in June 1913, and a fourth followed one month later. The war years, of course, scattered the class, and offered them full employment in the way of troop trains and the like; and steadfastly working on through difficult post-war years, all ten 'C8s' contrived to qualify for Southern Railway passenger green livery. By 1931 they were still working in the West Country. Then, in March 1933, two of them, Nos.298 and 299, were posted from Salisbury to Feltham, whence they occupied themselves on a wide range of goods and shunting duties around London. By now, though, time was running out for the class; and the other eight were withdrawn between then and 1936. The Feltham pair, possibly less harassed, carried on until No.299 was taken out of service in August 1937. Having completed a total of 973,117 miles, No.298 followed it five months later and soon, the only trace of the 'C8s' one could find at Eastleigh Works was tenders from Nos.290–296. They were duly attached to Urie 'S15' 4-6-0s to enable their own 5,000 gallon tenders to be passed on to 'Remembrance' Class rebuilds.

Reverting once more to Nine Elms affairs at the turn of the century, it seems that even as the 'C8s' were being built, Drummond was preparing plans for an improved class of 4-4-0. Externally, the 'T9s', as they were styled, looked little different from the 'C8' engines, but in fact, they embodied a larger firebox and a longer wheel base and 1⅛in tubes were installed in lieu of the 1¾in ones previously employed. In due course seven firms in all tendered for their construction and the lowest bid, that of Dübs & Co. at £2,945 per engine and tender, was accepted on 16th March 1898. A few weeks later, when Drummond added firebox water tubes to his specification, an amended price of £3,200 was agreed. Thus, 30 'T9s' were delivered to Nine Elms between February 1899 and January 1900, and were given running numbers 702 to 719 and 721 to 732. A rather special 'T9' which Dübs & Co. built for show at the 1901 Glasgow Exhibition was also added to LSWR stock, as No.773, in December 1901 once Dübs agreed to reduce their asking price from £3,525 to £3,200.

In the meantime, before even the first of the Dübs engines entered traffic, a further twenty 'T9s' had been ordered from Nine Elms works at £2,285 apiece; and Nos.113–122 and 280–289 were out-shopped, ready for the road, by February 1900. These differed by having conventional fireboxes, a simplification which reduced engine weight, by nearly two tons, to 46 tons 4 cwt. A final fifteen, Nos.300–305, 307, 310–314 and 336–338, which were further delivered from Nine Elms in 1901, reverted, however, to the use of firebox water tubes; and back went their engine weight to 48 tons 17 cwt. Still, considering that this series also introduced the LSWR's new double bogie, 4,000 gallon tender, their building costs, at £2,399 per engine and tender, were still substantially lower than those of the Dübs 'T9s'. These last fifteen also introduced wider cabs and splashers, which latter encompassed both driving wheels and coupling rods, while, at last, steam sanding replaced gravity. Two of them, Nos.337 and 338, entered service with both vacuum and Westinghouse brakes.

Production in 1901 of two completely new corridor trains for West of England express service, together with a considerable tightening of Bournemouth line schedules, set the stage appropriately for the 'T9s'. Like true artistes, they took full advantage of the limelight. Free running and economical on coal, they soon endeared themselves to LSWR footplate men and, ere long, were dubbed 'Greyhounds'. Little did the same men know that the *true* justification for that nickname would emerge twenty years later - once the whole class was superheated. Whatever, 25 of the 'T9s' were allocated to Nine Elms by 1902, and the remaining 41 were spread over West Country sheds in varying proportions. These ranged from ten each at Salisbury and Exmouth Junction to one at Dorchester.

The opening years of the twentieth century were busy ones for the LSWR, and many a working day saw a dozen or more boat specials pull out from Waterloo. Inevitably, Class 'T9s' played a prominent role in the frequent double heading which ensued. Then came a much more significant event in 1910, when the transfer of LSWR's Nine Elms locomotive workshops to more commodious new premises at Eastleigh was completed. Truly an astonishing manifestation of Dugald Drummond's determination and planning skills at the age of seventy, Eastleigh Works served his successors well. It certainly found full employment during the war years which followed.

Once peace was restored, by which time R. W. Urie had been in command of locomotive affairs for seven years, the LSWR found itself well supplied with express locomotives, but deficient in motive power for semi-fast activities. Urie responded by superheating the more modern Drummond 4-4-0 classes. The 'T9s' turn for this treatment began in April 1922, when No.314 emerged from Eastleigh Works with an extended smokebox, stove pipe chimney, new copper firebox, nineteen inch cylinders and an 'Eastleigh' superheater of Urie's own design. Another 29 followed suit by May 1924, before Urie's successor, R. E. L. Maunsell, took the bolder step of fitting all 66 'T9s' with *his* brand of superheater. The latter process took four years to complete.

Superheating certainly revitalised the 'T9s'; for what had previously been competent enough engines now became superlative machines which were capable of handling anything but the heaviest express duties. It was, no doubt, this factor, plus the number of Urie 4-6-0s it inherited, which persuaded the SR to embark on a complicated reshuffle of tenders in 1925, when ten 'T9s' lost their 'water carts' to Drummond 'L11' Class 4-4-0s and received six-wheeled tenders from '700' Class 0-6-0s in exchange. The object of the exercise was to permit the employment of 'T9s' on the Eastern Section, where some turntables were rather short. In similar vein, six more 'T9s' acquired smaller tenders from 'K10' 4-4-0s in 1928 to enable them to work on the Central Section. For operational reasons, all, too, had their prominent chimney capuchons cut down. Indeed, by June 1932 plain stovepipe chimneys were adopted as standard practice on practically all 'T9s'. The mere handful which escaped such treatment included No.119, a Nine Elms 'T9', which was frequently called into use for Royal and other prestige specials.

The outbreak of World War II in September 1939, soon saw more 'T9s' move westward. Exmouth Junction's allocation, for one, increased substantially within months, and by 1941 four 'T9s' were even lent to the LMS for use on their Somerset & Dorset Section. Fortunately, the whole 'T9' Class survived war service. Peacetime, however, brought its own complications, for an acute national shortage of coal in 1947 obliged the Southern Railway to earmark 110 locomotives for conversion to oil fuel. Equally perversely, a chronic shortfall in imported oil less than twelve months later reversed the situation, and the SR's programme was abandoned. Thirteen 'T9s' had, however, already been converted to oil-burning and their eight-wheel tenders now bore 1,600 gallon oil tanks. Generators, bolted to the left-hand running plate by the smokebox, had also been added to supply electric lighting. Most worked local passenger services in this guise, and were as popular as ever. Then, purpose served, all

When 'T9' No.119, still carrying its short capuchon, entered Eastleigh Works, midway through 1925, it was given special attention as a 'Royal' engine. Apart from receiving a superb green livery, metal work was highly burnished, and superheater snifting valve caps were even chromium plated. In a final touch the Royal coat of arms was also affixed to the leading splashers. *(Author's Collection)*

On 6th May 1939, however, No.718 was the 'T9' chosen to head the Royal Special as it passed through Clapham Junction, en route to Portsmouth Harbour, on the first stage of a Royal Tour of Canada and USA. *(Southern Railway)*

Right:
Its brief oil-burning mission long-since accomplished, 'T9' No.280, officially taken out of service in May 1951, lies at Eastleigh awaiting final disposal. The generator which provided electric light shows clearly in this study. So, too, does the 1,600 gallon oil tank atop her tender. *(Steamchest)*

Below:
As they pause en route to Sheffield Park in September 1963, the ex-Caledonian Railway single wheeler, No.123, and No.120, the restored 'T9', provide a thought-provoking backcloth to the passage of somewhat more modern traction. *(Steamchest)*

Stationed at Dorchester by 1931, 'K10' No.136, still in original form, pilots a SR Class N15X 4-6-0 through Wareham station. One of the first six to be withdrawn, No.136 was taken out of service in January 1947. *(Steamchest)*

were laid aside in store by October 1948 and remained there, sadly neglected, until they were condemned in April and May 1951.

In the late Spring of 1948 eight 'T9s', now running, of course, under British Railways auspices, were transferred to Stewart's Lane, whence for the next two years they tackled Chatham line services with barely diminished zeal. The summer of 1950 even saw several back on LSWR main line activity, thanks to the withdrawal of Drummond's 'T14' 4-6-0s. Then, in March 1951, withdrawals started and by December 1952 only 38 'T9s' remained. A slight easing of the situation ensued, with only seven more withdrawn by the end of 1957, but subsequent heavy inroads left only one 'T9', No.30120, intact by September 1961. Fortunately, this engine was taken into Eastleigh Works for preservation and has since become a highly prized working member of our National Collection, wearing a variety of (mostly appropriate!) liveries during recent years.

Reverting now to Nine Elms activities much earlier in the century, Drummond of course, did not rest on his laurels with the 'T9s'. Having provided his Company with adequate numbers of goods and passenger engines, he now addressed himself to the LSWR's lack of purely mixed traffic locomotives. Thus, with his earlier highly successful Caledonian Railway 'Gourock Bogies' very much in mind, he drew up plans for the production of 40 very similar small-wheeled, inside-cylinder 4-4-0s. Duly classified 'K10', and soon to be nicknamed 'Grasshoppers' on account of their liveliness and versatility, they emerged from Nine Elms Works in thirteen monthly batches between December 1901 and 1902. Basic dimensions were as for Drummond's earlier 'C8s', except that driving wheels were now 5ft 7in in diameter. Running numbers, though, were not in sequence, but wandered randomly between 135 and 394. Thirty 4,000 gallon tenders had been ordered for their use, but these went instead to Class 'T9' and 'C8' engines which, in turn, sur rendered their smaller six-wheeled 3,500 gallon ones. Thus, new 3,500 gallon tenders wee fitted to the first ten 'K10s' built. No.343, shopped from Nine Elms in December 1901, rang additional changes by entering traffic with an experimental water-tube boiler. Although this added 2½ tons to the engine weight, subsequent trials pleased Drummond and producing enhanced fuel consumption. The locomotive gave so much trouble maintenance-wise, however, that Nine Elms Works was not sorry to fit a conventional boiler in December 1906.

Transferred to the Southern Railway's Eastern Section in June 1925, then later moving to Reading, 'K10' No.388 demonstrates the stove pipe chimney it acquired as a result. Refitted with a Drummond pattern chimney at Derby Works during World War II and returned to the Southern Railway fold in March 1945, No.388 was finally taken out of service in April 1947. *(Author's Collection)*

The 'K10s' soon found ready and popular employment on mixed traffic duties all over the LSWR system. During the First World War, for instance, three were transferred to Guildford to take over munition trains as they came off the SECR's Redhill line. Thence, usually double-headed, they went on to Portsmouth to meet the Naval Dockyard's near insatiable appetite. Again, No.394 was sent to Reading in February 1918 and was loaned to the GWR for eleven days. At Grouping, all entered Southern Railway stock and, two and a half years later, ten 'K10s' spent eight months on the Eastern Section, relieving a motive power shortage there. Their tall Drummond chimneys accordingly replaced by shorter stove pipes, and footsteps slightly set in, they worked from Gillingham on Victoria and Dover semi-fasts. More tender exchanges ensued between 1925 and 1928, in course of which seven 'K10s' found themselves the proud possessors of eight-wheeled tenders.

According to this picture, taken in August 1951, 'K10' No.385 appears to have arrived at Ashford Works for scrapping. Closer inspection of the photograph, however, reveals the existence of the number 384 on the locomotive's dingy black cabside. The truth was that although No.385 had already been scrapped in January 1949, its tender continued to run behind No.384 for some considerable time to come. *(Author's Collection)*

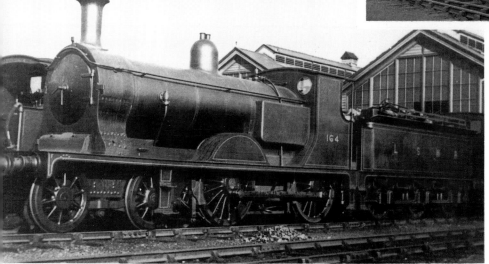

'L11' No.164, ready to leave Nine Elms Works in October 1903, carries the cabside numerals which Drummond introduced about this time. A Fratton engine for most of its life, No.164 acquired an eight-wheeled tender in November 1926 when one of Drummond's 4-2-2-0s, No.371, was scrapped. The 'L11' ultimately graduated as BR No.30164 before withdrawal came in September 1951. *(Author's Collection)*

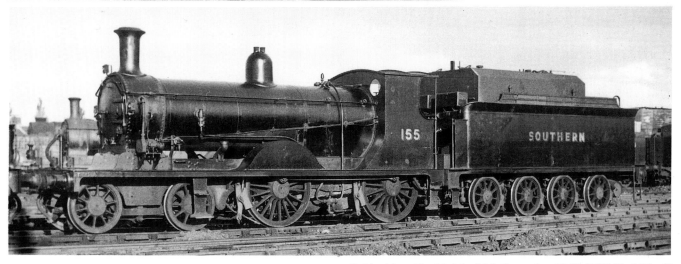

Laid aside at Eastleigh by 11th September 1948, 'L11' No.155 still carries the oil tank and generator it acquired eleven months earlier. The short footstep added to the rear of the tender was a typical Bulleid touch. No.155, meanwhile, lingered on in store until a merciful release came in March 1951. *(P. M. Gates)*

Inevitably, World War II years brought further changes. In May 1939, for instance, a start was made in removing smokebox wingplates; and all but five 'K10s' were denuded thus before withdrawal came their way. Rather curiously, though, three of the ten which had acquired stovepipe chimneys to work on the Eastern Section in Southern Railway days had standard Drummond chimneys refitted in 1944–46. Even more curiously, No.388, one of five transferred to the LMS Midland Division on long term loan in November 1941, had its chimney replacement effected at Derby Works! Another 'K10', No.394, loaned to the War Department in September 1941, spent the best part of a year working at various WD depots.

'K10' withdrawals commenced in January 1947 with six casualties; and three more joined them by the end of that year. Withdrawals then accelerated, and by November 1950 only two, Nos.384 and 389, remained. The latter succumbed in July

1951: the former spent its last month performing casual duties on the Somerset & Dorset line before it, too, was withdrawn in August.

Heartened by the success and undoubted popularity of his 'K10s', Drummond resolved to introduce a larger version. Thus, 40 mixed traffic 'L11' Class 4-4-0s were built at Nine Elms between April 1904 and May 1907. The fact that none were built during 1905 can be attributed to Drummond's ill-starred venture into six-coupled express locomotion that year. The 'L11s', meanwhile, though modelled faithfully enough on the

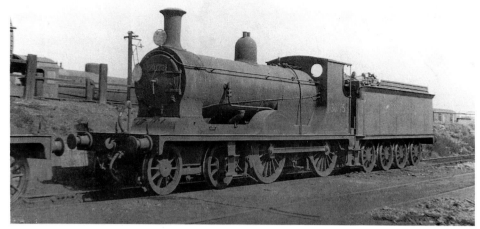

Devoid now of its water tube firebox, but otherwise unchanged, Class 'S11' No.401 was photographed at Exmouth Junction in July 1921. Less than a year later it attended Eastleigh Works to have an 'Eastleigh' superheater fitted. The beneficiary also of the Maunsell superheater in April 1930, No.401 duly entered BR stock; but was never renumbered before withdrawal came in August 1951. *(Steamchest)*

'K10s', differed by incorporating a larger firebox and a longer wheelbase. Provision of a water-tube firebox, at the expense of 4½ tons'extra engine weight, increased the total heating surface by 300sq ft, but tractive effort remained, as with the 'K10s', at 19,756lb. Twenty of the 'L11s' were fitted additionally with duplex feed pumps. These fitments, however, were always very unpopular with LSWR men and Urie had them removed once he took over at Eastleigh. Forty new eight-wheeled tenders were also built for 'L11' use, but in the event only nine received them. The rest had to be content with second-hand six-wheeled tenders from 'C8' and 'T9' locomotives.

The 'K10s' were lively enough engines, but the 'L11s' proved to be even livelier. Concentrated initially at the larger sheds — Nine Elms, for example, had fifteen — they soon made a name for themselves on secondary passenger and main line goods duties. As before, the analogy with winged insects appealed to the enginemen, and ere long the 'L11s' were dubbed 'Large Hoppers', as opposed to the 'K10s', the 'Small Hoppers'. Two, Nos.440 and 441, were Westinghouse fitted in May 1910, and retained both vacuum and Westinghouse brakes well into Southern Railway days. During World War I, 'L11s' also handled much of the busy passenger traffic on the Portsmouth line.

At Grouping, the entire class entered SR stock. None, however, were ever superheated; though by 1928 all except the two Westinghouse fitted 'L11s' acquired eight-wheeled tenders. Many more were stationed at West Country sheds by 1931 and, eight years later, the classic Drummond smokebox wingplates

began to disappear as new smokeboxes were fitted. Again, during World War II, the 'L11s' found no shortage of ready employment. In 1947 the national coal shortage mentioned earlier saw eight of them converted to oil burning. Like the 'K10s', they were laid aside once normality returned and were never used again. Years later, however, their electric light generators found a new use activating radio receivers on ex-USA tanks which were employed at Southampton Docks.

In the event, all 40 'L11s' survived to enter British Railways stock, but only sixteen of them had 30000 added to their running numbers. First withdrawals, those of Nos.439 and 440, came in May 1949; then further inroads in 1950 and 1951 so decimated the ranks that by the beginning of 1952 only five were left. These did not linger long, and No.411, the last to be withdrawn, went in April that year.

In March 1903 Drummond acted swiftly on a growing conviction that his 'L11' chassis, coupled with larger boiler, cylinders and driving wheels, might well undertake West of England express services with similar expedition. He immediately placed an order for ten such heavy duty 4-4-0s; and Nine Elms responded nobly by placing 'S11' Class Nos.395–404 in traffic

Seen at Bournemouth shed on 7th June 1941, 'S11' No.397 bears evidence of the capuchonless chimney and Maunsell superheater which became standard fitment in post-Grouping years. *(Author's Collection)*

What with its short stove pipe chimney, Maunsell superheater, and fresh BR livery, 'S11' Class No.30397, seen here at Basingstoke in 1950, looked good for another twenty years yet. Unfortunately, appearances were deceptive, and the locomotive was withdrawn in November 1951. *(H. C. Casserley)*

before the year was out. Their combination of 5ft boiler, 19in × 26in cylinders and 6ft 1in coupled wheels duly impressed contemporary railway circles. Initially, the first-built, No.395, went to Exmouth Junction and No.399 stayed at Nine Elms, while the remainder of the class were sent to Salisbury. Halfway through 1904, however, Exmouth Junction found itself with five, and the remainder were distributed between Plymouth and Salisbury. A *Railway Magazine* comment earlier that year made clear the status the 'S11s' were enjoying:

"The Italian Royal Special on November 10th was hauled between Portsmouth and Basingstoke by No.399, sister engine to No.395 (which hauled the French President's train from Victoria to Aldershot). The engine was tastefully decorated. The particular class to which both belong seems to be doing excellent express work, and have an extremely strong and massive appearance, with the long high-pitched boiler and tiny chimney characteristics now becoming so fashionable on some of our leading railways."

The First World War years saw little change in 'S11' activities, other than the posting of Nos.400/1/3 to Eastleigh shed, whence they undertook a deal of local goods and mixed traffic duties. Urie, meanwhile, was determined to improve the class and in November 1915 he made a start on fitting the 'S11s' with non-water tube fireboxes. War conditions, however, made this a protracted process and, two years before it was completed, Urie also commenced installing 'Eastleigh' superheaters. Again, the process took time and July 1922 arrived before all ten 'S11s' were so equipped.

Removal of the Drummond water-tube fireboxes and the fitting of 'Eastleigh' superheaters reduced total heating surface to 1,349sq ft and increased engine weight by 1¾ tons; but it vastly improved the performance of the 'S11s'. They were even deployed on Waterloo–Portsmouth services, quite a gruelling task, until Maunsell's 'King Arthurs' began to arrive on the scene. So, back to the West Country went seven of them while Nine Elms kept three for semi-fast Portsmouth services. All duly entered Southern Railway stock at Grouping, and were given the usual passenger green livery. Earlier superheating had provided them with capuchoned chimneys, but now, as new chimneys were required and a start was made in fitting Maunsell superheaters, the capuchon was abandoned.

Throughout the course of World War II, the 'S11s', living up to their reputation as 'born gypsies', wandered far and wide. By the end of 1941, for example, all ten could be found working on the jointly-owned SR/LMS Somerset & Dorset Section where, classified '2P' by the LMS locomotive management, they acquired tablet exchange apparatus for use on the latter's single-line section. After that, they ran elsewhere on the LMS system as operational demands dictated and most underwent repair at Derby Works some time or other during 1943/44. No.397 even showed up at Bow Works in April 1943 — before joining two other 'S11s' at Peterborough a year later. Things settled down by May 1945, however, and all ten migrants returned to the parent fold. Exmouth Junction again had the lion's share with six. The 'coal/oil' scare of 1947 next cost two of them, Nos.395 and 397, their eight-wheeled tenders and, quite patently, the mechanical condition of all was poor by now. None the less, all ten 'S11s' were taken over by British Railways in 1948 and all but two were renumbered. The short stovepipe chimney,

though, that four of them acquired under BR auspices hardly improved the appearance of these already weary engines and it came as no surprise that nine 'S11s' were withdrawn during 1951. For some reason, the sole survivor, No.30400, was given a second coat of British Railways black paint at Eastleigh Works in July 1952 and, to the delight of many, it worked on quite actively until it was called into Ashford Works for scrapping in October 1954. By that time it had accrued a very respectable 1,336,661 miles.

Dugald Drummond was not a patient man at the best of times; but one suspects he probably excelled himself in the run up to June 1904, when, exactly one year after the first 'S11' entered service, Nine Elms Works completed construction of No.415, a new 'L12' Class 4-4-0. More modern motive power was urgently required to handle heavy Bournemouth and Salisbury express traffic — and this was Drummond's answer. Nine Elms dutifully maintained the momentum, and out-shopped nineteen more, Nos.416–434 by March 1905. The 'L12s', in fact, were really 'S11s' with 6ft 7in coupled wheels. Cylinders, as before, were 19in × 26in and total heating surface 1,550sq ft; though the provision of larger driving wheels, of course, reduced tractive effort to 17,673lb as opposed to the 'S11s' 19,400lb. The 'L12s', too, were nearly two tons heavier at 53 tons 19 cwt. Inevitably, water-tube fireboxes made their reappearance and feed pumps, operated by steam, were installed instead of hot water injectors — though both features were removed by Urie a decade later. Fitted with Drummond's patent balanced crank axles, the 'L12s' also dispensed with driving wheel balance weights. In all, they were beautifully proportioned engines and, fortunately, their performance was as handsome as their appearance.

Initial allocation of the 'L12s' saw Nine Elms receive ten and Salisbury five, with the remainder being divided between Bournemouth and Exmouth Junction mpds. Their arrival was fortuitous, though; increased competition from the Great Western in the way of American passenger traffic was putting LSWR men very much on their mettle. Nor did the 'L12s' let them down — except for one early morning on 30th June 1906, when No.421, running late on a London-bound boat express, dashed through Salisbury Station's notorious curves at something like 60mph for some inexplicable reason. The result was the LSWR's worst ever disaster, wherein 28 people, including No.421's unfortunate crew, lost their lives. Resultant damage repair and compensation cost the LSWR a total of £32,854.

Ironically, No.421 was one of the first two 'L12s' superheated by Robert Urie in 1912 and 1915. War conditions, however, delayed resumption of the process until February 1918, and June 1922 arrived before the last was dealt with. By then all but No.421 had been fitted with new capuchoned chimneys; and what with their extended smokeboxes, the 'L12s' looked larger

The date is November 1925, the place Eastleigh, and the existence of a snifting valve high on No.432's smokebox indicates that the 'L12' has been duly fitted with a Maunsell superheater. The absence of chimney capuchon, however, is a relic of previous superheating, five years earlier, in February 1920. *(Author's Collection)*

The last of the 'L12s', No.30434 was, despite its short stovepipe chimney and six-wheeled tender, a popular choice when the Enthusiasts Club ran its Hants & Sussex Tour in 1953. *(Steamchest)*

Basingstoke 'L12s', meanwhile, were employed on Waterloo slow trains and Portsmouth services, while those at Nine Elms handled a similar mix of Salisbury and Lymington activities. Then, as might be expected, the World War II years brought full and quite indiscriminate employment to all and 1946 arrived before shed allocations reverted to normal.

Still intact, the class entered British Railways stock in January 1948, when, reassuringly, all but one were reliveried in lined black. No.430, the sole exception, surprised no one by being taken out of service in March 1951. A more sombre fact of life emerged, however, when seventeen more 'L12s' followed suit by the end of the year. The penultimate survivor, No.30415 hung on to January 1953 — though No.30434 raised something of a flutter by visiting Eastleigh Works ten months earlier. Fortunately, the main objective was to have its eight-wheeled tender replaced by a smaller 3,500 gallon one from 'K10' No.329. Thence, No.30434 re-entered traffic, and the Reading branch witnessed most of its subsequent activities — until February 1955, when, having completed 1,490,604 miles, it was finally summoned to Eastleigh Works and was broken up eight months later.

In view of the frustrating years Drummond subsequently spent in trying to develop a successful 4-6-0, it was perhaps poetic justice that the year 1912 should witness the emergence of his finest 4-4-0, the 'D15' Class. Five, Nos.463–467, were

than ever. Happily, while their fuel and water consumption showed a distinct improvement, their flair for speedy running remained unimpaired.

During 1921, and again in 1926, a shortage of locomotive coal obliged three 'L12s' to operate temporarily as oil-burners. Then, halfway through 1925, ten were transferred to the SR's Eastern Section to relieve a locomotive shortage there. Apart from being given rather ugly heavily capuchoned stove pipe chimneys for the purpose, all ten also lost their eight-wheeled tenders to sundry members of the 'L11' and 'K10' classes. Fortunately, the 'L12s' were well received by South Eastern & Chatham men, and were looked after at Ashford Works as circumstances required. Most of them had a subsequent spell on Central Section metals before Maunsell commenced resuperheating the class in May 1925.

Drummond's 'L12s' were well spread over Southern Railway sheds by the end of 1932. Fratton had eight, Nine Elms and Basingstoke four each, Brighton three, and Bournemouth one. Mid-Sussex electrification in 1938, however, saw Fratton lose seven 'L12s' to Brighton and Stewart's Lane; and three of the latter's quota soon found work on the Chatham line.

Superheated in March 1916, 'D15' No.E466 looked more impressive than ever in early Southern Railway days, when it was photographed heading a Southampton express in the summer of 1925. *(Author's Collection)*

built at Eastleigh Works early that year at a cost of £2,800 each; and five more, Nos.468–472, followed by December at a slightly increased cost of £2,835. Well worth the money, they were superlative engines, both in finish and pedigree. Their boilers were larger than any previously used on a Drummond 4-4-0 and not only were piston valves used for the 19½in × 26in cylinders, but, most unusually, Walschaerts valve gear was employed. Boiler pressure was initially pitched at 200psi and all the usual Drummond hallmarks (i.e. firebox cross water tubes, smokebox steam dryer, duplex pumps, and steam reverser) were present. Even the 4,500 gallon tenders trailed by the 'D15s' had previously run behind members of his 'T14' 4-6-0 Class. Equally intriguingly, No.463, the first-built 'D15', was given a deep-toned hooter in place of the usual whistle — presumably as an evocation of a visit Drummond made to his old Caledonian Railway haunts in April 1911. The hooter, one might add, remained with No.463 until October 1939, when it was removed — lest it should be mistake for an air raid siren!

Rostered straight away for Salisbury and Bournemouth express work, the 'D15s', with their ability to run freely and speedily, were an instant success and the original allocation, whereby Nine Elms had six and Bournemouth and Salisbury two each, lasted to 1925. Urie, meanwhile, superheated the lot between May 1915 and September 1917, which process, apart from providing new 20in cylinders, an extended smokebox, and a non-water tube firebox, involved lowering working pressure to 180psi. Superheating reduced the total heating surface to 1,515sq ft, but added a useful 1,500lb towards a final tractive effort of 20,100lb.

The years 1925–26 saw further developments, for not only were all ten 'D15s' refitted with Maunsell superheaters, they also inherited six-wheeled 3,500 gallon tenders from '700' Class 0-6-0s prior to being despatched to Fratton shed, whence they worked the Waterloo–Portsmouth services until 1931. Once Class 'U1' moguls took over, however, the 'D15s' reverted almost exactly to their old shed allocations, and concentrated mainly on Portsmouth to Salisbury activities.

It seems to be an axiom of twentieth-century life that major wars inevitably bequeath social unrest, coal shortages and strikes and Britain was no exception. In 1921, for instance, 'D15' No.470 ran as an oil-burner for two months — and again for five months in 1926 because of the General Strike. Came World War II and No.463, equipped this time with the 'Mexican' trough oil system, re-entered service in September 1947 with an oblong-shaped 1,250 gallon tank mounted on its tender. Three months later, a turbo-generator was added for the purpose of illuminating headlights and cab. Interestingly, as an oil-burner it proved to be very popular with footplate men and for the next

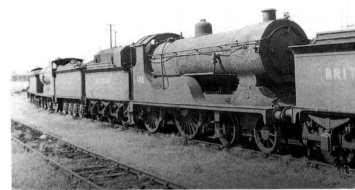

ten months it handled Portsmouth, Salisbury and Bournemouth semi-fast trains with distinction, until the restoration of near normal conditions saw it laid aside, with others, at Eastleigh.

Withdrawals continued, and four more 'D15s' were taken out of service in 1952. Nevertheless, a trio of 'D15s', Nos.30464/7/71, continued to cock a snook at Fate by taking the place of Maunsell 'U' Class 2-6-0s on Lymington ten-coach services during the summers of 1953 and 1954. All, though, vanished by September 1955. The sole surviving 'D15', No.30465, a Nine Elms engine, managed to work one Waterloo–Lymington train in the summer of 1955 before it, too, was withdrawn in January 1956. Broken up at Brighton, at least it went with final tally of 1,553,885 miles.

And perhaps our story of 'The Scottish 4-4-0' should end there — on a triumphant note for Dugald Drummond. In view of his remarkable, if tempestuous, contribution to the development of the classic inside-cylindered 'Scottish' 4-4-0, few people could have grudged him a long and peaceful retirement. Alas, it was not to be. He was still in charge at Eastleigh at the age of 72, when an accident, largely of his own making, badly scalded his leg and feet. Gangrene followed, again due to neglect and impatience. Amputation had to be effected on 7th November 1912, and poor Drummond died one day later at his home in Surbiton. Appropriately, he was buried at Brookwood with many other London & South Western men. Ironically, the last of his gallant 'D15s' had not even left Eastleigh Works.

Class D11/2 No.6388 *Captain Craigengelt*, a sturdy 1924 product of Kitson & Co., Leeds, pauses at Falkirk (High) Station before taking the 3.45pm Aberdeen–Glasgow express on to Queen Street. The date is July 1932, at which time the 'Scottish Director' had nearly 30 more working years ahead of it before twelve months storage at Parkhead culminated in official withdrawal in July 1961. (A. R. Martin)

Chapter 10
THOUGHTS IN RETROSPECT

WHERE *HAVE THE YEARS GONE!* It is extremely sobering to reflect that one must be at least approaching four score years to be able to conjure up personal memories of the Scottish 4-4-0 in its prime. But what memories they are!

Born in 1917 into a typical Central Scottish industrial environment, I was fortunate enough to be reared by two markedly Scottish prototypes: a mother, already well-versed in domestic service, who was prepared to spare no effort to advance her childrens' education and a father who, Border bred, had the foresight to eschew farm labour as a lad and seek, instead, comparatively secure employment with the North British Railway. A calm intelligent man, lacking only in ambition, my father loved his latter day job as an NBR/LNER goods guard and, though Fate ordained that I should enter Scottish banking in due course, I never ceased from childhood to share his enthusiasm for railways. For many years I even shared his good natured disparagement of things Caledonian — though, like him, I had no qualms in employing LMS trains from Falkirk (Grahamston) from time to time as and when the need for convenient access to Edinburgh or Glasgow arose — even at a tender age I well understood the conveniently flexible ethos of Company pride!

My home town, Falkirk, with its myriad of iron foundries, possessed two engine sheds: one, exclusively Caledonian, at Fouldubs, near Grangemouth — and a North British counterpart at Polmont. Both sheltered a healthy complement of locomotives, yet the only passenger engines either could muster was

a brace each of 0-4-4 tanks. These ferried back and forth all day on Larbert–Grangemouth and Grangemouth–Bo'ness branch service. For more stirring activity one had to haunt the ex-NBR lineside at Falkirk (High) station (fully a mile from the Town centre), or spend equally instructive Saturdays near Larbert station, again a walk of some two miles distant. Needless to say, such schoolboy safaris, fortified, as they were, by the sandwiches my mother prepared, offered a grandstand view of both NBR and CR 4-4-0 activity.

Fortunately, my father's limited quota of free passes and Privilege tickets was sufficient to enable our family to enjoy many a summer holiday with farm labouring relatives who were scattered throughout the Border country. Thus soon, I was introduced to the magic of Edinburgh (Waverley) station. Little did I know then, however, that the distinctive cupola of the Old Town building, which overlooked us as we strolled along from the Caley station at Princes Street, pinpointed the presence of the Head Office of the Bank of Scotland — not only my eventual employer, but the very institution which offered such stiff historical resistance to Waverley's earlier expansion! Once inside that mighty station, however, observation of sundry NBR 4-4-0 types, as they bustled about their various duties, dissolved into a haze of pure delight. Father did not seem to mind that North Eastern 4-4-0s indulged in a healthy share of East Coast country passenger activity — so why should I? A little later, when Gresley 4-6-2s began to appear on the Scottish scene, my family loyalties, once NBR, now LNER, rose effortlessly to the occasion.

From another favourite vantage point, this time at Falkirk (High) Station's East end, Class D34 No.9242 *Glen Mamie* was captured in May 1935, heading a Fife express as it stepped out briskly for Falkirk High Tunnel. Built at Cowlairs in 1919, the 'Glen' ultimately served on the GNSR Section before being withdrawn in March 1960. (*Author*)

Later still, when I was in my teens, a bargain Saturday afternoon return fare to Glasgow of 1/6d (just over 7p in modern parlance) enabled me to further my music studies at the Scottish National Academy. Ergo, I soon familiarised myself with Glasgow's four main line stations into the bargain: St. Enoch Station produced my first sight of a Glasgow & South Western 4-4-0, Central Station offered a fresh quota of Caley 4-4-0s (as did Buchanan Street), while Queen Street, on the other hand, left indelible impressions of smoke and energy as NBR tanks manfully banked heavy LNER trains up Cowlairs Incline. Cowlairs Works loomed up on the left just as the track levelled out and the banker dropped off; but alert passing inspection invariably revealed some NBR 4-4-0 or other as it lay by the Works awaiting attention. St. Rollox Works, I soon discovered, was rather more coy in revealing its Caley activities — fortunately, knowledge acquired later in the art of applying for shed permits cracked that nut before it was too late!

Latterly, regular access to the *Railway Magazine*, by courtesy of one of my father's colleagues, so fired the ambitions of myself and a railway/music-loving crony that we undertook shed visits to Corkerhill and Hurlford, Kilmarnock in the mid-1930s — just in time to catch the few G&SWR engines which remained in circulation. By then, too, we had borne excited witness as Highland Railway 'Clans' and 'Castles' worked through Larbert; but not until we visited Perth in August 1934 did we see our first HR 4-4-0s, in the shape of Jones' 'Lochs' and Peter Drummond's 'Wee Bens'. Flushed with success, we quickly followed up with a shed visit to Aberdeen, both Ferryhill and Kittybrewster, and eagerly grasped our first opportunity to photograph GNSR 4-4-0s. What a year that was!

It has become quite commonplace for contemporary railway authors to deride Scottish steam locomotive development as lamentably failing to reach beyond the late Victorian era. G. J.

Churchward is often quoted by comparison; but such facile near-dismissal of the Drummonds and McIntoshs of this world calmly glosses over the fact that the mighty Great Western functioned in the richest areas of the UK and that all through history, the Scottish economy has, for a variety of reasons, lagged far behind that of its infinitely more prosperous Southern neighbour. During the depressions of the 1920s and 1930s, for instance, it was no mere coincidence that Scottish workers led the way in seeking new lives in Canada, Australia and New Zealand. My own impressions of Scottish locomen, gleaned over the same period, was that of a hardy intelligent breed who could never resist a challenge and were prepared to work outlandish hours, cheerfully and without complaint, in so doing. Loyalty to their respective Companies was never in doubt, despite the fact that both they and the said Companies were working on a proverbial shoestring. I doubt if ardent admirers of the GWR and LNWR will ever understand the completely different *mores* which traditionally dominated financial matters in Scotland. What, for instance, would such people make of the fact that when I was fortunate enough to join a Glasgow Bank as an apprentice in 1933, on the then prevailing three year salary scale of £30, £40, and £50, my own remuneration for the first ten days was carefully calculated at £20 a year until I reached the magic age of sixteen?(!). Yet, typical of Scottish exactitude, no one, least of all myself, turned a hair. I wonder, though — would an *English* Bank have stooped to such parsimony?

The 3.2 miles between Falkirk (High) and Polmont offered a popular sprinting ground for the NBR's lively 4-4-0s. In this view, taken in July 1931, Class D30 No.9500 *Black Duncan* is taking full advantage of level terrain as it speeds the 'Fifeshire Coast Express' (4.10pm Glasgow–Crail) on its way. (*A. R. Martin*)

Conversely, my oldest brother tells me that *his* earliest childhood memory is of my father being 'knocked up' at two in the morning to assist in piloting Caley drivers who found themselves on 'foreign' territory after the 1915 carnage at Quintinshill. I need hardly add that he turned out instantly and without demure. In later years, when he acted as guard on the evening goods trains which left Falkirk nightly for Berwick and Carlisle, the fact that he would be absent for the next 36 hours created no consternation in our family ranks. Certainly, when he left to go on duty, no Guardsman ever wore his uniform more proudly. The name Dugald Drummond frequently dropped from his lips and the superheated Reid J37 Class 0-6-0 which latterly conducted him on these long and arduous return trips was ever the apple of his

The scene is Larbert Station in June 1936. The Edinburgh portion of the 12 noon Oban express has been detached and McIntosh '43 Class' No.14451 waits to reverse back into the platform before leaving for Edinburgh (Princes Street), via Falkirk (Grahamston) and Polmont. Note the traditional Caledonian route indicator on the front buffer beam. (*A. R. Martin*)

eye. The K3 2-6-0s which superseded the J37s earned the same warm accolade. Meanwhile, across the street from us, a fellow goods guard served the Caledonian Railway and the LMS with the same unquestioning devotion. Who can doubt that the Scottish Railway Companies, for all their parlous finances, were thrice blessed in possessing such a workforce?

Even in the late 1930s, ex-Caledonian 4-4-0s still played a consistent role in double-headed trains which passed through Larbert. However, on one rare occasion in July 1935, this Aberdeen-bound express, with its motley collection of coaches, was headed by two LMS Compounds. The train engine is No.922 — built by Vulcan Foundry in 1927 and withdrawn in 1952. The pilot engine, No.939, was a Derby product of 1932, and lasted four more years, to 1956. *(Author)*

Changing times are reflected at Edinburgh Waverley's East end in August 1931, as D49 No.329 *Inverness-shire* and ex-NBR D30 No.9414 *Dugald Dalgetty* (the 'Shire's senior by fourteen years) move forward in tandem after bringing in a heavy express from Glasgow (Queen Street). *(A. R. Martin)*

Finances apart, another crucial factor which conditioned steam locomotive development in Scotland was the sheer geography of the county — ie the harsh climate and the curves and gradients which bedevilled almost every main line to the North and South. In such conditions, the flexibility of four-coupled engines became almost a prime necessity; and as loads became greater, the temptation to add a second locomotive seemed logical at the time. After all, the Midland Railway and, to a slightly lesser degree, the mighty LNWR, responded to overloading in exactly the same manner. Crewe graduated eventually by introducing various classes of 4-6-0 but, let's face it, Derby adhered firmly to its conservative line and doggedly pursued the four-coupled trail. It even ended on a note of triumph with Deeley's magnificent Compounds.

Again in the early 1930s, Holmes Class D31 4-4-0 No.9729 and a Raven 'Atlantic' remind us of congenial NBR/NER co-existence as they head an express fish train past the Anglo-Scottish Border, a mile north of Berwick. *(Steamchest)*

First sight of a Highland Railway 4-4-0 came in August 1934, when 'Wee Ben' No.14410 *Ben Dearg* strolled into Perth with a modest goods train. Built at Lochgorm in August 1900, this hardy little locomotive completed nearly 50 years of active service before bowing the knee, second last of its class, in December 1949. *(A. R. Martin)*

One must concede, though, that locomotive developments at Swindon were ever closely watched, and often copied, by many lesser companies. Swindon, on the other hand, tucked away peacefully in Wiltshire, was perspicacious enough to ensure a smooth progression of house-trained Locomotive Superintendents over the century of the Great Western's independent existence. Thus, the names of Joseph Armstrong senior,

William Dean, G. J. Churchward, and C. B. Collett still trip facilely off the tongue of any railway historian — would that Scotland had experienced the same good fortune! As it was, in that sorely straitened area the perennial problems of lack of capital and despicable salaries guaranteed an almost constant turmoil and turnover of talented engineers. It was therefore no surprise that Dugald Drummond, the most controversial of them all,

Similarly, a first visit to Aberdeen in July 1935 yielded this study of ex-GNSR D40 No.6847 *Sir David Stewart* as it paused at Aberdeen General's North end before backing in to resume further duties. One of six which were supplied by the NB Locomotive Co. (Works No.22561) in 1920, it perished as BR No.62275 in December 1955. *(A. R. Martin)*

having set his immortal NBR 4-4-0 pattern in 1877, defecting to the Caledonian four years later, wandered further afield before finding his *metier*, in terms of secure financial backing, 400 miles further South at Nine Elms and Eastleigh. Even then, ironically enough, his attempts to graduate from 4-4-0 to 4-6-0 design met with a strange lack of success. Likewise, though J. F. McIntosh on the Caledonian Railway made a better cut at designing 4-6-0s, is it not the fame of his 'Dunalastair' 4-4-0s which still resounds in the corridors of railway history? On the NBR, both Holmes and Reid were gifted men — but both laboured under tough management and acute financial stringency. Yet, while Reid's massive NB 'Atlantics' may well have raised critical eyebrows in 1906, what possible role could *The Great Bear*, Churchward's acclaimed masterpiece, have played on Scotland's main lines? Meantime, Scottish 4-4-0s were scuttling about all over the country, functioning as all things to all men — Scottish locomen loved them.

One final thought occurs: the versatility of Scottish labour and its ability to create far beyond four-coupled machines is eloquently expressed by the fact that the City of Glasgow earned undying fame over a century and more by acting as host to a handful of locomotive manufacturers. Consider the table below and reflect on the huge variety of overseas engines which flowed therefrom. Many of them were giants. Indeed, the output of Glasgow's five famous names, at 27,000 units, constituted well over one third of the total steam engines built by all main UK contractors over the years 1831–1964. During that period the Scottish operating Companies themselves built 2,500 in their own workshops. The two major Companies, the CR and NBR, of course, were responsible for 2,000 of them.

GLASGOW LOCOMOTIVE CONTRACTORS AND THEIR OUTPUT

Name of builder	Date Span	Total Years	Locomotive Output
Sharp, Stewart & Co.	1833–1902	70	5,088
Neilson Reid & Co.	1838–1902	65	5,864
Dübs & Co.	1865–1902	38	4,485
North British Locomotive Co.	1903–1958	56	11,318
W. Beadmore & Co. Ltd.	1920–1931	12	393
Total Steam Locomotives Built — 27,148			

For good measure A. Barclay Sons & Co. Ltd., of Kilmarnock, subscribed a further 2,053 steam locomotives over the years 1859–1962. Yes, the Scottish Railway Companies may have clung too long to their 4-4-0 fixation — but the country itself has nothing to apologise for!

St. Rollox Works, 1938 and the end of the road for Jones ex-Highland Railway 4-4-0 No.14386 *Loch Tummel* is nigh. Outshopped from Dübs & Co.'s Glasgow Locomotive Works (Works No.3399) in July 1896, and rated LMSR Class 2P, the 'Loch' carried an ex-Caledonian boiler for ten years before withdrawal came in August 1938. *(Steamchest)*

Peter Drummond's ex-HR No.14422 *Ben a'Chaoruinn* and five sister 'Big Bens' came from the NB Locomotive Co.'s Glasgow workshops in 1908–09. Seen here at Balrnock shed in September 1937, and the last survivor of its class, No.14422 spent some months heating carriages before being scrapped in June 1938, having completed 831,860 miles during its working life. *(Author)*

I. NORTH BRITISH RAILWAY 4-4-0s

Designer	Class	Date built	Built by	Cylinders	Driving wheels	Bogie wheels	Boiler pressure lbs/sq in	Tractive effort lbs	No. of last survivor	Withdrawn	LNER Class
T. Wheatley	224	1871	Cowlairs	17in × 24in	6ft 6in	2ft 9in			224	1917	—
	420	1873	Cowlairs	17in × 24in	6ft 6in	3ft 4in			422	1918	—
D. Drummond	Abbotsford	1876–78	Neilson & Co	18in × 26in	6ft 6in	3ft 6in	150	13,770	1321	Nov 1924	D27
									487	1926	D28
	Abbotsford	1878	Cowlairs	18in × 26in	6ft 6in	3ft 6in	150	13,770	491	1926	D28
M. Holmes	574	1884	Cowlairs	17in × 26in	6ft 6in	3ft 6in	140	11,464	62072	Feb 1951	D31
	633	1884–95	Cowlairs	18in × 26in	6ft 6in	3ft 6in	150	13,770	62281	Dec 1952	D31
	729	1898–99	Cowlairs	18½in × 26in	6ft 6in	3ft 6in	175	16,514	62283	Feb 1951	D31
	592	1886–88	Cowlairs	18in × 26in	7ft 0in	3ft 6in	150	12,786	9596	Jly 1933	D25
	West Highland	1894–96	Cowlairs	18in × 24in	5ft 7in	3ft 6in	150	14,798	(10439)	Nov 1924	D35
	W/High Rebuild	1919	Cowlairs	19in × 26in	5ft 7in	3ft 6in	150	19,648	9695	May 1943	D36*
	Abbotsford (Rebuilds)	1902–04	Cowlairs	18¼in × 26in	6ft 6in	3ft 6in	175	16,514	10387	Sep 1926	D28
	317	1902	Cowlairs	19in × 26in	6ft 6in	3ft 6in	190	19,434	9325	Jly 1926	D26
W. P. Reid	Intermediate	1906–07	Cowlairs	19in × 26in	6ft 0in	3ft 6in	180	21,053	62451	Mch 1951	D32
	'Scott'	1909	NB Loco. Co.	19in × 26in	6ft 0in	3ft 6in	190	19,434	62411	Nov 1952	D29
	Intermediate	1909–10	Cowlairs	19in × 26in	6ft 0in	3ft 6in	190	21,053	62464	Sep 1953	D33
	'Glen'	1913–20	Cowlairs	20in × 26in	6ft 0in	3ft 6in	165	22,100	62469	Dec 1962	D34†
	'Scott'	1912–20	Cowlairs	20in × 26in	6ft 6in	3ft 6in	165	18,700	62422/8	Dec 1958	D30

Note: * Holmes 'West Highland' 4-4-0, rebuilt by Reid in 1919. † One preserved as NBR No.256 *Glen Douglas*.

II. NORTH BRITISH RAILWAY 4-4-0 TANKS

Designer	Class	Date built	Built by	Cylinders	Driving wheels	Bogie wheels	Boiler pressure lbs/sq in	Tractive effort lbs	No. of last survivor	Withdrawn	LNER Class
D. Drummond	'P'	1879	Neilson & Co.	17in × 26in	6ft 0in	3ft 6in	150	13,305	10390	Mch 1926	D50
	'R'	1880–84	Cowlairs	16in × 22in	5ft 0in	2ft 7in	140	11,170	10462	Aug 1933	D51

III. CALEDONIAN RAILWAY 4-4-0s

Designer	Class	Date built	Built by	Cylinders	Driving wheels	Bogie wheels	Boiler pressure lbs/sq in	Tractive effort lbs	No. of last survivor	Withdrawn	LMSR Class
G. Brittain	Dundee Bogies	1877	Neilson & Co.	18in × 24in	7ft 2in	3ft 4½in	140		1126	Aug 1910	—
	Oban Bogies	1882	Dübs & Co.	18in × 24in	5ft 2in	3ft 2in	130		14100/05	1930	1P
D. Drummond	Various	1884	Neilson & Co.	18in × 26in	6ft 6in	3ft 6in	150	14,720	14298	Jan 1930	
		1885	St. Rollox	18in × 26in	6ft 6in	3ft 6in	150		14304	1931	1P
		1889	St. Rollox	18in × 26in	6ft 6in	3ft 6in	150		14297	1928	1P
		1891	St. Rollox	18in × 26in	6ft 6in	3ft 6in	150		14309	Feb 1930	1P
	Eglinton	1886	Dübs & Co.	19in × 26in	6ft 6in	3ft 6in	150		(14296)	1925	1P*
	Gourock Bogies	1888	St. Rollox	18in × 26in	5ft 9in	3ft 6in	150		(14109)	1930	1P
	Gourock Bogies	1891	St. Rollox	18in × 26in	5ft 9in	3ft 6in	160		14113/4	1930	1P
J. Lambie	13	1894	St. Rollox	18in × 26in	6ft 6in	3ft 6in	160	14,720	14309/10	1930	1P
J. F. McIntosh	Dunalastair	1896	St. Rollox	18¼in × 26in	6ft 6in	3ft 6in	160	15,096	14315/6	Oct 1935	2P
	Dunalastair II	1897/8	St. Rollox	19in × 26in	6ft 6in	3ft 6in	175	17,850	14333	Sep 1947	2P & 3P
	Dunalastair III	1899/00	St. Rollox	19in × 26in	6ft 6in	3ft 6in	180	18,411	(54434)	Apl 1948	2P & 3P
	Dunalastair IV	1904–10	St. Rollox	19in × 26in	6ft 6in	3ft 6in	180	18,411	54439	Aug 1958	2P & 3P
	139	1910–11		20in × 26in	6ft 6in	3ft 6in	165		54441	Aug 1957	3P
	139	1912		20¼in × 26in	6ft 6in	3ft 6in	165		54446	Aug 1955	3P
	43	1913/14		20¼in × 26in	6ft 6in	3ft 6in	170		54458	Dec 1957	3P
W. Pickersgill	113	1916	St. Rollox	20in × 26in	6ft 6in	3ft 6in	175	20,400	54463	Dec 1962	3P
	928	1916	NB Loco. Co.	20in × 26in	6ft 6in	3ft 6in	175	20,400	54475	Jun 1961	3P
	72	1920	St. Rollox	20½in × 26in	6ft 6in	3ft 6in	180	21,435	54481/6	Mar 1962	3P
	82	1921	A/Whitworth	20½in × 26in	6ft 6in	3ft 6in	180	21,435	54495	Mar 1962	3P
	66	1922	NB Loco. Co.	20½in × 26in	6ft 6in	3ft 6in	180	21,435	54500	Mar 1962	3P

Note: * CR No.124 was built for Edinburgh International Exhibition of 1886, and was awarded a Gold Medal. The locomotive was named *Eglinton* in 1890.

IV. CALEDONIAN RAILWAY 4-4-0 TANKS

J. Lambie	1	1893/4	St. Rollox	17in × 24in	5ft 0in	3ft 2in	150		15025	Jun 1938	1P

V. GREAT NORTH OF SCOTLAND RAILWAY 4-4-0s

Designer	Class	Date built	Built by	Cylinders	Driving wheels	Bogie wheels	Boiler pressure lbs/sq in	Tractive effort lbs	No. of last survivor	Withdrawn	LNER Class
W. Cowan	28	1862–64	R. Stephenson	16in × 20in	5ft 1in		140			1920	—
	K	1866	Neilson & Co.	16in × 24in	5ft 6½in	3ft 0in	140	10,994	45A	Jly 1925	D47/2*
	L	1876	Neilson & Co.	17in × 24in	5ft 6½in	3ft 0in	150	13,298	52A	Jan 1926	D47/1†
	M	1878	Neilson & Co.	17½in × 26in	5ft 7in	3ft 0½in	150	15,152	6840	Jun 1932	D45‡
	C	1878–79	Neilson & Co.	17½in × 26in	6ft 1in	3ft 0½in	150	13,907	6803	Feb 1927	D39
J. Manson	A	1884	Kitson & Co.	17½in × 26in	6ft 0in	3ft 0in	150	14,100	6867	Oct 1932	D44
	G	1885	Kitson & Co.	17½in × 26in	5ft 6in	3ft 0in	150	15,382	6869	Nov 1934	D48
	N	1887	Kittybrewster	17½in × 26in	5ft 7in	3ft 1in	165	16,672	6805	Apl 1936	D46
	O	1888	Kitson & Co.	18in × 26in	6ft 0½in	3ft 9½in	165	16,296	6817	Feb 1945	D42
	P	1890	R. Stephenson	18in × 26in	6ft 0½in	3ft 9½in	165	16,296	6812	Jan 1938	D43
	Q	1890	R. Stephenson	18in × 26in	6ft 6½in	3ft 9½in	165	15,050	6875	Jan 1938	D38
J. Johnson	S	1893	Neilson & Co.	18in × 26in	6ft 1in	3ft 9½in	165	16,184	62225	Feb 1953	D41
W. Pickersgill	T	1895–98	Neilson & Co.	18in × 26in	6ft 1in	3ft 9½in	165	16,184	62241/2	Feb 1953	D41
	V	1899–1915	Neilson & Co. Inverurie	18in × 26in	6ft 1in	3ft 9½in	165	16,184	62264	Mch 1957	D40
T. E. Heywood	F	1920/21	Inverurie NB Loco. Co.	18in × 26in	6ft 1in	3ft 9½in	165	16,184	62277	Jun 1958	D40§

Note: * Dimensions as rebuilt by J. Manson in 1889–91. † Dimensions as rebuilt by W. Pickersgill in 1897–1901. ‡ Dimensions as rebuilt by W. Pickersgill in 1896–1904. § Preserved as GNSR No.49 Gordon Highlander.

VI. GLASGOW & SOUTH WEST RAILWAY 4-4-0s

Designer	Class	Date built	Built by	Cylinders	Driving wheels	Bogie wheels	Boiler pressure lbs/sq in	Tractive effort lbs	No. of last survivor	Withdrawn	LMSR Class
J. Stirling	6	1873–77	Kilmarnock	18in × 26in	7ft 1in	3ft 7in	140		15	Dec 1900	—
H. Smellie	Wee Bogies	1882–85	Kilmarnock	18¼in × 26in	6ft 1½in	3ft 0½in	140		138	1931	1P
	Wee Bogies	1882–85	Kilmarnock	18¼in × 26in	6ft 1½in	3ft 0½in	160		14118/20/3	Jun 1934	2P*
	153	1886–89	Kilmarnock	18¼in × 26in	6ft 9½in	3ft 7½in	120		14143	Nov 1935	1P
J. Manson	8	1892–04	Kilmarnock	18¼in × 26in	6ft 9½in	3ft 7½in	150	13,547	14195	Dec 1932	1P
	8	1892–04	Kilmarnock	18¼in × 26in	6ft 9½in	3ft 7½in	170		14170	Jly 1933	2P†
	336	1895–99	Dübs & Co.	18¼in × 26in	6ft 1½in	3ft 7½in	165		14220	Dec 1931	2P
	336	1895–99	Dübs & Co.	18¼in × 26in	6ft 1½in	3ft 7½in	170		14214	Nov 1932	2P‡
	11	1897	Kilmarnock	14½in × 26in (2) 12½in × 24in (2)	6ft 9½in	3ft 7½in	165	15,860	14509	Nov 1934	3P
	194	1899–01	Kilmarnock	18in × 26in	7ft 1in	3ft 7in	150		14234/6/9	1930	1P
	240	1904–11	Kilmarnock	18¼in × 26in	6ft 9½in	3ft 7½in	170		14260	Oct 1934	2P
	18	1907–12	Kilmarnock	18¼in × 26in	6ft 9½in	3ft 7½in	170		14366 14374/77	Oct 1932	2P
P. Drummond	131	1913	NB Loco Co.	19½in × 26in	6ft 0in	3ft 6in	180	21,009	14513	Dec 1937	2P
	137	1915	Kilmarnock	19½in × 26in	6ft 0in	3ft 6in	180	21,009	14521	Aug 1937	3P
R. H. Whitelegg	485	1921	Kilmarnock	18¼in × 26in	6ft 9½in	3ft 7½in	170		14270	Dec 1933	2P

*As rebuilt by R. H. Whitelegg in 1921–22. †As rebuilt by R. H. Whitelegg in 1920–21. ‡As rebuilt by R. H. Whitelegg in 1920–21.

VII. HIGHLAND RAILWAY 4-4-0s

W. Stroudley	5	1858	Hawthorns	17in × 24in	5ft 0in			11,791	7A	May 1899	—*
D. Jones	Duke	1874	Dübs & Co.	18in × 24in	6ft 3½in	3ft 9½in	140	13,219	67	1923	—
	Duke	1876–88	Lochgorm	18in × 24in	6ft 3½in	3ft 9½in	140	13,219	72/3/5	1923	—
	Skye Bogies	1882–01	Lochgorm	18in × 24in	5ft 3in	3ft 3in	150	15,552	14277/84	Jun 1930	1P
	Bruce	1886	Clyde Loco	18in × 24in	6ft 3in	3ft 9½in	160	14,100	14278	Jun 1930	
	Strath	1892	Neilson & Co.	18in × 24in	6ft 3in	3ft 9½in	160	14,100	14271	Aug 1930	1P
	Lochs	1896	Dübs & Co.	19in × 24in	6ft 3½in	3ft 3in	175	17,070	54385	Apl 1950	2P
P. Drummond	Ben	1898/9	Dübs & Co.	18¼in × 26in	6ft 0in	3ft 6in	175	17,890	54398	Feb 1953	2P
	Ben	1899/01	Lochgorm	18¼in × 26in	6ft 0in	3ft 6in	175	17,890	54409	Apl 1950	2P
	Ben	1906	NB Loco. Co.	18¼in × 26in	6ft 0in	3ft 6in	175	17,890	54416	Sep 1948	2P
	Large Ben	1908/9	NB Loco. Co.	18in × 26in	6ft 0in	3ft 6in	180	18,401	14422	Mch 1937	2P
C. Cumming	Loch	1916	NB Loco. Co.	19in × 24in	6ft 3½in	3ft 3in	175	17,070	14394	Sep 1936	2P
	Snaigow	1917	Hawthorn Leslie	20in × 26in	6ft 3in	3ft 3in	160	18,859	14522	Apl 1936	3P

Note: *Two 2-4-0s rebuilt by David Jones as 4-4-0s in 1873 and 1875.

VIII. HIGHLAND RAILWAY 4-4-0 TANKS

D. Jones	Yankee	1892/3	Dübs & Co.	16in × 22in	5ft 3in	3ft 0in	140	10,638 12,158	15014	Dec 1934	
	Ex-2-4-0T	1878–9	Lochgorm	16in × 24in	4ft 9in	2ft 7½in	140	12,715	15010	Nov 1933†	

Note: †Three 2-4-0Ts rebuilt by David Jones as 4-4-0Ts in 1881/2.

IX. LNER 4-4-0s IN SCOTLAND

Designer	Class	Date built	Built by	Cylinders	Driving wheels	Bogie wheels	Boiler pressure lbs/sq in	Tractive effort lbs	No. of last survivor	Withdrawn
J. G. Robinson	D11	1924 1924	Kitson & Co. Armstrong Whitworth	20in × 26in	6ft 9in	3ft 6in	180	19,644	62685	Jan 1962
H. A. Ivatt	D1	1911	Doncaster	18½in × 26in	6ft 8in	3ft 8in	170	16,074	(62209)	Nov 1950
N. Gresley	D49	1927–29	Darlington	17in × 26in	6ft 8in	3ft 1¼in	180	21,556	62712	Jly 1961*

Note: *Preserved as No.246 *Morayshire*.

X. LMSR 4-4-0s IN SCOTLAND

Designer	Class	Date built	Built by	Cylinders	Driving wheels	Bogie wheels	Boiler pressure lbs/sq in	Tractive effort lbs	No. of last survivor	Withdrawn
Sir H. Fowler	4P	1924–32	Various	19in × 26in (1) 21in × 26in (2)	6ft 9in	3ft 6½in	200	22,649	40920	May 1958*
Sir H. Fowler	2P	1928–32 1931–32	Derby Crewe	19in × 26in	6ft 9in	3ft 6½in	180	17,729	40670	Dec 1962

Note: *Compound 4-4-0s, based on earlier Midland Railway engines.

XI. SOUTH EASTERN RAILWAY 4-4-0s (JAMES STIRLING)

Designer	Class	Date built	Built by	Cylinders	Driving wheels	Bogie wheels	Boiler pressure lbs/sq in	Tractive effort lbs	No. of last survivor	Withdrawn
J. Stirling	A	1879/81	Ashford	18in × 26in	6ft 0½in	3ft 8in	140		67	Dec 1908
	F	1883/98	Ashford	19in × 26in	7ft 0in	3ft 9in	150		172	Dec 1930
	F1	1903/16	Ashford	18in × 26in	7ft 0in	3ft 9in	170		78 & 151	Feb 1949*
	B	1898	Neilson Reid & Co.	19in × 26in	7ft 0in	3ft 9in	160		A458	Dec 1931
	B	1898/9	Ashford	19in × 26in	7ft 0in	3ft 9in	160		A458	Dec 1931
	B1	1910/27	Ashford	18in × 26in	7ft 0in	3ft 9in	170		1443	Mch 1951†

Note: *Rebuild of Class F 4-4-0s. †Rebuild of Class B 4-4-0s.

XII. LONDON & SOUTH WESTERN RAILWAY 4-4-0s (DUGALD DRUMMOND)

Designer	Class	Date built	Built by	Cylinders	Driving wheels	Bogie wheels	Boiler pressure lbs/sq in	Tractive effort lbs	No. of last survivor	Withdrawn
D. Drummond	T7	Aug 1897	Nine Elms	15in × 26in (4)	6ft 7in	3ft 7in	175	22,030	720	Apl 1927*
	C8	1898	Nine Elms	18½in × 26in	6ft 7in	3ft 7in	175	16,755	298	Jan 1938
	E10	1901	Nine Elms	14in × 26in (4)	6ft 7in	3ft 7in	175	19,190	372/3	Apl 1927†
	T9	1899/01	Dübs & Co.	18½in × 26in	6ft 7in	3ft 7in	175	17,670	709/15/17	July 1961
	T9	1899/01	Nine Elms	18½in × 26in	6ft 7in	3ft 7in	175	17,670	120	July 1963‡
	K10	1901/2	Nine Elms	18½in × 26in	5ft 7in	3ft 7in	175	19,756	384	Aug 1951
	L11	1904–07	Nine Elms	18½in ×·26in	5ft 7in	3ft 7in	175	19,756	30411 & 437	Apl 1952
	S11	1903	Nine Elms	19in × 26in	6ft 1in	3ft 7in	175	19,400	30400	Oct 1954
	L12	1904–05	Nine Elms	19in × 26in	6ft 7in	3ft 7in	175	17,673	30434	Feb 1955
	D15	1912	Eastleigh	19½in × 26in	6ft 7in	3ft 7in	200	22,333	30465	Jan 1956

Note: *Divided drive 4-2-2-0 No.720. †Divided drive 4-2-2-0 Nos.369–373. ‡Preserved as LSWR No.120.

BIBLIOGRAPHY

British Locomotive Catalogue (1825–1923) — Bertram Baxter (Moorland Publishing)

A Biographical Dictionary of Railway Engineers — John Marshall (David & Charles)

Highland Railway Locomotives — J. R. H. Cormack & J. L. Stevenson (RCTS)

Locomotives of the LNER Parts 4 & 7 — (RCTS)

Locomotives of the LSWR — D. L. Bradley (RCTS)

The Locomotive History of the South Eastern Railway — D. L. Bradley (RCTS)

Scottish Locomotive History (1821–1923) — Campbell Highet (G. Allen & Unwin)

INDEX

4-4-0 LOCOMOTIVE CLASSES

CR

G&SWR

GNSR

HR

NBR

LNER

LMSR

SER

LSWR

4-4-0 TANK LOCOMOTIVE CLASSES

CR

HR

NBR

No.14336, the last-built 'Dunalastair 11' (St. Rollox, April 1898) looks resplendent enough in LMS passenger livery to earn J. F. McIntosh's posthumous pride. The locomotive itself outlived its creator by a quarter of a century, before going to the breakers in June 1939.